Education as the
Cultivation of Intelligence

The Educational Psychology Series

Robert J. Sternberg and Wendy M. Williams, Series Editors

Education as the Cultivation of Intelligence

MICHAEL E. MARTINEZ

University of California, Irvine

2000

LAWRENCE ERLBAUM ASSOCIATES, PUBLISHERS
Mahwah, New Jersey   London

The final camera copy for this work was prepared by the editors and therefore the publisher takes no responsibility for consistency or correctness of typographical style. However, this arrangement helps to make publication of this kind of scholarship possible.

Lawrence Erlbaum Associates, Inc., Publishers
10 Industrial Avenue
Mahwah, New Jersey 07430

Cover design by Kathryn Houghtaling Lacey

Library of Congress Cataloging-in-Publication Data

Martinez, Michael E.
    Education as the cultivation of intelligence / Michael E. Martinez.
        p. cm. -- (The educational psychology series)
    Includes bibliographical references (p.) and index.
    ISBN 0-8058-3251-3 (cloth : alk. paper)
        1. Learning, Psychology of. 2. Intelligence. 3. Education--Aims and objectives. I. Title. II. Series.
    LB1060 .M337 2000
    370.15'23--dc21
                                                            00-042189

Books published by Lawrence Erlbaum Associates are printed on acid-free paper, and their bindings are chosen for strength and durability.

Printed in the United States of America
10   9   8   7   6   5   4   3   2   1

For Stephanie

Contents

Preface

For many people, the word *intelligence* has a negative ring. The neat rank ordering of human beings implied by the word sounds ungenerous, confining to human potential, and possibly racist. Intelligence—at least as measured by IQ—dismisses the marvelous variation among people by forcing multiplied uniqueness into a single sterile number. How can that be right?

To me, however, the word *intelligence* has positive associations. It speaks of human potential and accomplishment. Intelligence helps explain *why* civilizations, cultures, inventions, and creative works of all kinds exist. Even so, intelligence is largely a mystery—but one that, if revealed, might unlock further creative and intellectual energies. Perhaps counterintuitively, a fuller understanding of intelligence might also address and help correct social inequities.

Does hope truly reside in intelligence? To test the possibility, we must appraise the research literature on the subject. We must also consider what role genetics plays in intelligence. That is the purpose of this book. My conclusion might seem paradoxical: Although genetics has an undeniable role in intelligence, heritability values do not impose limits on intelligence for individuals or societies. Instead, it is *experience* that is crucial in the formation of intelligence. This means that intelligence is learnable, and it is the quality of experience that determines the efficiency and effectiveness by which intelligence is learned. I will propose that education be redefined as all experiences that contribute to the formation of intelligence.

These themes are developed as follows: Part I of the book presents my claim that intelligence is important to valued social outcomes, and more so now than ever before in history. Part II addresses the question: What is intelligence? In this section, I present major and minor theories, some of which trace back to the late 1800s, others of which have emerged only in the last decade or two. The pivotal claim of this book—that intelligence is developed through experience—is exposited in Part III. In Part IV, the book concludes with a discussion of the implications of learnable intelligence for society.

Conventional beliefs about intelligence have too long been oppressors of the human spirit and antagonists of dignity and human potential. It is now time to see intelligence as a liberator—as a marvelously rich entity that helps explain the uniqueness of our species. To appreciate intelligence more fully is, I believe, to see a brighter future for all. It is to see possibilities for human expression as rolling forward indefinitely, proceeding in pleasing directions—possibilities whose hazy outlines we can barely perceive.

Acknowledgments

I am deeply grateful to the many people who have helped make this book possible. To begin, I owe much to the late Professor Richard Snow—first, for his suggestion that I write this book and, second, for his distinguished record of scholarship from which I have drawn many insights that are foundational to my argument. My colleagues Irving Sigel and Scott Wood provided helpful suggestions and encouragement in response to early drafts. Detailed critiques were made by series editor Robert Sternberg, and by technical reviewers David Lohman and Richard Mayer. The manuscript is much stronger because of their advice. Thanks go to LEA staff Naomi Silverman and Sondra Guideman for their kind and patient assistance in the pragmatic aspects of book writing and production. I am thankful to my fellow faculty and staff in the UCI Department of Education for their continuing interest and support of this project. Special thanks go to Dylan Le for his long-term assistance in all facets of the project, and to Anna Manring for her help in facilitating the preparation of camera-ready copy. Noel Arenain greatly improved the quality of illustrations. Philip Travisano generously contributed the illustration of the seed corn analogy, Fig. 6.1. Finally, I am thankful to my family, immediate and extended, for their dependable forbearance and encouragement, which have carried me through from beginning to end.

Part I

Introduction

1

The Age of Intelligence

In the fast-paced, technology-dense world indwelled by much of the earth's population, the supreme human resource is intelligence. That is because intelligence consists of the knowledge, skills, and strategies necessary to be effective in a world that is complex and information-rich, a world in which daily life consists largely in a concatenation of problems to be solved. Intelligence shapes the economic prospects of individuals, organizations, and nations. Intelligence also connects to the causes and potential solutions of deep-rooted social problems. My thesis is this: The intellectual abilities that are crucial to modern life, including economic viability and effectiveness in daily living, correspond to the cognitive functions that are reasonably called *intelligence*. Moreover, those intellectual abilities are learnable.

This differs radically from the conventional view that intelligence is invariant and determined by heredity. In this book, I present evidence that intelligence is not an innate, immutable, and strictly inherited capacity, but instead is a repertoire of learnable cognitive functions. And although genetics does have a role in shaping intelligence, the acquisition of competencies composing intelligence depends profoundly on experience. Tremendous economic and social implications follow. Most fundamentally, it becomes possible to reconceptualize the goals of education to embrace the cultivation of intelligence, and to redefine education as consisting in all those experiences, through the life span, that lead to its enhancement.

INTELLIGENCE AND THE ECONOMY

The rising importance of intelligence to work is demonstrated in the way that economists have redefined the job sectors composing the labor market. Long-recognized distinctions in the labor market—especially between "white-collar" managers and "blue-collar" laborers—are giving way to divisions that recognize the importance of intellect to contemporary work. One alternative typology of jobs was set forth by Reich (1992), who divided the labor market into three sectors: symbolic-analytic workers, in-person workers, and routine production workers (cf. Stewart, 1997). In modern economies, the most important and rewarding of these is the symbolic-analytic sector, which comprises workers who specialize in "problem solving, problem-identifying, and strategic-brokering" (Reich, 1992, p. 177). The symbolic analyst is a professional problem solver whose work consists of tasks that are novel and complex, that resist routinization, and that entail the

1

gathering and transformation of information in symbolic form. These task characteristics—problem solving, complexity, and symbolic information—have strong associations with the qualities of thinking collectively called intelligence.

The division of the labor market proposed by Reich explicitly recognizes the importance of intellect to work. Likewise, a U.S. government report on workplace skills needed for the 21st century called for a "new set of competencies" that are predominantly cognitive. These "new" competencies include a foundation of literacy and personal skills, but also such thinking skills as problem solving, reasoning, and decision making—the "true raw materials" from which workplace competency is now built (Secretary's Commission on Achieving Necessary Skills, 1991, pp. vi, 17). More technical analyses also support the view that contemporary jobs can be differentiated according to their cognitive demand. In a factor analysis of jobs in the petrochemical industry, Arvey (1986) found that a "judgment and reasoning" factor accounted for almost half of the common variance in job similarity ratings.[1] This factor, according to Arvey (1986) "corresponds quite well to a general [intelligence] g factor" (p. 418). In another study, Hunter and Hunter (1984) found that the key organizing dimension of diverse jobs was their complexity. These analyses are consistent with the intuitive categories proposed by Reich, and with the hypothesis that both people and jobs can be compared along a similar intelligence axis.

The importance of intelligence to contemporary work is also demonstrated by the power of intelligence, measured as IQ, to predict job performance. It is important to note that the terms *IQ* and *intelligence*, although often used interchangeably, are in fact not identical in meaning. The difference is that IQ is a rough approximation, a convenient stand-in, for the diverse collection of powerful cognitive competencies to which we give the name *intelligence*. Whereas IQ is a test-based metric expressed as a single numeric value, intelligence is the underlying construct that is so complex it may never be understood completely. As a test-based metric, IQ is never a perfect predictor of job performance, and in some cases it is only a mediocre predictor (Wigdor & Green, 1991). However, it is hard to find a better one. Of all personal traits studied, IQ predicts workplace performance best (Schmidt & Hunter, 1998). The predictive power of IQ is strongest when correlations are "corrected" statistically (or disattenuated) for the imprecision of the job performance measure and for restriction of ability range.[2] Over a wide span of occupations, the mean predictive validity (disattenuated) of IQ on job performance is about 0.51 (Schmidt & Hunter, 1998).

The predictive validity of IQ increases as jobs become more complex (Hunter, 1986; Hunter & Hunter, 1984). In one study, the range of disattenuated validity coefficients extended from 0.23 for low-complexity jobs to 0.58 for high-complexity jobs (Gottfredson, 1997; Schmidt & Hunter, 1998). Hunter and Hunter (1984) obtained similar results: Correlations between cognitive tests and job performance ranged from 0.27 to 0.61, with higher validity coefficients associated with more intellectually demanding jobs.[3] These studies suggest that it is possible to order jobs, job families, and job holders along a cognitive dimension defined by information-processing complexity, and that this dimension can account for variation among jobs in their demand qualities, as well as variation among people in job success (Arvey, 1986).

INTELLIGENCE, EDUCATION, AND ECONOMIC REWARD

IQ tests were not originally designed to predict workplace performance. The first intelligence tests, devised about a century ago by the Frenchman Alfred Binet, were constructed for the purpose of predicting success in school. Commissioned by the Paris public school system, Binet invented IQ tests to separate failing students into two groups: those who had the ability to succeed in regular classes and those who were mentally challenged and needed special instruction. IQ proved to be effective in making that distinction, and continues to be a successful, although not perfect, predictor of academic success, correlating about 0.50 with academic achievement (Brody, 1992; Hunt, 1995; Neisser et al., 1996).

Why should IQ have any predictive power at all in forecasting success—career or academic? The answer is that it is not IQ (the number) that is important, although IQ-like tests clearly do function as socially important screening devices, but instead that IQ quantifies a more functionally relevant set of cognitive competencies that make success possible. When intelligence is viewed as a set of competencies, the implication is that intelligence also can be learned. That is, intelligence is not just an *input* to education, but also an *output*, or product, of educational experience (Snow, 1982a). When Binet invented the first IQ test, he saw intelligence as an important input to education in that students who were more intelligent (i.e., had higher IQs) were more likely to succeed. Since Binet's time it has become clear that intelligence is equally a product of education or, more exactly, of all experiences that have educational value. Actually, Binet himself understood this quite well. This view of intelligence—as a product of experience—sharply contrasts with preconceptions of intelligence as invariable and as determined by each person's DNA code.

One potent form of experience in engendering the cognitive competencies associated with intelligence is formal education. Reich (1992) regarded a university-level education as a crucial phase in the development of the symbolic analyst. The investment reaps rewards: College and postbaccalaureate education greatly increase the likelihood of high pay. Moreover, the wage premium that accompanies higher levels of education is growing. In 1979, the average annual pay for a "prime age" (30 to 59) male high school graduate was $37,800, and for the holder of a bachelor's degree, $53,600 (in constant 1996 dollars; Carnevale & Rose, 1998). Just 16 years later, in 1995, the annual earnings of the high school graduate dropped 18% to $31,000, whereas for the college graduate annual earnings rose 10% to $58,700.[4] In other words, during this 16-year period, the wage premium for a college education over a high school education more than doubled, rising from 42% to 89%. Table 1.1 illustrates the association of income with formal education. Representation in the wealthiest quintile rises sharply with education level. The negative slope associated with the poorest quintile tells the reciprocal story. Opportunities for work success drop off steeply with lower levels of education, so much so that by the 1990s "low skill level" could be reasonably interpreted to mean no college experience (Carnevale & Rose, 1998; Hunt, 1995).

In the future, prospects for economic reward are likely to depend even more on the type of work in which one engages. The reason for this, according to Reich (1992), is that the economy has evolved to the point where "the value of new designs and concepts continues to grow relative to the value placed on standard products," and because of this "the demand for symbolic analysts will continue to surge" (p. 225). This trend places some workers at risk. Routine production workers will find themselves increasingly confined to low-wage jobs and vulnerable to replacement by machines. This is the case even now. Robots are displacing workers whose jobs can be reduced to a sequence of movements controlled by machine actuators. And, increasingly, robots can be programmed to produce short runs of customized products demanded by consumers. Thus, despite the economic transition from high-volume manufacturing to low-volume customization, robots threaten to displace workers whose primary skill is the routinized manipulation of materials (Hunt, 1995). Compounding this economic jeopardy, the globalization of commerce means that routine production workers must now compete with workers in developing countries—workers whose costs of living are much lower and who are quite happy to work for a fraction of the American minimum wage (Reich, 1992).

TABLE 1.1
Educational Attainment and Income Quintile
Within the United States:1995

Education Level Attained	Income Quintiles	
	Lowest	Highest
9th to 12th grade (no diploma)	39.9	5.0
High school graduate	19.5	11.9
Some college, no degree	15.6	18.5
Associate degree	11.0	21.4
Bachelor's degree	6.1	39.2
Master's degree	4.2	51.9
Professional degree	3.6	66.3
Doctorate degree	2.2	61.2

Note. Adapted from *Statistical Abstract of the United States* (p. 470; Table 726), by U.S. Department of Commerce, 1997, Washington DC: US. Author. Public Domain.

Although global economic evolution portends a dire future for routine production workers, opportunities for symbolic-analytic workers will continue to expand. Where will this lead? According to Herrnstein and Murray (1994), the divergence of opportunity paths has already produced a two-tiered society, segmented into a "cognitive elite" and a cognitive underclass. The division arises from the compounding prosperity of an insular cognoscenti—Reich's symbolic analysts—and the economic descent of the routine production laborer. Although there is disagreement among economists about the degree and seriousness of the cognitive-economic rift in American society, the fact of increasing social fractionation along economic lines is not disputed.

INTELLIGENCE AND SOCIAL PROBLEMS

In the foregoing paragraphs, I drew a conceptual triangle whose corners are intelligence, education, and economic reward. A fourth concept, already implied, is the vast arena of social problems. Social problems are of course multidimensional, but one especially salient dimension is the perennial inequality associated with race and ethnicity. Inequality is manifest in marked differences between racial/ethnic groups in academic opportunity and attainment, occupational achievement, health, and physical safety. These differences are yoked to income inequalities. Among the wealthiest fifth of Americans, by annual income, White families have two to three times the representation of African American and Hispanic families. At the other end of the economic spectrum the pattern is reversed: African American and Hispanic families have more than double the representation of White families among the poorest fifth (U.S. Department of Commerce, 1997). Although African American families, and to a lesser degree Hispanic families, have gained representation among the wealthy, the median income of White families has been rising even faster (U.S. Department of Commerce, 1997).

Race-based inequalities are manifest in measures of symbolic-analytic attainment (i.e., cognitive test scores), and in experiences that produce symbolic-analytic ability (i.e., formal education). And yet, within groups, the functional associations among cognitive ability, education, and economic reward are comparable: Those who have higher levels of cognitive ability are rewarded economically, regardless of race. This has not always been the case. In the 1960s, the earnings of African American workers who scored high on cognitive tests were only about two thirds that of White workers who obtained comparable scores. But by the mid-1990s, the average income of high-scoring African American workers was at 96% that of Whites (Jencks & Phillips, 1998a, 1998c). If cognitive test scores approximate intellectual readiness for effectiveness in a complex world, then "raising black workers' test scores looks far more important than it did in the 1960s" (Jencks & Phillips, 1998a, p. 46).

Intelligence can purchase economic rewards for individuals, organizations, and nations. It may even help explain social inequalities associated with race. But the importance of intelligence to social outcomes extends further. At issue is survival. The supreme social conundrum, which has been called *the world problematique*, is the tangle of world problems bearing on the survival and safety of all living things, and includes the nightmare of nuclear annihilation and the threat of a poisoned biosphere (Botkin, Elmandjra, & Malitza, 1979). The enormity of world problems has long been recognized; what is new is a reconceptualization of the root cause of those problems and where to look for answers. Until recently, serious world problems have been managed tactically as crises. A conceptual turning-of-the-corner is recorded in the document *No Limits to Learning*, also known as the Club of Rome Report, which presents the crux of the world problematique as essentially a *human* problem (Botkin et al., 1979). To pinpoint the difficulty, it arises from the gap between the increasing complexity of problems faced by humanity and the human capacity to understand and solve those problems. That is, the origin and center of the world problematique is not "out there" in the world, but instead lies within. Its cause and solution are human and, substantially, cognitive. The Club of Rome Report invites the reader to lay aside assumptions about what constitutes a normal course of education, and to trade those in for "an entirely new enterprise" that recognizes the human mind as the key to both averting disaster and building a better world (Botkin et al., 1979, p. xv).

RECONCEPTUALIZING EDUCATION

Both economic rewards and social problems are linked to symbolic-analytic ability, which I identify with intelligence. Intelligence, in turn, is presented as a set of learnable competencies whose cultivation depends on experiences of high quality; that is, experiences that merit the descriptor *educational*. A programmatic implication is that the purpose of education could be recast to include the development of intelligence as a primary goal. By definition and by intention, intelligence could become a conceptual integration point for the purpose and design of all educational experiences and a standard for judging the quality of experience.

For many people, the idea that education could be concerned with the cultivation of intelligence is counterintuitive. Even for many psychologists, the term *intelligence* implies a monolithic and static ability that is genetically preset. Without saying that genetics is irrelevant to intelligence—it is not—there now exists a large body of data showing that experience (i.e., "nurture") plays a powerful role in the development of the intelligent human being. Not only data, but also new theory, especially cognitive information-processing psychology, have recast intelligence as consisting of learnable competencies that can be cultivated through experience. Binet himself saw intelligence as malleable through instruction, and *cultivation* was exactly the metaphor he chose to describe how intelligence could be taught, with the expectation of a rich harvest (Cronbach, 1984).

What is intelligence? As a first approximation, I define intelligence as a repertoire of learnable cognitive competencies that permit effectiveness in a complex, symbol-rich, and problem-oriented world. Of course, intelligence is much more than that. Concise definitions of complex phenomena, although useful as points of departure, necessarily oversimplify. This is the case with intelligence, partly because it is multifaceted, but also because differing theoretical perspectives have been applied to intelligence over the century or so that it has been studied seriously. Although these differing paradigms are often cast as competitors, they are more productively viewed as complements that together present a fuller picture than any single perspective (Sternberg, 1990a). Multiple points of view also permit intelligence to be described in terms that are comprehensive enough to explain interconnections with social outcomes, yet precise enough to say how experience can be designed to favor the inculcation of the intelligence repertoire; that is, to say how intelligence can be cultivated.

NOTES

1. Loading heavily on this factor were the job descriptors: "deals with unexpected situations," "able to learn and recall job-related information," and "able to reason and make judgments."

2. Correction for restriction of range is justified because successful applicants (or "incumbents") display less variation in job performance than would all applicants, if hired. Predictive validity should be descriptive of the entire applicant pool rather than the incumbents only.

3. Some writers have estimated the predictive validity of IQ to be much more modest, approximately 0.2, when variables are not corrected for unreliability or range restriction (Sternberg, 1996b). However, correction for restriction of range is defensible because the utility of IQ measures for personnel selection should be based on the total applicant pool, not the subset of those hired (see note 2). Correction for unreliability is more questionable, but can be seen as important if the objective is to estimate the *theoretical* importance of the aptitude (intelligence) to the criterion (worker success), in contrast with real-world selection based on test scores. Whether corrected for unreliability or not, the moderate correlations imply that factors other than IQ are at work in shaping workplace success (Sternberg, 1996b). Nonetheless, it is likely that each job has an associated requisite mental ability that permits acceptable performance. Above that threshold, other personal qualities contribute to superior performance (Hunt, 1995).

4. A comparable trend is found for female workers. During the same period (1979 to 1995), the wage premium for women with a bachelor's degree over those with a high school diploma rose from 56% to 87%.

Part II

What Is Intelligence?

2

Psychometric Models

The theory of mental measurement is based on the rather audacious idea that innumerable and multifarious differences among people can be compressed onto a single axis, and that people can be ordered along that axis by assigning each a number that has consistency and meaning, and that permits comparisons. This idea can be traced back to the late 19th century, to the laboratory of the Englishman Francis Galton (1869). Galton, a cousin of Charles Darwin, is credited with being the first to propose that intelligence is a unified mental ability, and with providing a methodological foundation for studying intelligence and other individual differences quantitatively (Jensen, 1982). Galton's methodology of quantification spawned the mental testing movement by way of Galton's American student, James McKeen Cattell.

The sort of quantification that interested Galton was of basic physical and psychophysical differences between people, such as head circumference, reaction time, and sensory acuity. Galton was perhaps motivated by the idea that the social stratification of British society was a natural (and Darwinian) consequence of genetic variation that produced corresponding variation in the traits Galton measured. He fully expected to find statistical associations between specific traits that differentiated common Londoners from the Fellows of the Royal Society (Jensen, 1982).[1] Such associations were not found, at least not by Galton, but in the pursuit of his own ideology-driven agenda Galton launched the scientific study of individual differences. His enduring contribution to social inquiry is the quantification of individual differences and methods to associate those differences with real-world external behavior. This has become the foundation for the entire psychometric orientation to the study of the human mind, and for much of social science research.

Galton's measurement of individual differences is one pillar of the psychometric paradigm; the other pillar is the correlation coefficient, a quantification of the degree of association between mental tests, or, for that matter, between any two variables. The correlation coefficient is important to the psychometric study of the mind, partly because it permits tests of hypotheses concerning the legitimacy of general intelligence as a psychological trait. The reasoning is that if general intelligence is *real*, then it ought to extend to performances on a wide range of mental tests, and that contribution ought to be manifest as an array of positive correlations between tests. However, if intelligence is a fiction, then correlations between tests ought to be zero—that is, detecting high ability in one area would be of no utility for predicting high ability in another. It is at this conceptual point that another Englishman, Charles Spearman, raised Galton's methodology to a new level by analyzing correlations between mental tests, thus subjecting the hypothesis of general intelligence to empirical verification.

UNITY AND DIVERSITY

Around the beginning of the 20th century, Spearman (1904) began to accumulate evidence that the existence of general mental ability, implicitly conceptualized as a unified entity, was supported by a preponderance of positive correlations among mental test scores—a pattern called the *positive manifold*. The finding that cognitive tests tended to correlate positively with each other was evidence that a single mental ability was affecting performance, to a greater or lesser degree, on each one. Spearman did not use the word *intelligence* to identify this ability, but preferred the more scientifically precise denotation, *general mental ability*, which he symbolized by *g*. An important construct in intelligence theory, *g* belongs with IQ and *intelligence* as terms that point to the same general phenomenon, but that have differences in exact meaning. The entity *g* is now typically operationalized as a mathematically identified factor, specifically the unrotated first principal component of a collection of diverse cognitive tests (Thompson & Plomin, 1993), or as the highest-order factor in a hierarchical factor analysis (Jensen, 1992b). Empirically, the *g* factor is important because it typically accounts for more than half of the common variance in tests of cognitive ability (Carroll, 1997). It was the demonstration of a positive manifold, combined with the statistical procedure known as *factor analysis* (also invented by Spearman), that demonstrated the statistical unity of *g* and which lent scientific credibility to the ancient intuitive notion of intelligence.

Today, the testing industry has retained the idea that meaningful comparisons can be made between persons on a common scale, whether that scale is intelligence, verbal ability, or some other construct. Because mental test scores tend to follow, approximately, the normal distribution, "standard scores" (including IQ) are usually reported in terms of their position within the normal distribution. More specifically, standard scores report the proficiency of an individual in terms of standard deviations units from the mean. On a standard scale, both the numeric value of the mean and the numeric span of one standard deviation are arbitrary. As shown in Figure 2.1, for example, IQ scores have an assigned mean of 100, and a standard deviation value of about 15. Other cognitive tests differ in the values that are assigned to standard scores, but all are fungible to the language of means and standard deviations.

Not everyone accepted Spearman's proposal that cognitive ability has a statistical and conceptual unity. E. L. Thorndike was an early proponent of the view that cognitive ability was not unified (R. M. Thorndike & Lohman, 1990). L. L.

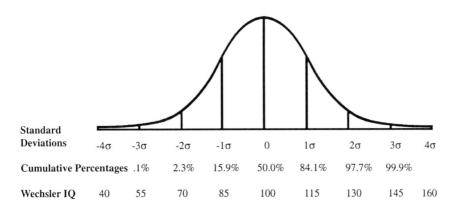

Standard Deviations	-4σ	-3σ	-2σ	-1σ	0	1σ	2σ	3σ	4σ
Cumulative Percentages	.1%	2.3%	15.9%	50.0%	84.1%	97.7%	99.9%		
Wechsler IQ	40	55	70	85	100	115	130	145	160

FIG. 2.1. The normal curve, standard deviations, and IQ equivalents.

Thurstone's (1938) rejection of a general factor was more widely recognized; Thurstone argued that intelligence consisted of a small set of independent primary mental abilities. Like Spearman, Thurstone factor analyzed cognitive tests to investigate the structure of mental abilities but, contrary to Spearman, Thurstone found clusters of independent abilities rather than a unified g. Upon completing a major factor analysis of cognitive tests, Thurstone (1938) concluded, "So far in our work we have not found the general factor of Spearman" (p. vii).

The question of whether intelligence is unitary or multiple has been a point of contention among intellectuals through the centuries. Socrates saw intelligence as basically unitary, whereas Plato and Aristotle saw intelligence as multiple (Snow, 1982a). Benjamin Franklin adopted the former view; Thomas Jefferson the latter. The controversy continues to the present. On the side of a multiplicity of factors is J. P. Guilford. Guilford (1967, 1988), like Thurstone, rejected the proposal of a single overarching g. Guilford's Structure of the Intellect (SOI) organized cognitive abilities into a content X operations X product matrix, rendered pictorially as a cuboid (Figure 2.2). Each small cube within the larger structure represented a separate cognitive ability described by the independent combination of the three dimensions.

The validity of Guilford's theory depended on evidence for the existence of the postulated abilities, and whether those abilities were statistically uncorrelated with each other and therefore truly independent. Guilford was partially successful in finding supportive evidence, but in the end the theoretically elegant SOI was not vindicated. Guilford's theory was criticized from at least two bases. First, Guilford's claim that there is no general mental ability was disputed, partly on the basis of Guilford's own data. Guilford (1964) pointed out that, in his analysis, 17% of intertest correlations were near zero (between -.10 and +.10). However, the claim is actually more damaging to the SOI model than supportive, because the converse

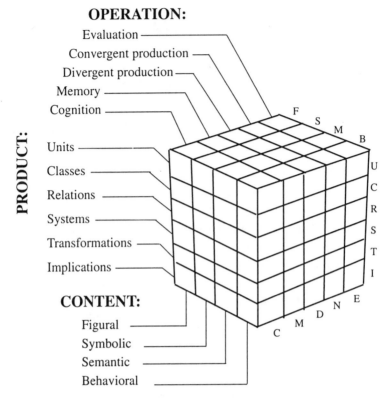

OPERATION:
Evaluation

Convergent production

Divergent production

Memory

Cognition

PRODUCT:

Units

Classes

Relations

Systems

Transformations

Implications

CONTENT:
Figural

Symbolic

Semantic

Behavioral

FIG. 2.2. Structure of the Intellect. From *The Nature of Human Intelligence* (p. 63), by J. P. Guilford, 1967, New York: McGraw-Hill. Copyright 1967 by McGraw-Hill Companies. Reprinted with permission.

is that 83% of the correlations were *moderate* to *high* (Brody, 1992). Apparently, Guilford's data could not escape the "empirical fact" of the positive manifold (Jensen, 1992b, p. 272).[2]

Even more devastating to Guilford's theory was the criticism leveled against his methodology. Guilford used the Procrustean (or Cliff) method of factor analysis (Cliff, 1966, cited in Guilford, 1985). The name of the technique invokes the mythical figure Procrustes who graciously offered his guests lodging, but cut off their legs (or stretched them) if the guests' legs did not fit their beds precisely. Likewise, in the Procrustean method of factor analysis, hypothesized factor loadings are preset by the investigator, and the data are forced to the model and a goodness-of-fit index is computed. Unfortunately for Guilford, Horn and Knapp (1973) used the Procrustean method to test a *random* model and found comparable goodness of fit for the random model and for Guilford's SOI. This strained the credibility of both Procrustean analysis and the Structure of the Intellect model. The Horn and Knapp result may have been pure coincidence; later, other investigators tested a large number of chance-generated models using the same methodology and found that these models generated poor fits to data (Elshout, Van Hemert, & Van Hemert, 1975, cited in Guilford, 1985). But the damage was already done and Guilford's SOI never gained wide acceptance among intelligence theorists. However, the SOI was later modified in a way that is relevant to the evolution of hierarchical models: Guilford (1981, 1985) eventually conceded the existence of second- and third-order hierarchic factors, although not g.

The best known modern version of a multiple view of intelligence is Gardner's (1983) theory of multiple intelligences. Gardner's theory is described and critiqued more fully in chapter 4. For now, I will note that Gardner's theory, like Thurstone's and Guilford's, has contributed substantially to an appreciation of the breadth of abilities underlying intelligent thought and action. Gardner (1983) proposed a theory of independent intelligences that is supported by data from several sources, including the circumscribed effects of some brain injuries. According to some psychometric theorists, however, Gardner's proposal of autonomous cognitive abilities, like Thurstone's and Guilford's, neglects evidence that intelligence has substantial unifying qualities (Brody, 1992; Carroll, 1993; Eysenck, 1998; Messick, 1992).

THE HIERARCHICAL MODEL

Data pointing to the unifying qualities of intelligence eventually led Thurstone to abandon his tenet of independent mental abilities. Analyzing correlations among first-order factors, Thurstone isolated a second-order general factor. In a remarkable recantation of his earlier doctrine, Thurstone concluded that "our findings seem to support Spearman's claim for a general intellective factor" (Thurstone & Thurstone, 1941, p. 26). Eventually, Spearman also moved away from his original position to acknowledge the existence of "group factors" (Carroll, 1996; Spearman & Wynn Jones, 1950). What happens when two opposing theorists each acknowledge that the other has been right all along? Thurstone's isolation of a general factor and Spearman's acknowledgment of group factors in fact led to a productive synthesis of both models; in Cattell's (1987) words, "the Spearman and Thurstone findings were reconcilable; and with mutual illumination" (p. 30). The reconciliation of the ostensibly competing truths of the unity and diversity of mind is accomplished in a single structural model, which is the hierarchical organization of mental abilities. The accommodation of unity and diversity within a single structural model is illustrated in Figure 2.3.

Proposed by such early researchers as Holzinger (Holzinger & Swineford, 1939, cited in Gustafsson, 1999) and Burt (1940), and developed further by Vernon (1950) and Cattell (1971), hierarchical models now dominate psychometric theories of intelligence. They represent something of a consensus about the structural organization of cognitive abilities, with general ability (or abilities) positioned

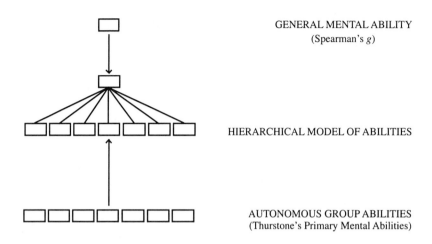

GENERAL MENTAL ABILITY
(Spearman's *g*)

HIERARCHICAL MODEL OF ABILITIES

AUTONOMOUS GROUP ABILITIES
(Thurstone's Primary Mental Abilities)

FIG. 2.3. The hierarchical structure of intelligence, which accomodates properties of unity and diversity.

near the apex of the hierarchy and narrower abilities subtended below (Brody, 1992; Eysenck, 1998; Messick, 1996). Confidence in the basic validity of the hierarchical structure is evident in the words of Gustafsson and Undheim (1996), who claimed that "the empirical evidence in favor of a hierarchical arrangement of abilities is overwhelming" (p. 204).

The case for a hierarchical organization of cognitive abilities was bolstered by Carroll's (1993) massive analysis of more than 460 data sets, some of which were those originally built and analyzed by Spearman and Thurstone. Carroll's unified structural model of cognitive abilities, which derives from this analysis, is shown in Figure 2.4. At the superordinate position is psychometric *G*, which is "conceptually equivalent to Spearman's *g*" (Carroll, 1996, p. 2). Below *G* lie several broad second-stratum factors that include fluid intelligence and crystallized intelligence. Below the second-stratum factors are the narrower first-stratum factors that derive directly from test score intercorrelations. The lines connecting *G* with the second-stratum factors are unequal in length; the line lengths correspond, approximately, to the degree of association between *G* and the second-stratum factors. Note that *G* is most strongly associated with the factor known as fluid intelligence, and secondarily with crystallized intelligence. Fluid and crystallized intelligence are two fundamental, and to some degree complementary, aspects of intelligence. A deeper analysis of this complementarity advances the process of attaching meaning to the grand construct of intelligence, and along with the hierarchical organization of abilities the fluid-crystallized distinction represents a major structural discovery in the psychometric tradition.

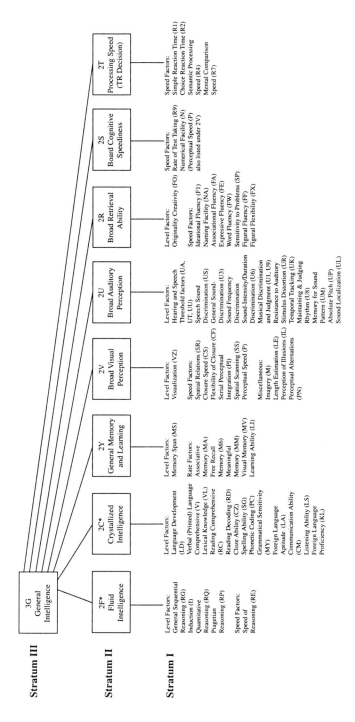

FIG. 2.4. The structure of cognitive abilities. From *Human Cognitive Abilities: A Survey of Factor-Analytic Studies* (p. 626), by J. B. Carroll, 1993. New York: Cambridge University Press. Reprinted with the permission of Cambridge University Press.

If the hierarchical model of cognitive abilities is correct, it becomes clear that IQ is a numerical estimate of the most general of these abilities, those residing near the apex of the hierarchy. It is also clear that IQ cannot be precisely equated to intelligence, nor even to g. Rather, IQ is "simply an effort to attach a number to the complex phenomenon of intelligent behavior," a quantification that is sometimes revealing, sometimes misleading, but "never . . . the phenomenon itself" (Perkins, 1995, p. 32). The idea that intelligence as tested (IQ) and intelligence as demonstrated in real-life situations are related but not identical entities can be traced at least to Hebb (1949), and probably also to Binet, the originator of the intelligence test, who regarded the index of mental age (a precursor to IQ) as a mere convenience. To acknowledge the limitations of IQ is not to deny its importance, for in fact no other psychological concept in intelligence theory is as robust (Perkins, 1995). Indeed, apart from socioeconomic status, few other variables in social science research have as much theoretical, empirical, and historical importance as IQ.

Yet intelligence itself, although partially captured by IQ and by g, remains far less understood than either. Notwithstanding Boring's (1923) operationalist and circular point of departure—that intelligence "is the capacity to do well on an intelligence test" (p. 35)—there is much more to intelligence than is revealed in performance on IQ tests. This point was made forcefully by Gardner (1983), and is accepted by most specialists in the field. Intelligence also transcends the structural relations identified in hierarchical psychometric models. Many theories have been proposed to expand the conceptualization of intelligence beyond the range of the somewhat narrow and artificial (but not valueless) tasks posed on IQ tests. Some of these theories will be considered in chapter 4.

FLUID AND CRYSTALLIZED INTELLIGENCE

Cattell first distinguished between fluid and crystallized intelligence in 1941, and the identities of these two factors was subsequently elaborated by Cattell (1963) and Horn (1968). The distinction between fluid and crystallized intelligence has proven to be one of the more powerful organizing distinctions in intelligence theory. Roughly, it is the difference between intelligence as potential and intelligence as achievement (Hebb, 1949). Fluid intelligence, as a kind of capacity or potential, is most clearly manifest in novel, complex, and challenging environments. Cattell (1987) saw fluid intelligence as the ability of an individual to apprehend "complexity of relationships," and to act on them "when he does not have recourse to answers to such complex issues already stored in memory" (p. 115). In other words, fluid intelligence is that flexible and versatile form of intelligence manifest in situations that call for adaptation in the face of complexity (Larson, 1990). It is not domain bound, but "formless" (Horn, 1967, p. 23), and "directable to almost any problem" (Cattell, 1987, p. 97).

In Carroll's (1993) hierarchical model, fluid intelligence is the second-stratum factor that is closest to general intelligence. The two may even be equivalent (Gustafsson, 1999). According to Gustafsson and Undheim (1996), "the correlation between the second-order Gf [fluid] factor and the third-order G factor is so close to unity that they must be considered identical" (pp. 198-199). Although not all theorists (e.g., Carroll) agree with this conclusion, fluid intelligence and *g* must be considered, at the least, very close cousins. In contrast to fluid intelligence, crystallized intelligence is the ability to acquire knowledge and knowledge possessed. It is intelligence that takes shape or is *crystallized* as a person acquires knowledge (often domain knowledge in verbal form) and integrates that knowledge with information already stored in long-term memory. Whereas fluid intelligence is functionally manifest in novel situations in which prior experience does not provide sufficient direction, crystallized intelligence is the precipitate of prior experience and represents the massive contribution of culture to the intellect.

Fluid and crystallized intelligence are functionally related in that fluid intelligence is often understood to be the raw material for the formation of crystallized intelligence. Cattell's (1987) investment theory describes fluid intelligence as undifferentiated capacity that, when invested through education, experience, and effort, "flow[s] into" organized knowledge in the form of crystallized intelligence (Horn, 1967, p. 23). According to Cattell, "One can think of [fluid intelligence] as describing the power of a *process* and [crystallized intelligence] as being the *product*, resulting from [fluid intelligence] and experience" (p. 297). If crystallized intelligence is a product of experience, then it is modifiable by that experience. Crystallized intelligence depends on "the individual's unique cultural, educational, and environmental experiences" (Benton & Roberts, 1988, p. 142).

Fluid intelligence, by contrast, seems closer to inborn capacity and therefore less subject to modification. Indeed, Cattell's (1987) own view is that fluid ability is largely related to biochemical efficiency in the cortical cell mass, or even a function of the total cortical cell count (Cattell, 1963). A genetically driven biological basis is heavily implied. However, not all theorists agree. Many now believe that fluid intelligence is as much a product of experience as crystallized intelligence. Cronbach (1977), for example, declared that "fluid ability is itself an achievement" that reflects the "residue of indirect learning from varied experience" (p. 287). And according to Horn (1985), "There are good reasons to believe that Gf [fluid intelligence] is learned as much as Gc [crystallized intelligence]" (p. 289). Moreover, heritability values for fluid and crystallized intelligence are approximately equal (Gustafsson & Undheim, 1996; Scarr & Carter-Saltzman, 1982).

CONCLUSION

The fluid/crystallized distinction and the hierarchical structure of abilities begin to define intelligence from the viewpoint of the psychometrician. These are conceptual advances. More fundamentally, psychometric research has established the meaningfulness of intelligence as a psychological construct. But it is the analytical power of another paradigm—information-processing psychology—that begins to unpack the inner workings of intelligence, and presents them in sufficiently precise, process-defined terms such that the deliberate cultivation of intelligence becomes a plausible goal of education. We now turn to this perspective.

NOTES

1. See Scarr (1997) for a contemporary model that links socioeconomic status to genetic variation relevant to intelligence.

2. The percentage of all correlations below +0.10 (including slightly negative correlations) was somewhat higher: 24%. However, both values (17% and 24%) are likely to overestimate the frequency of non-positive correlations among mental tests. The reason for this is that Guilford (1964) himself constructed these tests, and in doing so made a "frank effort to achieve minimal correlations between every pair of tests of two different factors" (p. 402). In other words, the tests were designed to produce the same effect that Guilford was submitting to empirical verification.

3
Information-Processing Models

In the second half of the twentieth century, scientific psychology transformed radically. The fundamental transition was a rejection of Skinner's (1938) behaviorism, and a return to the study of thinking, reasoning, and memory—topics that engaged scholars in the early days of psychological inquiry. In the new cognitive psychology, these processes took theoretical center stage. The most prominent manifestation of the new paradigm is the brand of psychology known as *cognitive information-processing theory.* In this theory, or family of theories, the mind is modeled as an information-processing system that receives information through the senses, and that represents, transforms, stores, communicates, and acts on that information. Informational-processing psychology has led to a different view of intelligence than that gained within the psychometric framework. In particular, information-processing models have "unpacked" the IQ to reveal complexity that is hidden in composite test scores. As a result, intelligence can now be seen more clearly as a collection of competencies that are acquired through experience, rather than as a mysterious latent power.

COGNITIVE ARCHITECTURE

The early information-processing psychologists recognized that human cognition depends on different kinds of memory structures. Two types of memory seemed to have special importance: short-term memory and long-term memory (Atkinson & Shiffrin, 1971). Short-term memory was seen as constrained in capacity to a small number of meaningful units or "chunks" of information (Miller, 1956). Short-term memory was also ephemeral—information that was not actively maintained or "rehearsed" was rapidly forgotten. In short-term memory, new information continuously streamed in as old information exited, either by being filed into long-term memory or by slipping away into oblivion. These parameters—small capacity and short duration—implied that humans have severe limitations in their ability to handle complex information (Simon, 1969).

In more recent years, the conceptualization of short-term memory has evolved considerably. Because short-term memory not only stores information but is also the locus of processing, it is now referred to as *working memory* (Baddeley, 1986, 1992; see Fig. 3.1). The reformulation of short-term memory as working memory acknowledges its function as a mental workspace as well as its capacity to hold different kinds of information in separate stores. In Baddeley's (1986) model, a

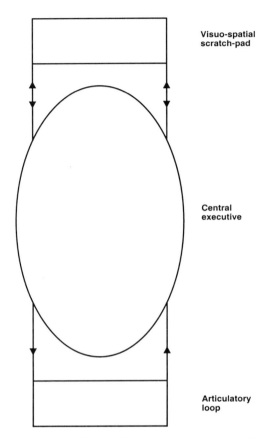

FIG. 3.1. The Baddeley and Hitch working memory model, from *Working Memory* (p. 71), by A. Baddeley, 1986, Oxford: Clarendon Press. Copyright 1986 by Oxford University Press. Reprinted by permission of Oxford University Press.

visuo-spatial "scratch-pad" and an articulatory loop temporarily hold imagery and phonological information, respectively. A modality-free central executive controls attention, reasoning, and learning. There are strong associations between working memory and intelligence. For example, performance on working memory tasks improves as a function of development, mirroring increases in mental age and chronological age (Thorndike, 1984).[1] In adults, individual differences in working memory capacity correlate significantly with IQ (Baddeley, 1986; Kyllonen & Christal, 1990).

Long-term memory is the repository for that vast information stockpile that defines what we know: words, images, strategies, procedures, and innumerable assemblages of knowledge. Long-term memory is the mind's warehouse. Its capacity is, for all practical considerations, unlimited. The duration of long-term memory is probably unlimited except by neural degeneration. Once an idea is recorded in long-term memory it may stay there permanently, although retrieving it may prove difficult. A schematic for the basic cognitive architecture is depicted in Figure 3.2. The top portion of the diagram is Baddeley's working memory model; the bottom portion represents long-term memory. The efficient movement of information between long-term and working memory is vital to intellectual functioning. To move information from volatile working memory to long-term memory produces the trace we call *learning* (or storage). *Remembering* (or retrieval) entails moving information in the opposite direction, from long-term memory back into the consciousness of working memory. Effective cognitive functioning depends on the efficient cooperation of memory storage and symbol processing, and both psychometric theorists (e.g., Carroll, 1993) and cognitive scientists (e.g., Hunt, Frost, & Lunneborg, 1973) have found ties between these memory transfer functions and *g*.

The box symbolizing long-term memory depicts some of its important features. For example, knowledge is stored in idea networks, called *schemas*, that organize past experience and that anticipate and structure current experience (Bartlett, 1932; Marshall, 1995). Knowledge stored in schemas can assume different forms, or representations. In Fig. 3.2, a simple schema is shown for the concept *one third*, which is represented in three ways (Lesh, Post, & Behr, 1987). These are all *declarative* representations that specify knowledge that is essentially factual in nature (Anderson, 1985). Complementing declarative knowledge is *procedural* knowledge, which guides thought in the form of "if-then," or condition-action statements. The triggering of related ideas within schemas has been modeled by the mechanism of spreading activation, in which thinking about one idea causes nearby nodes to become "activated." This means that related nodes, or ideas, become primed in such a way that they require only incremental activation to reach a threshold and enter consciousness or trigger action (Anderson, 1983; Collins & Loftus, 1975).

As noted, knowledge in long-term memory is represented and stored in various forms. In Anderson's (1983, 1996) ACT theory, a general theory of cognition within the information-processing framework, knowledge representation relies on at least two perception-based codes—images and temporal strings—although other perceptual codes (e.g., olfactory, kinesthetic) probably exist (Lohman, 1989). In addition to these perception-based codes, ACT posits an abstract, meaning-based code that dominates long-term memory and that acts as a lingua franca between the lower-level perception-based codes. Memory representations in ACT are therefore hierarchical, with mode-specific representations controlled by higher-order, mode-general representations. This mode-specific–mode-general hierarchy seems to correspond to Baddeley's working memory model of an executive and mode-specific "loops" or "scratch-pads."

A more interesting parallel for intelligence theory is that the general-specific hierarchy of ACT also conforms to psychometric models of cognitive abilities (Lohman, 1989). For example, perception-based representational forms map onto

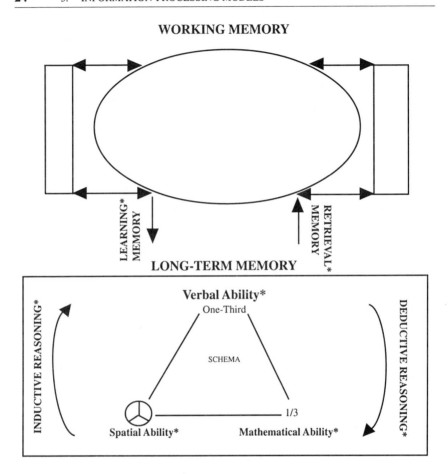

WORKING MEMORY

LEARNING* MEMORY

RETRIEVAL* MEMORY

LONG-TERM MEMORY

INDUCTIVE REASONING*

DEDUCTIVE REASONING*

Verbal Ability*
One-Third

SCHEMA

1/3

Spatial Ability*   Mathematical Ability*

FIG. 3.2. A model of human information processing. Asterisks indicate key parameters indentified through psychometric research. The working memory component is from *Working Memory* (p. 71), by A. Baddeley, 1986, Oxford: Clarendon Press. Copyright 1986 by Clarendon Press. Adapted by permission of Oxford University Press.

factors long recognized by psychometricians. Verbal ability and spatial ability are well-established factors underlying general intelligence; neuroscientists have corroborated their independence and importance by identifying each with a separate neural circuitry (Dehaene, Spelke, Pinel, Stanescu, & Tsivkin, 1999). More recently, Carroll (1993; also, Guilford, 1967) confirmed the importance of numerical representations and their manipulations among psychometric factors. However, mode-specific cognitive abilities alone cannot explain complex performance. Complex cognition, even within a single perceptual form such as mental rotation, draws heavily on *g*. Interpreting these psychometric findings in terms of Anderson's ACT theory, perception-based representations map onto lower-level factors, whereas facility in creating and transforming more abstract representations that transcend specific codes is captured by *g* (Lohman, 1989).

Cognitive information-processing theories such as Anderson's ACT have triumphed over behaviorism and opened the mind's black box. Although Watson (1913) and Skinner (1990) denounced theorizing about mental life as too subjective to be scientific, a new array of research tools and perspectives has permitted entree into the inner workings of mental life. As a result, the nature of intelligence has been illuminated. Cognitive information-processing psychology permits one to pose the question: "What lies behind the positive manifold?" (Perkins, 1995, p. 39). Using such research techniques as the analysis of verbal protocols, eye-tracking data, and reaction times, investigators have disaggregated complex intellectual performances and built process models of cognitive functioning that describe mental events on a second-by-second basis (Newell & Simon, 1972). When a new model is transmuted into a computer program, the resulting "hypothetical robotology" embodies a formal theory of cognition (Hunt, 1995). In their more elaborate forms, such programs are said to exhibit "artificial" intelligence (Laird, Newell, & Rosenbloom, 1987).

ELEMENTARY COGNITIVE PROCESSES

The contrasting theories of Binet and Galton lead to a fundamental question about the nature of intelligence: Is intelligence primarily a reflection of lower-order parameters, such as speed of processing (Galton's view), or of higher-order complex cognition (Binet's view)? Most of intelligence theory has been based on the Binetian conceptualization that intelligence is expressed most clearly as controlled, complex cognition. However, Galton's paradigm is also alive and well. Jensen (1982), Nettlebeck (1987), and many others have found moderate correlations between performance on elementary cognitive tasks and measured IQ. Jensen (1992b) estimated that reaction time measures taken from different elementary cognitive tasks yield a multiple correlation with psychometric *g* somewhere between -0.50 and -0.70. These correlations (typically "disattenuated" for restriction of ability range) have led theorists to reexamine the association of intelligence with more basic processing.

Individual differences in reaction time have been recognized since at least the early 1800s (Jensen, 1982). Psychological tasks and equipment have been developed to measure individual differences in reaction time to within a tiny fraction of a second. In a *simple* reaction time task, a subject lifts a finger from a button when a light turns on, and the elapsed time is recorded. A *choice* reaction time task involves the same basic procedure, but involves additional lights that add informational complexity. In the 1950s, a relationship was discovered connecting reaction time and complexity. This relationship, formulated in Hick's (1952) Law, is that choice reaction time is a linear function of informational complexity in bits (base 2 logarithm) of the number of alternatives. Later, Roth (1964, cited by Jensen,

1982) discovered that people differed in the slope of this function, and that the individual reaction time slope was negatively related to IQ. Absolute reaction times also correlate negatively with IQ.

Other manifestations of elementary cognitive tasks have similar relationships with psychometric intelligence. For example, inspection time tasks require a subject to make a judgment about simple stimuli after a brief exposure. The most common inspection time (IT) task involves a brief glimpse (less than 120ms) at two vertical lines that differ slightly in length (about one degree of visual angle), and a judgment as to which is longer. Other IT tasks involve brief exposure to simple stimuli of different sorts, such as pairs of tones that differ in pitch, or pairs of vibrating keys placed under fingertips and activated in variable order (Nettlebeck, 1987). These tasks are likely to tap somewhat different processing mechanisms than those called on in the simple and choice reaction time tasks. For inspection time tasks, disattenuated correlations with g are approximately -0.50, although Nettlebeck (1987) reported lower median correlations, between -0.30 and -0.40. Actual correlations may be even lower. In one study, investigators recruited a representative sample of the population, ensuring a broad cognitive ability distribution and removing the justification for disattenuating correlations (Crawford, Deary, Allan, & Gustafsson, 1998). They found rather modest associations between inspection time and intelligence (uncorrected r = -0.28 for full scale WAIS-R IQ, and r = -0.30 for the Performance (fluid) scale). Of greater theoretical interest is that the same investigators found that IT measures correlated more strongly with the group factor Perceptual Organization (which was orthogonal to g) than to g itself.

The standard interpretation of correlations between g and elementary cognitive tasks is that psychometric g is at least partly explained by mental efficiency parameters that reside at a basic, even neuronal level (Deary & Stough, 1997). The real explanation, however, may be more complicated. Although there are often substantial correlations between g and simple cognitive tasks, even stronger correlations can be found between g and within-person *standard deviations* of reaction times (Jensen, 1992b). In a study by Larson and Saccuzzo (1989), the disattenuated correlation between reaction time and g was -0.16, but the disattenuated correlation between g and the intra-individual standard deviation of reaction times was -0.46. As Jensen (1992b) recognized, whatever mechanism is responsible for variation in the standard deviations may also play a role in producing variation in the reaction times. One possibility is that this variation reflects individual differences in random "noise" or errors of transmission in the nervous system. However, a "higher-order" explanation is also possible, which is that both reaction times and their standard deviations are related to the consistent application of attention over time. Self-regulatory abilities involving the sustained focus of attention may contribute to higher test scores as well as to more consistent reaction times. If this is the case, intermittent lapses in attentional control would contribute to variation in the standard deviation of reaction times and to slower average reaction times. Reaction time per se, aggregated over many trials, would then be epiphenomenal to the more substantive connection between cognitive self-regulation and *g*.

Task complexity is another consideration. As elementary tasks become more complex, correlations between *g* and reaction time increase (Jensen, 1992b). Therefore, it is not so much pure speed that explains *g*, but speed in the face of a significant information load. Generalizing from their own data, Larson and Saccuzzo (1989) inferred that the general cognitive characteristics underlying intelligence must include (a) the ability to demonstrate consistency in cognitive performance, and (b) the ability to handle a high information load—that is, complexity—effectively. Stated differently, intelligence depends on focused attention that spans both time and informational complexity. "Intelligent individuals," Larson and Saccuzzo concluded, "can more flexibly and consistently reconfigure the 'contents of consciousness'" (1989, p. 23). This interpretation is theoretically quite distant from that of Jensen, who interpreted chronometric data as reflecting parameters of neural efficiency rather than self-regulation.

COGNITIVE ANALYSIS OF PSYCHOMETRIC TASKS

In a synthesis of research bridging information-processing theory and psychometric theory, Pellegrino and Glaser (1979) distinguished between cognitive correlates and cognitive components research. *Cognitive correlates* research entails quantifying performance on "paradigmatic" tasks of the psychology laboratory. The resulting estimates of information-processing efficiency are then related to psychometric measures of cognitive ability, such as IQ.

In research that is prototypical of the cognitive correlates approach, Hunt and his colleagues related the efficiency of access to semantic memory to scores on tests of verbal ability (Hunt et al., 1973). The investigators measured the efficiency of semantic access by using the name identity/physical identity (NIPI) task, in which letter pairs are presented on a screen. Letters pairs can be the "same" in either physical identity (e.g., AA) or name identity (Aa), or they can be different (e.g., AB). Respondents simply indicate "same" or "different" without making finer distinctions. Not surprisingly, physical identity matches are fast and easy, whereas name identity matches take longer. The parameter of interest is the difference in reaction time between name matches (Aa) and identity matches (AA). This difference is thought to reflect the efficiency of semantic access because retrieving a letter's name cannot be made on the basis of perceptual characteristics alone. Hunt found that the efficiency of semantic access was related to aggregate scores of verbal ability, suggesting that verbal ability consists at least partly in the efficiency of semantic access.[2] The larger significance is that a global psychometric variable (verbal ability) was linked empirically to a specific, and presumably constituent, cognitive process (semantic access).

Whereas the cognitive correlates approach led to connections between parameters of cognition and global task performance, the objective of *cognitive components* research is to isolate and measure stages of information processing that compose performance on psychometric test items. The rationale for this method is that aggregate performance on test items is an expression of how well the constituent cognitive components can be assembled into a coordinated strategy, and a function of the efficiency of the individual components (Sternberg, 1977, 1980). In this approach, performance on a test item is broken down into individual information processes, called *components*, and efficiency parameters for those components are estimated for each person.

One way of isolating cognitive components is the subtractive methodology. This involves presenting several versions of a problem by systematically removing segments from the whole task. For analogy items, such as those taking the form A:B::C:D, item fragments such as A:B::C:, A:B::, or A alone, are "precued" to the subject, and then followed by the remainder of the item. A response latency is measured from the time all item elements are presented to the time the subject responds. This time represents the processing of item elements *not* presented in the precued item fragment. By comparing response times for partial and complete items, it is possible to estimate the efficiency of the constituent components. Efficiency parameters for individual components can then be compared statistically to global performance on psychometric tests. These comparisons sometimes show that individual differences in global performance can be explained by variation in certain key components, and that individuals differ in their facility with those components. Like cognitive correlates research, studies of cognitive components have contributed to the idea that global performance on tests of cognitive ability is not impenetrable, but can be explained by the proficient exercise and coordination of more molecular processes.

Other research on psychometric tasks has explored the role of cognitive self-regulation and goal management on performance. Some of this research has been directed toward understanding performance on Raven's Progressive Matrices, which is probably the single best measure of fluid intelligence (Snow, Kyllonen, & Marshalek, 1984). In Raven's Matrices, an incomplete pattern of shapes is displayed on a 2 x 2 or 3 x 3 grid (see Fig. 3.3 for an example). The examinee studies the pattern on the grid, infers rules describing the pattern, and then selects from among eight options the element that best completes the grid. Because Raven's Matrices is a prototypical test of fluid intelligence, and because fluid intelligence is close to the essence of general intelligence, an analysis of performance on Raven's provides a window to understanding *g*.

Cognitive analyses of Raven's Progressive Matrices have shown that variation in performance can be accounted for largely in terms of subjects' ability to manage complex goal structures (Carpenter, Just, & Shell, 1990). Embretson's (1995) hybrid cognitive-psychometric methodology likewise identified the importance of general control processing to Raven performance. Complex goal structures

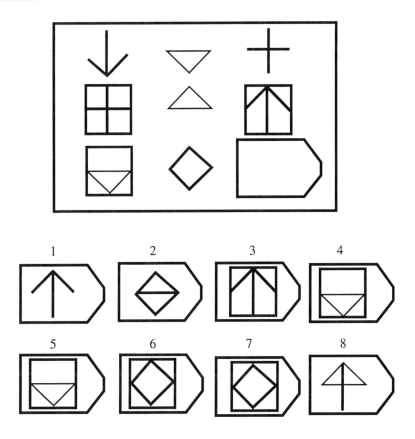

FIG. 3.3. A problem similar to those in Raven Advanced Progressive Matrices. (The correct answer is 5.) From "What One Intelligence Test Measures," by P. A. Carpenter, M. A. Just, & P. Shell, 1990, Psychological Review, 97, p. 407, Figure 2. Copyright 1990 by the American Psychological Association. Reprinted with permission.

must be managed within the processing constraints imposed by the cognitive system. These constraints include the amount of complexity that the thinker can tolerate at any one time, which in turn is a function of working memory capacity (Halford, 1993; Larson & Saccuzzo, 1989). Some of the more complex Raven items place "a formidable information-processing burden on short-term memory" (Hunt, 1995, p. 101). This working memory bottleneck was identified years earlier by Bereiter and Scardamalia (1979), who found that 86.5% of the variance on Raven item difficulty could be accounted for by an item's M-demand, a construct strongly related to working memory load.[3] The strong tie between performance on Raven's Matrices and the ability to manage demanding goal structures reflects a more general relationship between fluid intelligence and working memory capacity.[4]

THE INTELLIGENCE REPERTOIRE

Cognitive research has shown that intelligence is not a monolithic and hopelessly mysterious entity, but instead is a collection of information-processing functions that underlie the molar factors identified in the psychometric paradigm (Anderson, 1996; Carroll, 1976; Jacobs & Vandeventer, 1972; Resnick, 1976; Thorndike, 1984; Whimbey, 1975). The global trait of intelligence can be understood as "simply the collection of cognitive skills [a] person possesses" (Hunt, 1986, p. 105)—that is, a learned repertoire (Ackerman, 1996). The constituents of that repertoire are information-processing functions that can be identified and measured, as well as compared statistically to more global measures of cognitive ability.

The intelligence repertoire does not consist of a single kind of cognitive function, such as knowledge or skill or the ability to learn. It is, rather, a richly diverse mixture. Snow (1986, p. 136) described the repertoire as a "very large bank of cognitive processing components and chunks of organized knowledge from which samples are drawn. . . . The bits and pieces of the bank can be described as S-R bonds, information processing components, schemata, plans, learning sets, generalization tendencies, knowledge systems in semantic networks, productions in production systems, or all of these" (p. 136). These diverse competencies are placed under a common rubric, *intelligence*, because they have wide applicability and are differentially held and used in any population. Stated differently, for functions to be considered part of the intelligence repertoire, they should possess qualities of generality across situations and variability across persons (Ohlsson, 1998). This opens the possibility that there are cognitive functions that meet these criteria but have not yet been recognized. Not only cognitive functions, but certain affective and conative (i.e., motivational and volitional) characteristics might meet these criteria and thus constitute "broad sense" intelligence.

Speculations that intelligence might consist of a cognitive repertoire actually trace back to the early part of the 20th century. Thomson (1916), a psychometrician, recognized that a collection of independent cognitive skills could give the impression that general mental ability is functionally monolithic. To prove his point, Thomson demonstrated statistically that properties of unity among tests of mental ability (i.e., Spearman's g) need not be attributed to a single monolithic ability, but could instead result from each test *sampling* from a larger set of differentiated abilities (or functions, components, etc.). In the latter case, observed positive correlations among tests (i.e., the positive manifold) would reflect overlap in the cognitive functions sampled by tests. Like Thomson, Humphreys (1989) spoke of intelligence as a repertoire whose most important functions lie closest to the centroid—that is, closest to psychometric g.

Snow (1980a; Snow & Lohman, 1984) elaborated the Thomson/Humphreys hypothesis, demonstrating that differences in intelligence consist not only in what functions are available to an individual, but also in how those functions are selected, ordered, and reordered if necessary in the course of performance. Thus, individual differences are manifest not only at the *construct* level, as they are in psychometric theory, but also at the level of *components* and *strategy* within the information-processing framework. Individual differences in strategy can be rather global. Spatial tasks, for example, may be mediated by the generation and transformation of mental imagery, but they can also be mediated linguistically (Cooper, 1982). Even though there may be important differences between people in global strategy, intelligence performance is also mediated by within-person differences in strategy shifting and learning from item to item (Snow & Lohman, 1989). Snow's research led to the view that intelligence consists not only in the possession of constituent functions, but also the ability to sample, assemble, reassemble, and control information-processing components (Snow, 1992).

The monitoring and control of one's own thinking is variously referred to as *metacognitive* or *executive control* (Brown, 1978; Flavell, 1979). Executive control refers to the conscious deployment and evaluation of cognitive competencies. Executive functions establish goals, select and order relevant knowledge, and track progress toward goals, switching strategies as needed. Metacognition is a related concept that refers to the awareness that permits such control. Sternberg's (1985a) componential subtheory of intelligence identifies metacomponents as information processes that select and control other components, as well as monitor their effects. Many other investigators have likewise proposed that self-regulatory aspects of cognition are close to the essence of intelligent thought (Belmont, Butterfield, & Ferretti, 1982; Campione, Brown, & Ferrara, 1982; Snow, 1992).

Executive or metacognitive functions lend a hierarchical structure to information-processing models. In Sternberg's model, metacognitive ability stands at the apex of the information-processing pyramid, directing lower-level and more specific components. The hierarchical ordering of information-processing functions establishes a rough congruence with hierarchical psychometric models. Both acknowledge a differentiation of functioning between higher-level aspects of intelligence, which have an executive role and cross-situation generality, and lower-level aspects, which are used locally and are responsive to situational demands. It is sensible, therefore, that the cognitive functions described by the terms *executive* or *metacognitive* have been identified with individual differences corresponding to psychometric *g* (Sternberg & Gardner, 1982).

CONCLUSION

Having contrasted the psychometric and cognitive frameworks for understanding human intelligence, it is tempting to ask: Which is correct? The answer is *both,* but for different reasons. The structure-oriented psychometric approach defines the landscape of cognitive abilities. The process-oriented cognitive perspective elucidates mechanisms—the time-dense mental operations that manipulate, store, and retrieve information—that are responsible for intelligent thought and action. The two perspectives triangulate on their common subject. An understanding of intelligence requires a macro view of structural properties provided by psychometric theory alongside the micro-level unpacking of mechanisms made possible by information-processing theory. These two paradigms are dominant and foundational; however, even their union does not exhaust the meaning of intelligence. Other, "emergent" models—some conjectural, some dependable— can push our understanding of intelligence to still higher levels.

NOTES

1. It is not completely clear why working memory performance improves as a function of development. It may result from increases in memory capacity that reflect brain maturation, but it might also reflect the gradual accumulation of mnemonic strategies or greater familiarity and organization of relevant knowledge (Chi, 1978).

2. However, Hogaboam and Pellegrino (1978) failed to replicate this finding. Lohman (1994) argued that weak or inconsistent results in this research paradigm may reflect misconceptualizations about the relationship between individual slope parameters (e.g., reaction time regressed onto item demand features such as angle of mental rotation) and aggregate performance. According to Lohman, most individual variation in total scores will not be accounted for by the regression slope, but instead by differences in the vertical height of the regression line as indexed by the intercept. Whereas differences in the intercept help explain variation in performance between persons (the traditional variable of interest in psychometrics), slope differences help account for the much smaller variation in the person x item interaction (the "error" term). Lohman's critique goes further to suggest how cognitive psychology and psychometrics can interact profitably and avoid dead-end research paths.

3. Guinagh (1971) found that digit span (a proxy for working memory) mediated the trainability of performance on Raven's Matrices. Among African American children with a low digit span, training in Raven concepts produced no gains, but Raven performance improved dramatically among African American children with a high digit span.

4. Correlations between g and working memory capacity increase as processing load increases. For example, the correlation between backward digit span and IQ is higher than that of forward digit span and IQ, and can account for more than twice as much IQ variance (Jensen, 1992b; Jensen & Figueroa, 1975).

4

Emergent Models

The information-processing perspective transformed intelligence theory because it led to a more molecular view of intelligent functioning than was possible within the psychometrician's theoretical framework. Information-processing psychology helped researchers identify the cognitive elements of intelligent functioning and describe their operations and interactions. Yet, to many investigators, the reconceptualization of intelligence did not go far enough. It still seemed to have a narrow quality, partly because it was often aimed at explaining those information-processing competencies that facilitate success on tests of cognitive ability—hardly ends in themselves. The parochial quality of the psychometric paradigm was largely inherited by cognitivists because they, too, restricted the phenomena of interest to a rather narrow range of tasks and contexts (Cattell, 1987).

For cognitivists, the initial concentration on psychometric tests was defensible because it connected their efforts to the instruments that for nearly a century had been the basis of serious theoretical and empirical work on intelligence. Tests had become (and still are) the most accepted way of operationalizing intelligence and its quantification as IQ. Also, cognitive tests *do* predict real-world attainments with moderate success, even though considerable residual variance remains unexplained. The variance in valued outcomes not absorbed by psychometric tests hints that mechanisms other than those captured by IQ tests are at work, and some of these might legitimately be considered aspects of broad-sense intelligence. In the language of this book, the intelligence repertoire is larger than that evoked by IQ tests or quantified in IQ scores.

In response to limitations in the range of phenomena studied in the psychometric and cognitive paradigms, other approaches to intelligence have emerged. These approaches have led to a greater appreciation of an expanded range of functions constituting intelligence, the range of performances recognized as intelligent, and the relevance of context and culture. New research methods, including brain imaging, also contribute to a more complete understanding of intelligence. A sampling of these emerging perspectives is reviewed in this chapter.

GARDNER'S THEORY OF MULTIPLE INTELLIGENCES

The best-known contemporary model of independent abilities is Gardner's (1983) theory of multiple intelligences. Gardner proposed the existence of eight "relatively autonomous" intelligences: linguistic, logical-mathematical, spatial, musical, bodily-kinesthetic, interpersonal, intrapersonal, and naturalist (Gardner, 1983, p. 203; Gardner, Kornhaber, & Wake, 1996). A brief description of each of the intelligences is presented in Table 4.1. In addition to these, Gardner (1997) left open the possibility of additional intelligences, such as an "existential" intelligence identified by deep concern with and insight into questions of meaning and existence. In proposing separate intelligences, Gardner rejected the idea of a unifocal g that cuts across disparate forms of cognitive functioning. This conceptualization of intelligence is "Thurstonian" in orientation, although not in methodology. Multiple intelligences (MI) theory can be seen as a modern-day version of the independent factor theories of E. L. Thorndike and Thurstone in the early 1900s, but is based on a different set of epistemological tools.

In a considerable break from past epistemologies used to understand intelligence, Gardner conjoined methods and findings from several disciplines to construct a theory that has broadened traditional accounts of what constitutes intelligence. Gardner drew from many data sources, but primary among these is the neurological phenomenon of selective impairment. In brain-injured patients, cognitive impairments are sometimes circumscribed such that other cognitive abilities retain normal functioning. For example, a brain injury might disrupt musical competence but leave logical, language, and other functions unharmed; if so, Gardner would take this as evidence for the neurological independence of musical intelligence. The selective impairment methodology assumes that intelligences can be mapped onto different regions of the cerebral cortex, and in fact Gardner found some evidence for the anatomical separability of intelligences (Gardner & Hatch, 1989).

Another stream of evidence for MI theory is the variety of adult roles and, especially, the expert end-states valued by cultures. A poet, for example, is the apotheosis of linguistic intelligence; a sculptor displays a honed form of spatial intelligence. The existence of cross-cultural differences in the relative valuation of intelligences is yet another line of evidence for Gardner's distinctions. For example, Gladwin's (1970) study of sea navigation in Micronesia demonstrated how a focused ability (spatial) can be indispensable to achievements of high prestige within a culture. The master navigators of the Puluwat atoll can steer an outrigger sailing canoe over hundreds of miles of open ocean. To do this, they rely on a system of celestial navigation of their own invention, and pass on the secret knowledge of sea navigation only to those young men who are invited into the guild.

Two peculiar kinds of expertise are the conspicuous talents of prodigies and idiots savants. To Gardner, the existence of children who develop impressive levels of musical talent precociously is evidence for the independence of musical intelligence. Among idiots savants, functioning is uniformly *sub*normal except in the focal area of talent. For example, some idiots savants (or autistic savants or simply savants), having heard a complex musical piece only once, may be able to reproduce it flawlessly on a piano (Sloboda, Hermelin, & O'Connor, 1985). Yet,

Table 4.1
The Eight Intelligences

Intelligence	End-States	Core Components
Logical-mathematical	Scientist, mathematician	Sensitivity to, and capacity to discern, logical or numerical patterns; ability to handle long chains of reasoning
Linguistic	Poet, journalist	Sensitivity to the sounds, rhythms, and meanings of words; sensitivity to the different functions of language
Musical	Composer, violinist	Abilities to produce and appreciate rhythm, pitch, and timbre; appreciation of forms of musical expressiveness
Spatial	Navigator, sculptor	Capacities to perceive the visual-spatial world accurately and to perform transformations of one's initial perceptions
Bodily-kinesthetic	Dancer, athlete	Abilities to control one's body movements and to handle objects skillfully
Interpersonal	Therapist, salesperson	Capacities to discern and respond appropriately to the moods, temperaments, motivations and desires of other people
Intrapersonal	Person with detailed, accurate self-knowledge	Access to one's own feelings and the ability to discriminate among them and draw on them to guide behavior; knowledge of one's own strengths, weaknesses, desires, and intelligences
Naturalist	Botanist, geologist, archaeologist	The ability to distinguish among, classify, and use features of natural and artificial environments

Note. From "Multiple Intelligences Go to School: Educational Implications of the Theory of Multiple Intelligences," by H. Gardner and T. Hatch, 1989, *Educational Researcher, 18*(8), p. 6. Copyright 1989 by the American Educational Research Association; reproduced with permission from the publisher. The description and end-states for the last-listed intelligence, naturalist, are taken from the Project SUMIT website (http://pzweb.harvard.edu/SUMIT/MISUMIT.HTM) and Gardner ,1997.

the savant is no genius—typically, his or her "expertise" is inflexible and unoriginal.[1] Nonetheless, the stunning prominence of a single ability against a field of general impairment was seen by Gardner as evidence for the independence of its referent intelligence.

As further evidence for independent intelligences, Gardner cited the module-based development of symbol systems used to represent and communicate ideas. For musical and linguistic intelligence, these symbol systems are obvious: musical notation and written language. Logical-mathematical intelligence is supported notationally by an elaborate system of symbols, equations, and operations. Other intelligences have lesser-known symbol systems or none at all, but according to Gardner the generation of a supportive symbol system is only a tendency, not a requirement.

Gardner's theory of multiple intelligences is significant methodologically and theoretically because it reaches beyond the parochiality of much psychometric and cognitive research on intelligence. Cattell (1987), in a frank commentary on his own methodology, admitted that psychometrically defined intelligence has been "systematically biased" and "sadly uninformed by imaginative safaris into new areas" (p. 128). Gardner's theory goes a long way toward remedying this bias. MI theory also has practical implications. Schooling and Western culture generally are strongly skewed toward certain kinds of intellectual expression, especially linguistic and logical-mathematical intelligence. Other aspects of intelligence are neglected or ignored, possibly squandering talent. To the degree that educational systems can recognize and develop the full range of abilities represented by diverse intelligences, individuals—indeed, all of society—will benefit.

Yet is MI Theory really so different from what psychometrically oriented researchers proposed long ago? Psychometric theorists have long acknowledged that g cannot tell the whole story of intelligence, and that subordinate group factors certainly exist (Boring, 1923). These factors might be sensibly described as "relatively independent," because their degree of covariation is moderate (but real). In fact, at least three of Gardner's intelligences—logical-mathematical, linguistic, and spatial—can easily be mapped onto the psychometric hierarchical model because these three identify major group factors that have been recognized since the time of Thurstone.[2] Even interpersonal intelligence and musical intelligence have identifiable counterparts in the psychometric tradition. According to Eysenck (1998), "It is difficult to understand what Gardner is saying that is not covered by the orthodox hierarchical model" (p. 109).

As Eysenck implied, Gardner was justified in highlighting group factors, because a theory of g alone could never be a complete theory of intelligence (however, cf. Jensen, 1998). What Eysenck's comment missed is that Gardner made the much bolder claim that general intelligence is not warranted as a scientific construct. On Gardner's proposal—that multiple intelligences are both autonomous and sufficient—research spanning decades speaks to the contrary. Hundreds of data sets have revealed substantial covariation among logical, linguistic, and spatial abilities. Gardner's own data are mixed on the question of autonomy. Although one study showed a modest degree of statistical independence among intelligences, another study revealed substantial intercorrelation (Gardner & Hatch, 1989). In Project START, Callahan and colleagues conducted a factor analysis of four MI-based scales, finding support for the validity of logical-mathematical and linguistic scales, limited support for a spatial scale, but no support for an independent interpersonal intelligence (Callahan, Tomlinson, Moon, Tomchin, & Plucker, 1995). In a more direct test of MI theory using confirmatory factor analysis, Callahan et al. found that the data conformed better to a hierarchical model than to an MI model of uncorrelated latent variables.[3]

Does *g* exist? On this question, some of the data cited by Gardner actually support an affirmative answer. Whereas most of Gardner's intelligences can be identified with specific areas of the brain, logical-mathematical ability is anatomically diffuse, spread over a large region of the cortex. Logical-mathematical ability seems to correspond functionally to the general mental ability factor identified by psychometric researchers, and its anatomical diffusion may reinforce claims for its functional generality (Gustafsson & Undheim, 1996; Messick, 1992). Gardner himself acknowledged uncertainty about the independent status of logical-mathematical ability, owning that it might be "some kind of supra- or more general intelligence" (Gardner, 1983, p. 159). His more recent description of logical mathematical intelligence as the ability to appreciate and use abstractions made the comparison with general mental ability even more direct (Gardner et al., 1996).

According to Messick's (1992) critique of MI theory, Gardner used psychometric evidence selectively in highlighting data that support the existence of separable intelligences, but downplaying evidence for their common variation. Gardner suggested that common variance among mental ability tests, which is evidence for *g*, is an artifact of tests' reliance on "skill in taking short-answer, paper-and-pencil tests" (Gardner et al., 1996, p. 213). However, this proposal seems weak. First, it does not explain relations exhibited within hierarchies both horizontally (similar abilities cluster) and vertically (higher factors involve more general functions related to abstraction, complexity, and the induction of pattern). Second, it is not intuitively compelling that a century's worth of predictive associations between IQ and educational, job, and social outcomes can be chalked up to individual differences in test savvy. Third, it is simply not true that tests of cognitive ability are always confounded with paper-and-pencil administration—many of the better-known intelligence test batteries involve performance or spoken responses by examinees. The weight of evidence for a hierarchical organization of abilities far outweighs the evidence for autonomous abilities proposed in MI theory. The convergence toward a hierarchical model with *g* at the pinnacle, and with primary abilities serving to "define" *g* (Cattell, 1987), is all the more plausible because it arose from different theoretical starting points (e.g., Spearman's and Thurstone's). To Messick (1992), "The invoking of autonomous mental modules as opposed to a hierarchical structure of abilities would appear to be simply counterfactual" (p. 371).

On this point, Gardner himself has equivocated. When addressing the issue of *autonomous* intelligences, Gardner (Gardner, Kornhaber, & Wake, 1996, p. 203) employed the hedge "relatively," leaving the reader unsure of what he meant. "Relatively autonomous" might well describe group factors in the hierarchical model—their intercorrelations are, after all, only moderate. But perhaps the issue was not really crucial for Gardner. Indeed, it seems that Gardner was less concerned with being a good Thurstonian with regard to the emptiness of *g* than with emphasizing the breadth of cognition and performances that can be called intelligent, and with recognizing that intelligent thought and behavior are profoundly embedded within cultures. On these counts, Gardner succeeded.

Despite these criticisms, Gardner's theory is a vital contribution to intelligence theory in many respects. Undoubtedly, MI theory has been good for education by emphasizing that students differ in important ways, and that those differences are relevant to instructional decisions. Equally important, Gardner challenged, with intellectual integrity and healthy consequence, the orthodoxy of the psychometric "establishment," whose adherents will, at times, candidly acknowledge the parochialism of their own framework and methodology (Anastasi, 1986). Gardner's expansion of constructs and research methods are major contributions to the study of human intelligence.

STERNBERG'S THEORY OF SUCCESSFUL INTELLIGENCE

Sternberg's (1996c) theory of successful intelligence posits the existence of three aspects of intelligence that operate jointly to produce success. In this theory, success is defined with respect to an individual's own standards and the sociocultural context. The theory is meant to expand traditional conceptualizations of intelligence by recognizing that individuals vary in many ways—not just in their IQ scores—that are relevant to personal success. The theory of successful intelligence recognizes *analytical* intelligence as the set of abilities associated with success in academic environments, and in solving abstract problems. Analytical intelligence therefore connects Sternberg's theory with traditional accounts of intelligence that correspond to proficiencies tapped by IQ tests.

Two other forms of intelligence, creative and practical, enlarge the meaning of intelligence and its power to account for diverse manifestations of success, as well as the corresponding diversity of human characteristics responsible for success. Practical and creative intelligence also have weaker statistical associations with SES and racial/ethnic background than does analytical intelligence (Sternberg, 1998c). *Creative* intelligence entails skills and attitudes that enable a person to transcend the existing order to produce something new and culturally significant.

According to Sternberg (1999), creative intelligence is manifest in problem situations that are relatively novel, especially those that require a person to escape the entrenchment of scripted ways of thinking and acting. Measures of creative intelligence correlate only weakly with analytic ability and, unlike analytical ability, creative intelligence does not appear to have much general or cross-domain utility, but rather is domain specific. This finding differs from much of the research literature in which creativity is simplistically presented as an expression of creative personality characteristics. True creativity depends on the accessibility of richly interconnected knowledge in the domain of creative work (Ochse, 1990; Simonton, 1996).

Finally, *practical* intelligence refers to competencies that produce success in real-life situations, such as in the home or on the job. It is manifest in a person's ability to adapt to, select, and shape real-world environments. As Sternberg operationalized practical intelligence, it often takes the form of tacit knowledge that is acquired incidentally through experience, rather than taught directly. This tacit knowledge might include unspoken rules or skills necessary for success, such as how to move up in an organization, how to gain favor, or how to shield oneself from the crossfire of office politics—hence, it has high adaptive value. There is evidence that people differ dependably in their propensity to pick up tacit knowledge of this kind in everyday settings. There is also evidence that the measures of practical intelligence, such as one designed for corporate managers, have low statistical associations with analytical intelligence but predict success in the workplace more readily than do conventional tests of intelligence.

Sternberg's constructs of creative and practical intelligence, although welcome expansions of broad-sense intelligence, are somewhat lacking in clarity and defensibility. One potential problem is that the strong domain dependence of creativity makes it difficult to see how creative intelligence conforms to any reasonable sense of *intelligence*, because the word *intelligence* implies something more general. Also, creative intelligence is described by Sternberg as being best measured by performance on tasks that are "relatively novel" (Sternberg, 1999). However, creativity seems less a reflection of task characteristics than of the responses to a task. Raven's Matrices are novel for many examinees, and yet it is difficult to interpret successful performance on the Raven as creative. On the other hand, a person might be presented with a very conventional task, such as washing dishes, and invent a highly creative solution to it. The key dimension would seem to be the nonentrenchment of the *solution*, not of the task itself. Finally, the strong association of tacit knowledge with practical intelligence seems puzzling. Competent performance in any realm—analytical, creative, or practical—might be supported by knowledge that is acquired incidentally and held in tacit form. For example, it is easy to see the metacomponents that steer analytical intelligence as largely tacit.

Sternberg saw the three forms of successful intelligence—analytical, creative, and practical—as being subserved by their own information-processing components. The idea of components was elaborated in Sternberg's triarchic theory of intelligence (1985a), a theory that predates the theory of successful intelligence and is now subsumed by it. In developing the *componential* subtheory, Sternberg's ideas and research techniques helped shape inchoate processing theories of intelligence, partly by introducing analytic methods into a domain that had long been dominated by psychometric methods (see chap. 3). According to the componential subtheory, intelligent thought can be broken down into constituent processes that Sternberg called *components*. A component is a basic information process—a one-step transformation of information that requires a processing time on the order of seconds or fractions of a second. Reading a single word, for example, could constitute a component. The subtheory specifies that performance on even a single test item is psychologically complex, and that an analytic understanding of that performance can be gained from subdividing aggregate performance into steps.[4]

The *contextual* subtheory recognizes that what is called intelligent thought and behavior depends on the particular cultural context, a point that cultural psychologists have pressed for decades. The idea is that a person thinks and acts intelligently when behavior is adaptive or has survival value within a particular setting. Also, intelligence is not passive adaptation to the demands of that context, but can involve the selection and shaping of environments in "a process of reciprocal transformation with the environment" (Ochse, 1990, p. 216). Contextual intelligence includes tacit knowledge about the unwritten rules of success in a particular environment.

In the *experiential* subtheory, Sternberg proposed that intelligence is exercised most clearly in two seemingly opposite situations. The first is novelty, which requires adaptation through problem solving and insight (cf. Larson, 1990). This proposal is closely linked to the theory of fluid intelligence, which also recognizes effective functioning in the face of novelty as a sign of intelligence. At the other end of the experiential continuum, intelligence is also exercised when a person employs skills adeptly in familiar situations with little conscious effort. Sternberg (1985a) explained that "complex tasks can feasibly be executed only because many of the operations involved in their performance have been automatized. Failure to automatize such operations, whether fully or in part, results in a breakdown of information processing and hence less intelligent performance" (p. 71). It is therefore at the poles of the experiential continuum—extreme novelty and extreme familiarity—that intelligence is most clearly observable. The pole corresponding to familiar situations is satisfied by knowledge, skills, and schemas that have been automated. The novel end of the continuum depends more heavily on executive processes. Viewed another way, the subtheory recognizes the hierarchical arrangement of cognitive processes, and the complementarity of higher- and lower-level elements. The subtheory is *experiential* in that what is considered novel or familiar depends on the experiential history of the person.

Sternberg's theory of intelligence has evolved considerably over time, and there has been a major shift in emphasis from his earlier triarchic theory (componential, experiential, and contextual) to his more recent and more inclusive theory of successful intelligence (analytical, creative, and practical). The newer theory subsumes the older. For the reader of Sternberg's books and papers, it is sometimes hard to see how these various constructs relate to each other. Sternberg is now clear that he has only one theory of intelligence, the theory of successful intelligence. It is also fairly clear that all aspects of successful intelligence are subtended by cognitive components as modeled in the componential subtheory. Sternberg has had less to say, however, about the status of the contextual and experiential subtheories. One has the impression that they point to important aspects of human intelligence, and seem to map onto creative intelligence (task novelty) and practical intelligence (tacit knowledge, environment selection and shaping); but these earlier subtheories have receded to the theoretical wings, whereas other, presumably more explanatory aspects (i.e., creative and practical intelligence), have moved to center stage.

CONTEXTUALIZED INTELLIGENCE

The idea of contextualized intelligence gives due recognition to specific situational knowledge, whose importance has often been ignored in traditional theoretical accounts. Contextual theories reject the historical and everyday meaning of intelligence as cognitive capability that cuts across a wide swath of diverse situations. A generalized version of the context argument is that what is considered intelligent behavior depends on the particular culture within which thought and action occur. In non-Western countries, for example, people are sometimes more likely to classify common objects by function (e.g., knife goes with orange) rather than by taxonomic category (e.g., knife goes with fork), opposite to what a typical Western person would do. Glick's (1975) famous observation is pertinent here. Glick studied the performance of a Liberian Kpelle tribesman on a sorting task. Twenty items were laid out on the floor—five items each of food, clothing, tools, and cooking utensils—and subjects were asked to sort the items in a way that made sense to them (Cole, Gay, Glick, & Sharp, 1971). Glick (1975) recounted:

> When the subject had finished sorting, what was present were ten categories composed of two items each—related to each other in a functional, not a categorical manner. Thus, a knife might have been placed with an orange, a potato with a hoe, and so on. When asked, the subject would rationalize the choice with such comments as, "The knife goes with orange because it cuts it." When questioned further, the subject would often volunteer that a wise man would do it this way. When an exasperated experimenter asked finally, "How would a fool do it," he was given back sorts of the type that were initially expected—four neat piles with foods in one, tools in another, and so on. (pp. 635-636)

This anecdote makes the point vividly: What is considered rational behavior can differ radically across cultures (Glick, 1975). Important questions follow. How legitimate are inferences drawn from measures of cognitive ability when they are used in cultures that do not share the experimenter's assumptions on what constitutes intelligent thought and behavior, and on which tests are scored? What is the relative adaptive value of competencies in one culture with respect to another?

Working with children from rural Kenya, Sternberg (1998c; Sternberg et al., in press) investigated the relationships between tacit knowledge of local herbal medicine, measures of vocabulary in English and Dholuo (the language spoken in the children's homes), academic achievement, and fluid intelligence (using Raven's Matrices). Perhaps surprisingly, traditional knowledge of herbal medicine was found to correlate *negatively* with English vocabulary, even after controlling for children's age and SES. Traditional knowledge also correlated negatively, but not significantly, with both Raven's scores and mathematics achievement. Negative correlations between cognitive tests are rare; they are also theoretically important because they violate the assumption that a general factor applies to all such tests. One way of accounting for these findings is to see them as the result of trade-offs in the investment of finite time, and therefore acquired knowledge, associated with one culture (local) versus another (Western). If the degree of Western enculturation can be approximated as a unidimensional variable, it follows that the acquisition of local knowledge would compete with both a Western-style education and English vocabulary.

Larger patterns of cognitive competence that presumably constitute g may vary in importance from culture to culture. General cognitive functions may have more meaning in a complex technological society than in a "traditional" one. Anastasi (1986) thought it unlikely, for example, that societies lacking formal systems of education would exhibit the "widely generalizable cognitive skills" (p. 20) that are detectable through such techniques as factor analysis. Thus, not only does the *meaning* of intelligence vary across cultures, but possibly also its *meaningfulness*. Moreover, the meaning and meaningfulness of intelligence can change over time within a culture, and in individual people within cultures.

To say that culture is important is not to deny inborn predispositions to process information in particular ways. Fodor's (1985) modularity theory is based on evidence that low-level processing of sensory input, such as vision, is largely "hard wired." This is likely to be advantageous for the newborn who otherwise would have to bootstrap cognitive development from a tabula rasa. However, modularity theories are unlikely to explain the remarkable flexibility and creativity of the human cognitive system, which are better accounted for by the openness and receptivity of the mind to experience and therefore to culture (Karmiloff-Smith, 1992). Mind and cognition are profoundly cultural (Berry, 1974; Ceci, 1996). Cognitive anthropologists have pushed the argument further by saying that the mind can be properly understood only as the *interaction* of its neurological substrate (the brain) with the symbolic patterns that infuse all cultures. Intelligence, like cognition, is " 'cultured' all the way down" (Shore, 1996, p. 5). The degree to which the elements of the repertoire are common to cultures or are culturally distinct is open to investigation; some functions may have value across cultures and contexts, and may endure over time. Although it must be acknowledged that intelligence is rooted in culture and context, this does not preclude the possibility that within cultures, and even across cultures, some cognitive functions will have considerable breadth of applicability.

BIOLOGICAL THEORIES

By the reckoning of some neuroscientists, and perhaps by common sense, any complete theory of intelligence must eventually be reconciled with the brain sciences. In recent decades, there has been growing interest in linking intelligence to measures of brain functioning, or in exploring what Eysenck (1982) called the "new look" in intelligence measurement. Theories that probe the biological correlates of intelligence have assumed a variety of forms. In one class of explanations, g is viewed as a manifestation of individual differences in the "neural efficiency," expressed as nerve conduction velocity (Cattell, 1987). In apparent support of this claim, mild associations (r = approx. 0.45) have been found between IQ and the speed of signal transmission in the nerves of the arm and the hand (Vernon & Mori, 1992).

Associations between IQ and brain waves, recorded by an electroencephalographic (EEG) device, have also been found. EEG measures, in particular the wave form identified as P300, have yielded modest correlations with IQ. The P300 is an evoked potential recorded 300ms to 900ms after the presentation of a stimulus, such as a flash of light. Higher-IQ subjects tend to have larger, faster, and more complex P300s than do lower-IQ subjects, although these associations are not found consistently (Eysenck, 1998; Sternberg, 1994b). Another avenue of research is the identification of specific genes associated with high cognitive ability—genes that presumably give rise to individual differences at the level of neurons (Chorney et al., 1998).

Research on the linkages between cognition and the brain has gained precision through brain-imaging technologies. Functional MRI and PET scans allow researchers to chart associations between cognitive processing and brain physiology by mapping cerebral blood flow patterns and glucose metabolism. Imaging technologies have shown, for example, that mathematical calculation and estimation activate different brain circuits: Calculation activates areas associated with language, whereas estimation stimulates brain activity in areas responsible for spatial representation (Dehaene, Spelke, Pinel, Stanescu, & Tsivkin, 1999). In another imaging study, Haier and colleagues (1988) used a radioactive glucose analog to determine which brain regions were most active while subjects solved problems on Raven's Advanced Progressive Matrices. PET scans showed that brain activity was distributed throughout the cortex, but that posterior regions of the brain (the parietal and occipital regions) were especially active. Even more interesting was the relationship between glucose metabolic rates and Raven performance. In particular, *higher* Raven scores were associated with *lower* rates of glucose utilization in the brain areas responsible for performance. High-performing subjects seemed to be more metabolically efficient. In studies such as these, empirically derived mind-brain connections help anchor information-processing models to brain physiology.

Still, caution is needed. It is easy to draw unwarranted inferences from brain research to conclusions about human learning. Perhaps the most serious conceptual error is to see neurological mechanisms as driving all cognitive activity. This view ignores causation in the other direction—from cognition to changes in neuronal structure and function (Sternberg, 1994b). Mind and brain reciprocate. The brain's "wetware" affords a physical and electrochemical substrate for the mind's dynamic patterning of symbols, or what Perkins (1995) called "mindware" (Shore, 1996). Consciously controlled strategic thinking might be more sensibly viewed as propagating *downward* to more elementary information processing, and from there to brain function, than seen as moving strictly upward from cells to strategy (Hunt, 1986). In an arguably revisionist rejection of reductive physicalism or "microdeterminism," Sperry (1995) proposed that cognitive science might be seen as a flag carrier for other sciences. Complex systems—whether the human mind or the path of a molecule in a rolling wheel—often exhibit behavior in which causal control is tenably described as being both top-down and bottom-up.

A top-down interpretation is reinforced by data showing that neurological structure is "sculpted" by experience (Nelson, 1999). At least two mechanisms are responsible for this environment-to-brain effect. In experience-*expectant* development, the experiences that are typical of a species stimulate the overproduction (or blooming) of neurons, and guide their selective elimination (or pruning; Greenough & Black, 1992). In contrast, experience-*dependent* development describes idiosyncratic changes in synaptic structure within the individual organism. The first process occurs early in life (in humans, up to adolescence) and defines normal brain structure; the second is functional through most of the life span and differentiates one organism from the next, reflecting the uniqueness of individual experience (Cotman & Neeper, 1996). In infrahuman species, enriched environments have been associated with greater numbers of synapses, increased vascularization, and enhanced glial cell support in brain regions corresponding to the environmental enrichment. Rapid and profuse dendritic branching as a function of enriched experience has even been observed in adult and "middle-age" rats at nearly the level observed in youngsters.

Brain plasticity appears to be mediated by a class of molecules known as *neurotrophins*. Neurotrophins, such as nerve growth factors, can induce the proliferation of neurons and increased brain vascularization. As organisms age, neurotrophin levels tend to drop precipitously, but this is not inevitable. Neurotrophin levels rise in response to cognitive stimulation and physical exercise (Cotman & Neeper, 1996). Neurotrophins (NTFs) may also be responsible for the strengthening of neural pathways as a function of use. This process is illustrated in Figure 4.1. Panel A shows, in sequence, that the stimulation of a neuron can induce the production of neurotrophins, which are then sensed by the originating and adjacent neurons. The entire neural pathway is strengthened as a result. Panel B shows the larger context, namely that the organism's behavior, including learning and exercise, can stimulate the production of "plasticity factors," such as neurotrophins. The positive effects of neurotrophins on the system can lead to a second and more robust feedback loop in which the strengthened behavior induces the release of additional neurotrophins, leading to further neuronal enhancement.

Wachs (1996) saw the contrast between experience-expectant and experience-dependent development as helping to explain Scarr's (1992) contention that nonextreme or species-normal environmental variation is functionally equivalent, and therefore has little impact on normal development. Minimally sufficient

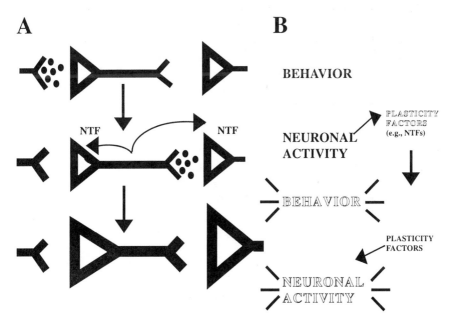

FIG. 4.1 Effects of growth factors: (A) Release of neurotrophic factors (NTFs) following neural stimulation, leading to enhanced neural growth and function; (B) Repetition of behavior leading to the release of additional plasticity factors and further strengthening of the neural pathways. From "Activity-Dependent Plasticity and The Aging Brain," by C. W. Cotman & S. Neeper, in *Handbook of the Biology of Aging* (4th Ed.) (p. 293) edited by E. L. Schneider and J. W. Rowe, 1996. Orlando, FL: Academic Press. Copyright by Academic Press, Inc. Reprinted with permission.

environmental support might well permit normal development of the experience-expectant type. However, *optimal* development may depend on experiences that are *not* typical of the species. Human cultures excel in inventing atypical experiences (Simon, 1969). Even within the range of human experience called "normal," there is tremendous variation in the type and degree of environmental enrichment; this variation, including experiences that are species-atypical, may produce important variation among people. High levels of talent development, for example, certainly depend on atypical experiences (Bloom, 1985).

Aside from unwarranted assumptions about the direction of causal control between mind and brain, brain research is often misconstrued when it is applied prematurely to educational problems. The aura of science surrounding brain research is attractive, and it is tempting to co-opt that glow for the realm of education. Unfortunately, scientific findings are often grossly overextended in the process. One notorious example involves the lateralization of brain function. Lateralization research has relied heavily on epileptic subjects whose corpus callosum, the major interhemispheric pathway, has been severed. Research on these subjects led to a fascinating discovery: The functions of the left and right hemispheres correspond, roughly, to linguistic versus spatial processing, and to analytical versus holistic processing (Reuter-Lorenz & Miller, 1998). But here, the application of science has run far ahead of the science itself. The tendency has been to spin off, prematurely, "theories" of learner types in which students are classified as right-brained or left-brained, and then to tailor instruction to accommodate those dubious distinctions. Other examples of the misapplication of neuroscience to education were documented by Bruer (1997). The tendency to misapply does not reduce the importance of neuroscience to an understanding of cognition, intelligence, and education. It is a reminder to be cautious, however, because in the past neuroscience research has been overextrapolated and distorted. Bruer (1997) appreciated that neuroscience *can* be bridged to education, but observed that the connecting bridge is usually made more sturdy if it is mediated by the interposed "island" of cognitive science.

THINKING DISPOSITIONS

Intelligent performance consists not only in the possession of important cognitive functions, but also in the propensity to use them. Tendencies to approach intellectual tasks in certain adaptive ways have been called *thinking dispositions.* They are, in essence, habits of mind that merge cognitive abilities with motivational and volitional tendencies. Conceptually, dispositions are similar to cognitive styles because they refer not to maximal capabilities, but instead to the optimal regulation of thought (Messick, 1994, 1996). Dispositions tend not to be recognized as readily as cognitive abilities, but have a quiet presence in all intellectual activity.

Some theorists have described global kinds of cognitive dispositions. Langer's (1997) construct of *mindfulness* represents a general awareness and critical engagement, and the ability to withhold an impulsive action or judgment (cf. Salomon & Globerson, 1987). Langer contrasted mindfulness with an endemic, uncritical mind*less*ness so often observed in everyday situations. Baron (1985) advanced a theory that explains lapses in rational thinking not as expressing an inability to think, but instead as reflecting insufficient *search*—that is, insufficient internal deliberation about the problem at hand. Baron argued that good thinking (or cognitive search) involves the generation of goals, possible actions to satisfy those goals (or ideas concerning what is possibly true), and evidence bearing on those possibilities. He presented evidence showing that, for most people and for much of the time, search is terminated prematurely.[5] The disposition to engage in cognitive search has a developmental aspect. As children mature, they tend to shift from a (prematurely) self-terminating strategy to one that is more nearly exhaustive. Of course, exhaustive search is not always warranted. Baron acknowledged it is possible to think *too* much about a problem—another kind of irrationality—but contended that human thinking is overwhelmingly biased toward *too little* search. Baron argued that if education were geared to develop the disposition to engage in more search, people would think and act more intelligently and find greater success in attaining valued goals, and so lead more satisfying lives.

A finer-grained theory of thinking dispositions was elaborated by Perkins, Jay, and Tishman (1993). Their taxonomy of dispositions includes: to clarify and seek understanding, to be planful and strategic, and to be intellectually careful. According to this theory, dispositions entail not only specific cognitive functions, such as the ability to seek clarity, but also conditions of use. Thus, the ability to *detect* fuzzy thinking should trigger the disposition to seek clarity. Paul (1993) advanced a functionally similar list of intellectual virtues, which includes a sense of justice, perseverance, integrity, humility, empathy, courage, confidence, and autonomy as these are expressed in the realm of thinking. It seems likely that such qualities of thought are facilitative not only on IQ test performance, but in making real-life decisions and taking actions that are "eco-logically" intelligent (Shore, 1996, p. 4). These descriptors imply that intelligence should be understood not just as the possession of certain knowledge or skill, but also as a more general pattern of intellectual life. It is perhaps in this sense that Anastasi (1986, p. 19) referred to intelligence as "a quality of behavior," and that Baron (1987) compared the teaching of intelligence to character education.

EMOTIONAL INTELLIGENCE

Theories of cognitive dispositions touch on a larger point: Many researchers now believe that to fully account for intelligent performance it is necessary to attend to emotional, motivational, and volitional aspects of thought. There is evidence, for example, that positive mood can enhance certain kinds of cognitive performance (Nantais & Schellenberg, 1999), and that anxiety can lead to performance decrements (Meichenbaum, 1972). It is therefore reasonable to view "broad-sense" intelligence as embracing emotional and motivational elements, rather than as a cool rationality devoid of feeling or desire (Snow, Corno, & Jackson, 1996; Sternberg, 1990b).[6]

Some writers have proposed that the ability to understand and control one's own emotional state is relevant to success and failure outcomes in many different contexts. The idea of a distinct *emotional intelligence*, entailing the ability to understand one's emotions and to use that information to guide thinking and action, was suggested as early as Thurstone (1924), formulated more precisely by Salovey and Mayer (1989-90), and popularized by Goleman (1995). It is easy to accept the importance of emotional controls in intelligent thought; of course, to say that these constitute an independent intelligence is a far stronger claim. Some commentators believe it is unwarranted. Eysenck (1998) maintained that the voluminous research literature on personality already addresses many of the claims associated with emotional intelligence. However, Mayer, Caruso, and Salovey (1999) presented evidence that emotional intelligence is factorially coherent and that it consists of definable competencies that develop with age and experience. On this basis, they argued that emotional intelligence meets the standards of a bona fide intelligence.

Questions about the legitimacy of emotional intelligence raises the larger question of how broad "broad-sense" intelligence should be. Most who have an opinion on the subject believe that intelligence has been conceptualized too narrowly in the past (Neisser, 1976). This does not mean that any adaptive behavior constitutes a separate and legitimate intelligence—yet, many speak and write as if that were true (e.g., note book titles touting the importance of "career intelligence," "competitive intelligence," and "sensual intelligence"!). Broadening what is meant by intelligence is a good idea, but an unbridled and fatuous proliferation of "intelligences" undermines whatever scientific gains have accrued over decades, and results in what Eysenck (1998, p. 109) called a "fundamental absurdity."

Research on emotional intelligence redresses an area of neglect. "Hot" cognitions, those involving emotions and intentions, have been paid short shrift in intelligence research. Perhaps the dismissal of emotion and related human characteristics as acausal epiphenomena stems from an intrinsic limitation of the cognitivist metaphor, the digital computer. Bruner (1990), one of the early cognitivists, lamented the dehumanizing consequences of taking the computer metaphor too seriously:

> With the mind equated to [a computer] program, . . . there could be no place for "mind" in such a system—"mind" in the sense of intentional states like believing, desiring, intending, grasping a meaning. . . . How could a belief, desire, or attitude be the *cause* of anything in the physical world? . . . So action based on belief, desire, and moral commitment . . . is now regarded as something to be eschewed by right-minded cognitive scientists. (pp. 8-9)

To recognize the importance of dispositions, personality characteristics, motivational tendencies, cognitive styles, and so on, is to acknowledge that intelligent thought and action cannot be accounted for solely in terms of "cool" cognitions.

DISTRIBUTED INTELLIGENCE

Intelligent functioning is "not the solo dance of a naked brain" (Perkins, 1995, p. 323), but instead employs numerous physical, social, and symbolic supports. Increasingly, psychologists have appreciated the importance of social and technological supports to intelligent thought and action (Bower, 1995; Salomon, 1993). Inventions of culture can amplify intelligence. Thought and action occur in a world that is "thick with invented artifacts" (Pea, 1993, p. 48), which not only amplify intelligence, but also embody and express intelligence in their own right. Some artifacts indirectly constitute the cognitive operations of inventors on users (Pea, 1993). Every learner is engulfed in a cultural surround that channels intelligence, simultaneously abetting and constraining its expression.

Elements of the external world constitute distributed intelligence when they can be linked meaningfully to the cognitive system of the user, and the user becomes more capable as a result. Digital computers and communications devices, sensor-effector technologies, and miniaturization are salient examples of capability-boosting technologies (Hunt, 1995). A less flashy information technology, radio, also has qualities that shape cognition, and is likely to have played an important role in transforming some preindustrial cultures to ones that are information rich and technology dense. Some low-tech inventions have had even more profound cognitive consequences. The invention of written text, in particular, forever changed human cognition (Ong, 1982). In contrast to the spoken word, the written word provides a stability to language that permits dissection and extended critique. Because the reader and writer are often physically and temporally distant, the writer is forced to be explicit to a degree that is not necessary and perhaps even counterproductive in everyday discourse.

Just as the invention of writing amplified the effectiveness of cultural transmission exponentially, the printing press added further potency to the accumulation of knowledge over generations, and introduced massive changes in thought forms. Printed text supported a form of discourse that had no historical precedent, namely the form of expository prose that is in reality an extended argument, and that assumes rational exposition from beginning to end. Extended formal discourse was foundational to the development of modern science and democracy. According to Olson (1976), "The use of extended prose statements which are logically independent is a technique of relatively recent origin—a technique that was closely, though not exclusively tied to the invention of printing. . . . Knowledge was an extended logical essay—an assertion examined and re-examined to determine all of its implications in a single coherent text" (pp. 195, 197). The existence of the printing press meant that complex and extended arguments could be set down in relatively permanent form to be pored over, tested, critiqued, and debated by people removed from the author in space and time. Its effects did not stop there. Extended discourse also paved the way for its intramental analog, the elaborate and nuanced schema of the expert.

Newer electronic technologies may be producing similar effects. Electronic communication has forged high-speed and almost uninterrupted person-person and person-knowledge connectivity. Communication via the internet combines the interactivity of speech and the reflectivity associated with writing and print, and may have unprecedented effects in molding the cognition of subsequent generations (Warshauer, 1999). Also, the parallels between hypermedia webs and long-term memory are striking: Each contains an enormous corpus of information in multiple representational forms, which is content addressable through direct indexing (rather than serial access), fully cross-linked and, within domains, partially hierarchically organized. The line dividing mind and information technologies is blurring.

Intelligent performance is strongly associated with the availability of performance-amplifying technologies and the ability to use those technologies adeptly (Salomon, 1993). Although the technology-cognition alliance has always existed, its strength is growing. It is becoming clearer that thinking about intelligence as independent of the surrounding culture, and especially the "prosthetics" afforded by that culture, is a mistake. Societal changes occasioned by the advent of microcomputers are perhaps the clearest examples of the new fusion, but the braiding of human and machine capabilities promises to become much more intimate in the future. Information-processing devices are not only becoming smaller and more interconnected, they are also being fitted as "wearable" technologies, just as wristwatches made timepieces wearable decades ago. Intercommunication between wearable technologies can be accomplished by special fibers woven into clothes or by skin conduction. Prototypes of "heads-up" video displays on eyeglasses and a computer carried in a belt already exist (Pentland, 1998). Technologies are also going subdermal. The familiar cases of pacemakers and cochlear implants are now being joined by such latecomers such as retinal implants and muscle actuators (Dunn, 1998). In one recent demonstration, researchers at Emory University developed a brain implant that permitted a paralyzed user to control a computer cursor simply by *thinking*. Technologies bridging humans and machines are often pursued with religious zeal (Noble, 1997). According to the president of Advanced Bionics, "We are going to make the blind see and the lame walk" (Dunn, 1998, p. 28). Such inventions are at once fascinating and frightening because in their logical extrapolation materializes the fantastic image of the man-machine cyborg.

Problems of social equity arise when there is unequal access to technologies that have qualities of cognitive amplification. Print, of course, has long divided societies into the literate and the nonliterate. Hunt (1995) declared that, in the age of information processing, "the aristocracy of this age will be the people who can solve new problems using the new technology" (p. 231). The new technologies are probably complicit in the bifurcation of society into the cognitive elite and all others. Paisley (1987) anticipated this when he noted: Future environments for applying literacy will provide extraordinary access to information, but only for those who understand the process of information seeking. They will provide extraordinary ability to generate and manage information. . . . In time, those who cannot apply literacy in such environments will not be regarded as literate" (p. 5). The segmentation of the world into the cognitive elite and those whose work will consist of routine performance will likely be determined, in part, by a person's access to and readiness to use amplifying technologies effectively.

EXPERTISE, GENIUS, AND CREATIVITY

Expertise and genius constitute highly valued end-states of effectiveness. The transition from novice to expert involves the expansion and extension of ability with a simultaneous contraction of domain focus. Expertise is, by definition, focused in particular domains, but this does not mean that there are no general characteristics of experts or similar paths followed in the development of expert knowledge and skill. Research has revealed such patterns in the cognitive and experiential history of experts across a wide range of creative expression. For example, expert performance requires an enormous body of domain knowledge (Larkin, McDermott, Simon, & Simon, 1980). Simon (1980) noted: "[One] thing that research on cognitive skills has taught us in recent years is that there is no such thing as expertness without knowledge—extensive and accessible knowledge" (p. 82). How much knowledge? Simon estimated that expertise in any field requires a mental fund of approximately 50,000 pieces of meaningful information (i.e., about 50,000 chunks) that can be quickly accessed and deployed. Building a knowledge base this size requires a huge investment of time. As Simon (1991) observed: 'The level of a world-class expert is never achieved with less than 10 years of intensive, round-the-clock effort" (p. 36). To rise to the level of world-class performance in any field seems to require a sustained commitment over a period of at least a decade.

There are also strategic differences between novices and experts in how knowledge is organized and used. Novices rely much more on general problem solving processes, whereas experts tend to use domain-specific heuristics (Hunt, 1995). Expert knowledge is also more compactly organized into chunks or automated procedures that can be retrieved or activated with little burden to working memory. The resulting reduction in working memory load may permit higher-order strategic or creative cognition. Ochse (1990, p. 242; Jensen, 1992b) observed that the "employment of well-established routines frees attention from basic procedures to focus on the unusual or unique aspects of complex tasks."

Finally, there are regularities in the path toward expertise. In fields as diverse as chess, wrestling, figure skating, and musical performance, aspiring experts tend to adopt a regimen of disciplined study that Ericsson (1996) called *deliberate practice*. Deliberate practice consists of activities designed specifically to improve performance, activities that may or may not be intrinsically enjoyable (Ericsson, 1996; Starkes, Deakin, Allard, Hodges, & Hayes, 1996). In the evolution of the world-class performer, deliberate practice, sustained over years, is a better predictor of expertise than are hints of initial talent (Ericsson, Krampe, & Tesch-Römer, 1993; but see Winner, 1996). A deliberate practice regimen requires the capacity to focus one's interest and efforts, and to structure time daily. The regimen typically consists of about 3 or 4 hours of concentrated practice per day, broken into blocks of about 90 minutes, and engaged in habitually (Ericsson, Krampe, & Tesch-Römer, 1993). Over many years, the practice routine can build a huge base of knowledge and skills, but does so in a manner that avoids exhaustion.

Cumulative engagement in deliberate practice not only distinguishes between novice and expert status, but also between degrees of expertise (Ericsson, Krampe, & Tesch-Römer, 1993). Among elite violinists, for example, skill level is strongly predicted by the number of hours of deliberate practice accumulated over years. Displays of precocious talent are also identified with sustained and intense practice regimens (Bloom, 1985). Regularity and intensity of deliberate practice may ultimately be explained by motivational and self-regulatory abilities that sustain the drive to practice for hours each day, year after year (Ericsson, Krampe, & Tesch-Römer, 1993). The impressive association between accumulated deliberate practice and attained level of expertise seems to demystify elite performance, and calls into question commonsensical notion of native talent. According to Ericsson (1996), deliberate practice has so much explanatory power that it leaves "little room for the influences of innate fixed capacities" (p. 30). Even child prodigies, by some observations, display scant evidence of exceptional promise before the initiation of a serious practice regimen (Bloom, 1985; Ericsson, 1996). Indeed, the widespread adoption of Suzuki violin instruction can make thousands of normal Japanese children seem like musical prodigies (Winner, 1996).

However, the hypothesis of innate talent has not been completely discarded. Asserting the reality of innate talent, Winner (1996) found that child prodigies in artistic drawing displayed not only obsessional interest and engagement in picture drawing—what she termed a "rage to master"—but also produced superior drawings even at early stages of involvement.[7] Similar patterns have been detected in other pursuits, such as chess and guitar playing: Precocity seems to be linked to unusual interest and drive, but also, at least in some cases, to hints of talent that preexist the establishment of a practice regimen. If Winner is correct, then deliberate practice, although presenting a parsimonious explanation for the development of expertise, and one that is hopeful for education and human potential, does not furnish a complete account.[8] Other objections can be raised against the cumulative practice hypothesis. It is possible, for example, that people with high ability (i.e., more talent) find it sensible and rewarding to engage in intense, sustained practice, whereas those who lack talent recognize the fact and either give up serious pursuit or reduce their level of commitment (Sternberg, 1996a).

What about genius? For centuries, explanations for creative genius have mainly taken the form of myth and superstition (*genius* is partly derived from the Latin word for "tutelary spirit" or "genie"). The tendency to ascribe individual differences in intelligence to inborn and unchangeable factors is doubly strong when it comes to explaining great creative minds. There is general agreement that high IQ does not equate to genius, for genius is demonstrated only in its product, namely, a profound contribution to human culture (*genius* is also traceable to the Latin for "generate"; Simonton, 1984). Some children may therefore be properly called prodigies, but never geniuses. Likewise, intellectual daring may be a component of creativity, but authentic creativity goes much deeper and, like genius, is more defensibly moored to the criterion of a revolutionary cultural product (Mumford & Gustafson, 1988; Ochse, 1990).

Like expertise, the even more rarefied phenomenon of genius has been the subject of serious study and speculation. Simonton (1996), for example, attempted to demystify genius, just as Ericsson did expertise. According to Simonton, the chances of producing a great work are a direct function of the number of works generated. Creative masterpieces typically represent only a fraction of total output. This fraction is stable throughout a career and, surprisingly, roughly even across persons. By this model, eminence is achieved through a random "equal-odds" process, which in turn is a function of prolific output. As with expertise, studies of outstanding creative achievement reinforce the essential quality of relevant knowledge that is "profusely interconnected" (Simonton, 1996, p. 245).

Massive experience contributes to expertise, but expertise only makes genius possible, not inevitable. The eventual genius must *pass through* expertise—expertise must be attained and then transcended (Ericsson & Charness, 1994). In other words, to think "outside the box" requires knowing what's inside the box very, very well. In Polanyi's (1958, p. 195) terms, there must be a "dwelling in" before there is a "breaking out." Supreme acts of creativity are discontinuities marked by the fusion and radical reorganization of existing knowledge (Kuhn, 1962; Mumford & Gustafson, 1988). At the highest level of creativity are those "transcendent products" that redefine a whole field (Briskman, cited in Mumford & Gustafson, 1988, p. 28).

CONCLUSION

The emergent theories surveyed in this chapter do much to expand the range of phenomena that are considered under the rubric of intelligence. These ideas can be interpreted according to the predictor-criterion models that have long dominated theories of intelligence. Psychometric theory postulates that tests sample from a larger hidden (or latent) ability or domain. This underlying ability is expressed not only on a test, but also in real-world criterial behavior that can also be sampled. One measure of a test's quality (i.e., its validity) is its ability to predict samples of criterial behavior. Emergent theories of intelligence enlarge on this basic model in two ways. First, the latent ability is not so hidden anymore. The black box has been opened and illuminated to reveal its unruly complexity and variegated nature. I have called the contents of this box the *intelligence repertoire*. The second contribution of emergent theories is that they enlarge and differentiate both intelligence (the predictor) and what it predicts (the criterion). On the criterion side, we can ask what kinds of thought and behavior truly manifest intelligence. Diverse performance realms might draw from differing facilitative functions. Criteria for success in different ecologies might overlap substantially, minimally, or not at all with the standard interpretation of intelligence. Once the criteria of effectiveness are understood more exactly, that understanding would result in a parallel appreciation for new and broader aspects of the intelligence repertoire, such as those described in this chapter. Thus, the expression of intelligence and the underlying proficiencies that permit intelligence at once become broader *and* more exact than in the original psychometric conceptualization. One implication is that the improved model can be used to enhance the underlying ability. That is, the predictor-criterion relation need not stop at prediction, but can advance to the higher level of *preparation* (Snow, 1996), which is to say *education* in its broader and truer sense.

NOTES

1. Sloboda, Hermelin, and O'Connor (1985) studied one musical savant, NP, an autistic man in his early 20s. In comparison to a professional musician of normal intelligence and comparable age, NP was much more adept at reproducing on the piano Grieg's Op. 47 no 3 ("Melodie"), and could play it almost flawlessly 12 minutes after first exposure. The error rate for the professional musician, by contrast, was 10 times that of NP. However, when both subjects were exposed to a

more unusual (although simpler) atonal composition, Bartok's "Whole tone scale" from Book 5 of *Mikrokosmos*, NP's attempts to reproduce the piece declined radically, whereas the professional musician was able to master the composition after three trials. In reproducing Bartok, NP's errors were "structure preserving," meaning that they tended to impose more conventional melodic structure onto the composition, suggesting that NP's "expertise [could] not survive outside [the] framework" of more conventional tonal structures (Sloboda, Hermelin, & O'Connor, 1985, p. 165). One possible interpretation of the savant's inflexibility is that high competence is developed in memory codes that are closer to perception, but that more abstract meaning-based representations are poorly developed (Anderson, 1983). This, in turn, would imply a more unified interpretation of mind.

2. Messick (1992) saw the possibility of convergence between MI theory and psychometric models of intelligence, and proposed that the multiple intelligences model could be accommodated within a hierarchical structure with little or no loss of its implications for education. In such an arrangement, the hierarchy would consist of "semi-autonomous ability complexes or modules, cross-connected by higher-order general processes" (p. 374). These abilities could be used to draw individual profiles of students' strengths and weaknesses, and even to redress the narrowness of school curricula that leads to the neglect of certain abilities and the overemphasis of others.

3. Project START investigators also tested the effectiveness of instruction based (somewhat loosely) on MI theory. Primary grade students from 16 elementary schools were divided into two treatment groups (MI instruction plus mentoring, MI instruction with no mentoring, total N = 256 students) and a control group (N = 86). Teachers of students in the treatment groups were trained to enrich and broaden instruction "via multiple intelligences" by, for example, developing and using "multiple activities for a single task goal" (Callahan et al., 1995, p. 71). The investigators found that "the intervention had no significant effect on the achievement on the treatment groups in any of the grades" (pp. 92-93). Although Project START may cast some doubt on the utility of general enrichment inspired by MI theory, it does not constitute a strong test of MI theory's applicability to education because it did not systematically match students' MI profile with instructional treatments (however, cf. Cronbach & Snow, 1977, for negative results obtained in similar interventions).

4. As an example, consider the analogy (Sternberg, 1985a), Lawyer : Client :: Doctor : _____. A solution of the analogy can be explained in terms of four components: *encoding*—each of the three terms of the analogy is entered into short-term memory, and each term is read and recognized; *inference*—the relationship between the first two elements, *lawyer* and *client*, is determined; *mapping*—the relationship between the first and third elements, *lawyer* and *doctor*, is determined; and *application*—the relationship between the first two elements is then applied to the third term to generate the ideal fourth term, completing the analogy. In order to explain composite item and test performance, each of the constituent components becomes an individual difference variable. In componential analysis, Sternberg's dependent variable of choice has been response time, which is the time needed by subjects to complete the analogy correctly. To obtain response times for individual components, Sternberg manipulated the analogies: Sometimes all of the analogy was given at once; at other times, part of the analogy was "precued" and the timed phase included encoding the new part of the analogy plus the response. By subtracting response times for partial sets from the response time for a complete analogy, Sternberg was able to estimate a response time for each item component. He then related the response times for components back to psychometric measures, such as aggregate performance on analogies, or to other cognitive abilities or measures of intelligence.

5. The premature termination of search is illustrated in Sternberg's (1977) componential analysis of analogy items. Errors in solving analogy problems were largely accounted for by "premature self-termination of information processing" (Sternberg & Gardner, 1982, p. 249).

6. "Broad-sense" intelligence has previously been proposed to include social intelligence. The notion that skilled social cognition constitutes one expression of intelligence can be traced to E. L. Thorndike in the early 20th century, and is an explicit element in Guilford's (1967) and Gardner's (1983) theories. Despite the intuitive rightness of the idea that people differ dependably in social cognition, and that these differences have important real-world consequences, there has been a great deal of difficulty establishing social intelligence as a legitimate form of intelligence that is distinct from an analytic intelligence (Salovey & Mayer, 1989-90).

7. Obsession may be a common characteristic of experts, prodigies, and idiot savants. If "expertise" in these forms is primarily structural, reflecting a large accumulation of knowledge and skill over time, then obsessional behavior with respect to the target domain might be necessary for the buildup of this knowledge base (cf. Jensen's (1996) vignette of the mathematician Ramanujan).

8. Howard Gardner pointed out that initial talent and eventual expertise are actually separable (Ericsson, Krampe, & Heizmann, 1993). It is the initial signs of talent that Ericsson maintained are not very predictive of future attainment. Even if novices differ greatly in initial talent (which they demonstrably do in many domains), this does not mean that those who show early promise will inevitably become elite or eminent as adults. Nor can we say that those who do *not* show initial promise will never display high levels of performance. However, initial levels of skill may influence opportunities for further training, including access to the best instruction (Ericsson, Krampe, & Heizmann, 1993). Besides referring to initial skill levels, the word *talent* might refer to the slope of the function relating proficiency to experience. Clearly, such slopes vary greatly among individuals, and in fact intelligence itself has been described in terms of the slope of accumulated learning against time. *Talent* might also refer to the individual asymptote of this function—something akin to "potential." Ericsson's thesis that deliberate practice can predict attained expertise better than do signs of initial talent challenges advocates of the talent view to be clearer about what they mean by *talent,* and to provide evidence for their views. It also suggests that although functions relating performance to experience may differ substantially across individuals, the shape and position of these functions might be moot if the "input" of concentrated, sustained practice varies among aspirants by orders of magnitude, rendering talent parameters (start or slope) ineffectual as predictors of success. Much the same argument can be applied to the cultivation of the intelligence repertoire. Parameters of individual functions relating the accumulated repertoire to experience will vary, but these too might matter much less than individual variation in the "input" of cumulative educative experience in the school and elsewhere.

5

A Model of Learnable Intelligence

Intelligence has been called a *superconstruct* because it embraces a grand span of cognitive and quasi-cognitive functions (Baltes, 1986). In this book, the elements of mental functioning that compose intelligence have been portrayed as competencies, and referred to collectively as a *repertoire*. Intelligence is a cognitive congeries. It is not *just* knowledge or skill, adaptivity or purposivity, competencies or dispositions, words or images: It is a federation of all of these and more. Cognitive competencies are unequal in their importance, and intelligence consists of a subset of cognitive functions—the *intelligence repertoire*. These are the functions that are most general and powerful in promoting effectiveness, and are differentially possessed and deployed by members of a population. Cognitive functions that lie within the intelligence repertoire will have both properties of generality across situations and variability across persons.

The dual characteristics of intelligence functions—generality across situations and variability across persons—establish criteria for defining the intelligence repertoire. As expressed by Ohlsson (1998): "We need to identify some component (or components) of the mind that is both a locus of generality and a source of individual differences" (p. 144). The task for theory builders is to characterize the identity of the intelligence repertoire, that "finite set . . . that constitute[s] the content of intelligence" (Jacobs & Vandeventer, 1972, p. 241). If *instruction* in the intelligence repertoire is desired, then a third dimension must be considered, which is that elements of the intelligence repertoire may differ in their modifiability. As Snow (1982b) observed, "Some aspects of intellectual aptitudes may be expected to be readily trainable and others not" (p. 29). To enhance intelligence, attention must be fastened on those functions that are general across situations and variable across people, but are also tractable, that is, responsive to intervention.

In this chapter, I outline a three-part model of intelligence, to which I give the name the 3E Model. This model is structured by the following three propositions:

1. Intelligence is fundamentally *entelic*, involving the pursuit of valued goals within a problem space. Because of this, problem solving (and problem finding) can serve as a general model for intelligence;

2. Intelligence is *efficient*, involving the skilled representation, transfer, and transformation of information within the human cognitive system. Key cognitive abilities as identified in the psychometric tradition are parameters that describe the efficiency of the information processing system;

3. Intelligence is *evaluative*, in that purposeful thought and action depend on the quality of schemas for knowledge, motivators, procedures, and goals, which in turn relies on internalized standards as to what constitutes a high-quality schema.

THE ENTELIC QUALITY OF INTELLIGENCE

Historically, psychology has been balkanized into differing theories and methodologies, with little cross-talk between camps (Cronbach, 1957). Research on cognition has similarly been splintered. Newell (1980) observed that research in the areas of reasoning, problem solving, and decision making "rarely give more than lip service to the results and theories from the others. What should be a unified scientific endeavor seems fragmented" (p. 694). Is there a way to unify research on cognition? According to Newell there is, and the unifying model he proposed places *problem solving* at the hub. Problem solving is the pursuit of a goal when the path toward that goal is uncertain. Typically, problem solving involves breaking a larger goal into subgoals, and through those subgoals incremental and often imperfect progress is made toward eventual success (Anderson, 1985; Newell & Simon, 1972). All of cognition, according to Newell, is fundamentally concerned with reasoning and decision making within a problem space. Problem solving, in turn, is fundamentally goal-directed behavior (Anderson, 1985; Newell & Simon, 1972). It is the purposeful or goal-driven aspect of intelligence, manifest as problem-solving behavior, that is emphasized in my term *entelic* (Greek *telos*: completion). The entelic aspect of intelligence recognizes nonpsychologists' understanding of what makes for an intelligent person (Sternberg, 1989). It is also a nod toward Maslow's (1968) holistic apprehension of larger human ends, which embraces the Greek ideal *arete*—a personal apprehension of "the true, the good, the beautiful" (p. 84).

Newell's hypothesis has been tested in the artificial intelligence device known as SOAR. SOAR uses a problem space as the generic representation for a wide range of information-processing tasks (Laird, Newell, & Rosenbloom, 1987). Arguably, it instantiates psychology's closest approximation to a grand unified theory. Within SOAR, problem solving, represented as heuristic search within a problem space, is adopted as "the fundamental organization of *all* goal-oriented symbolic activity" (Laird et al., 1987, p. 5). Decisions within the problem space are guided by the application of general heuristics (or weak methods), such as hill climbing (i.e., make a move that increases the value of the current state). General heuristics have special importance in situations that are knowledge-lean, in which prior knowledge does not help much. Such situations are highly descriptive of tasks that demand fluid intelligence.

Intelligence theorists have long recognized parallels between problem-solving ability and intelligence (e.g., Gardner, Kornhaber, & Wake, 1996; Resnick & Glaser, 1976; Rowe, 1985), and especially fluid intelligence. Sternberg (1985a), for example, noted that "the kinds of behaviors that constitute the problem-solving factor are very similar to what Cattell (1971) and Horn (1968) have referred to as 'fluid ability' " (p. 60). Intelligence and problem solving are fundamentally *extrapolative*, both inwardly as cognition and outwardly as behavior, building on what is already known and bridging into the unfamiliar. Fluid intelligence, identified as close to or equivalent to g, is demonstrated in environments that are complex, novel, or incomplete in their informational structure. Similarly, cognitive models of problem solving depict the human capacity for transforming the internal world of representations, and the external world of people and objects, toward purposeful ends, especially when reaching those ends cannot be accomplished by the straightforward application of known algorithms. In psychological essence, humans are "problematizing being[s]" (Getzels, 1979b, p. 9). The cognitive overlap of problem solving and intelligence, including choice among alternatives in uncertain situations, "point to problem solving as a key model for intelligent adaptation" (Belmont, Butterfield, & Ferretti, 1982, p. 148).

In proposing that problem solving can serve as a general model for cognition, the phenomenon of *transfer* must be considered.[1] Transfer is the application of knowledge learned in one situation to a new and different situation. The role of transfer in problem solving is clear: Intelligent action must depend on what is already known, and yet existing knowledge is not completely sufficient. In learning also, new knowledge must be bridged to existing knowledge, implicating transfer (Butterfield, Slocum, & Nelson, 1993). Because transfer is descriptive of both learning and problem solving, there is a convergence of constructs—problem solving and transfer are both manifestations of a more general pattern. Both accommodate thought and action in unfamiliar circumstances. Both imply a cognitive extension beyond what one already knows or can do, a cantilevering into the unknown and untried. Both also address the paradox that although intelligence is manifest in meeting challenges never before encountered, it also draws deeply on accumulated experience and its dividend, knowledge.

At least as typically conceptualized, however, problem solving is still not fully able to account for intelligence because it does not answer the all-important question of what problem to solve. It is necessary to simplify a world "teeming with dilemmas" into problems that are deemed worthwhile and solvable (Getzels, 1979a, p. 167). Perhaps it is on this point that existing theories of intelligence are most inadequate, because real-life intelligence is exercised in the *choice* of problems to which finite time and energy are allocated. In the psychological laboratory or in the examination hall, problems are prefabricated; but "in the real world, intelligence is as much problem finding as it is problem solving" (Snow, 1980b, p. 196). The term *problem finding*, probably introduced first by Mackworth (1965), refers to the identification and formulation of the most promising problems, those most worth pursuing. If targeted problems are trivial or inconsistent with more general purposes and values, the resulting actions cannot be called intelligent. Problem *finding* must therefore be incorporated into any comprehensive model of intelligence.[2] The ability to select problems worth solving—that is, consistent with one's purposes and capabilities—has primacy within the intelligence repertoire.

An expansion of the terms of intelligence to include problem finding is consistent with Sternberg's (1985a) proposal that intelligence involves not just adaptation, but also the selection and shaping of environments. Most studies of problem solving have proceeded "as if questions and problems, like the weather, were just there naturally" (Getzels, 1979a, p. 1267). These are formalized or "well-structured" problems, whose criteria for success can be clearly defined and whose solution requires only "practicable amounts of computation" (Simon, 1973, p. 183). Real-world problems, however, are ill-structured in that problem definition and success criteria are fuzzy, and the problem space consists of an indefinitely large number of possible states. Moreover, ill-structured problems are not always presented to the problem solver, but sometimes must be discovered or intentionally created (Arlin, 1989b; Getzels, 1979a). The ability to discover and formulate significant problems may have special significance in advanced stages of psychological development: Problem finding has been hypothesized to characterize a postformal "fifth stage," for which formal operations is necessary but not sufficient (Arlin, 1989a).[3] It may be the case that problem finding is best conceptualized not as an ability, but instead as a propensity or disposition supported by certain values (Jay & Perkins, 1997). There is evidence that, given appropriate instructional scaffolding, problem-finding behavior can be enhanced (Jay, 1996).

Polanyi (1958) has even proposed that the recognition of a problem "which can be solved and is worth solving is a discovery in its own right" (p. 120). Galileo, for example, recognized that light might not travel instantaneously, but instead with finite and measurable speed. Unfortunately, he did not have access to the tools and techniques that would address this possibility. Nevertheless, the problem had been found. Einstein commented that "Galileo formulated the problem of determining the velocity of light, but did not solve it. The formulation of a problem is often more essential than its solution. . . . To raise new questions, new possibilities, to regard old problems from a new angle, requires creative imagination and marks real advance in science" (Einstein & Infeld, 1938, p. 95).

THE EFFICIENT QUALITY OF INTELLIGENCE

I have described intelligence as entelic, manifest as problem solving and problem finding. The entelic quality describes the general form of intelligence. But intelligence also depends on qualities of the human information-processing system. The system can be characterized by a relatively small number of key parameters that describe its efficiency. These efficiency parameters are concerned with the transformation, storage, and retrieval of information. More completely, it is through representational forms, such as words and images, and the operations on these representations, that the entelic quality of intelligence becomes possible. Without information processing, there is no problem solving.

Insights into the parameters that govern information processing can be gained from the psychometric analysis of cognitive abilities. The theoretical units of psychometric models are *factors*—cognitive entities that have psychometric coherence. Findings from psychometric research have much to say about the content and structure of abilities composing intelligence. In this section, I highlight certain key factors derived from Carroll's (1993) larger array. Factors composing the reduced set are identified as *key* abilities if they satisfy four criteria: strong replicable evidence for their existence, robust correlations with general intelligence (3G), strong associations with the broad group factors of Carroll's Stratum II, and sufficiently delimited breadth so as to permit the construction of a cognitive model.

Key cognitive factors are identified in Table 5.1. These are organized by three facets: *reasoning, representation*, and *memory*. The faceted quality of cognitive abilities has turned up repeatedly in the history of research on intelligence, as is illustrated by the theories of Guilford (1967), Cattell (1987), and Snow and Lohman (1989). Guilford's theory represents an attempt to apply psychometric findings to understanding the cognitive system. Thus also in my account, I assert that the key psychometric factors align with key efficiency parameters of human information processing. In Fig. 3.2, these are indicated by asterisks. Most of the identified factors have already been modeled in information-processing terms (e.g., in Denis & Tapsfield, 1996; Sternberg, 1985b). In the following paragraphs, I provide brief descriptions of the three facets and their constituent factors.

Reasoning

Reasoning, and especially inferential reasoning, has traditionally been placed at or near the center of what is meant by *intelligence* (Carroll, 1993). The subsumed complementary factors of induction and deduction are, in turn, the best understood forms of inferential reasoning (Nickerson, 1986b). Both induction and deduction have strong empirical connections to general intelligence, and both have been featured in thinking skills curricula, such as Project Intelligence. Inductive and deductive reasoning contribute to the quality of representations by providing mechanisms by which representations can be extended to make them more complete, accurate, and internally consistent. They are the yin and yang of intelligent reasoning.

Inductive reasoning is the ability to generalize (or induce, or educe) patterns, to reason "from parts to wholes, from a few to all, from the particular to the general" (Nickerson, 1986b, p. 70). Of all the first-stratum cognitive ability factors identified in the psychometric tradition, inductive reasoning is closest to the essence of fluid intelligence (Cattell, 1963). Gustafsson's (1999) hypothesis that fluid intelligence and *g* are equivalent gives special importance to inductive reasoning— it may lie at the heart of *g*. In cognitive terms, intelligence is substantially concerned with the ability to find order in complexity by inducing patterns. Raven's Matrices, which is often said to be the best available measure of fluid intelligence and

TABLE 5.1
Key Psychometric Factors/Information Processing Parameters

Factor or Composite	Carroll's Terminology	3G Load	2G Associations (Loads)	Thurstone Factor
		Reasoning		
Inductive reasoning	Induction	0.57	Fluid intelligence (.64)	Reasoning
Deductive reasoning	Sequential reasoning	0.41	Fluid (.55); crystallized (.69)	Deduction*
		Representation		
Verbal ability	Verbal ability	0.49	Crystallized intelligence (.71)	Verbal comprehension
Mathematical ability	Quantitative reasoning	0.51	Fluid intelligence (.65)	Number
Spatial ability	Visualization	0.57	Visual perception (.67); fluid (.62)	Spatial visualization
		Memory		
Working memory	Memory span	0.36	Fluid intelligence (.54)	—
Learning memory	Associative memory	0.43	General memory and learning (.66)	Memory
Retrieval memory	Ideational fluency	0.38	Broad retrieval (.68); fluid (.60)	Verbal fluency
	Originality/creativity	0.37	Broad retrieval (.58)	

* Thurstone's factor labeled "D" corresponds to deductive reasoning, but was not presented as a primary mental ability.

Note: Data are from Carroll (1993).

psychometric *g*, is predominantly a test of induction. The historical importance of induction (or eduction) is expressed in Spearman's (1927) well-known definition of intelligence as the eduction of relations and the eduction of correlates.

The logical complement to inductive reasoning is *deductive* reasoning. If induction entails finding order or pattern within a complex field, deductive reasoning is the extension or application of that pattern to its necessary implications. Deductive reasoning involves reasoning from premises to conclusions, often in a series of steps (Carroll, 1993). Many common errors of thinking are essentially missteps in the deductive process (Nickerson, 1986b). Like inductive reasoning, deductive reasoning contributes to representations by making them more complete and coherent.

Representation

The human mind does not record sense experience directly, but rather it registers and selectively archives a highly processed and meaning-centered version of experience (Martinez, 1999). Representations are schematic in that they do not fully capture the external environment, but only selected features of the environment according to their perceived importance and meaning. Because representations are what the mind thinks about, they are central to any circumspect account of cognition and intelligence. Both psychometric and cognitive research traditions have reinforced the importance of representations to mental life, and both provide insights into the identity and nature of the most common forms of representation.

Representation involves the use of proxies—symbols and symbol systems, semiotic signs, and idealized analogical models—to understand and act on the external environment (Eisner, 1997). The idea that cognitive abilities can be identified with symbols systems has been advanced in several psychometric models, including the content dimension of Guilford's (1967) Structure of the Intellect, Cattell's (1987) agencies, and the sectors of Snow's (Snow & Lohman, 1989) radex model. In these and other accounts, two classes of representation are recurrent: verbal and spatial. A third representational form, quantitative, has been less reliably identified in psychometric studies, but was vindicated in Carroll's (1993) near-definitive analysis, as well as Gardner's (1983) account of adult end-state intelligences.

Besides its formal identification in psychometric research, *verbal* ability is recognized in commonsensical notions of what an intelligent person is like (Sternberg, 1990a). Psychometrics can provide some specificity. The factor I highlight in Carroll's model is strongly identified with facility in comprehending printed language. Why should printed language figure so prominently in verbal ability? Perhaps because print is typically more demanding than everyday speech, presenting greater syntactical complexity and a broader vocabulary range.

Like verbal ability, *spatial* ability has been identified as a major factor of intelligence in diverse models and theories. In cognitive terms, spatial ability involves the ability to search, apprehend, generate, and manipulate two- and three-dimensional analog representations (Kosslyn, 1980). Spatial ability is process-intensive, requiring little in the way of stored knowledge, although it does have its own elaborate rules of syntax (Hoffman, 1998). The functional importance of spatial ability across diverse cognitive performances, including those that are not obviously spatial, is increasingly appreciated. For example, spatial ability might help a reader build a dynamic "situation model" of the text, experienced vicariously as if the reader were actually in the narrative (Lohman, 1996; Zwaan, 1999). Image-based mental models also contribute to understanding and expertise (Ericsson, 1996; Perkins, 1992), especially in science domains. The ability to visualize mentally is now recognized as an essential workplace competency (Secretary's Commission on Achieving Necessary Skills, 1991). Anecdotally, mental imagery has long been associated with creative thinking and scientific discovery, as is evident in Einstein's own introspections (Ghiselin, 1952).

It has long been known that there is a substantial mean gender difference, favoring males, in the form of spatial ability that involves complex mental rotation (Neisser et al., 1996; Okagaki & Frensch, 1994). Hormones may be involved. Vernon (1948) found that spatial skills increased dramatically among males between the ages of 14 and 20. Some studies have demonstrated that, even among males, testosterone levels are positively correlated with spatial ability, and that testosterone supplementation can enhance spatial performance. But spatial ability has been shown to be responsive to relevant experience. For example, Härnqvist (1968) found an upward shift of spatial ability among students in a vocational education curriculum. Like all abilities, spatial ability responds to interventions aimed directly at its development (Kyllonen, Lohman, & Snow, 1984). The visually demanding computer game Tetris has even been shown to enhance spatial ability in both males and females (Okagaki & Frensch, 1994).

A third representation form, *quantitative*, involves reasoning about mathematical properties and relations. Its essence is not advanced mathematical skill as such, but the ability to conceptualize the world in mathematical terms, as might be manifest in selecting the appropriate arithmetic operations to solve a problem. Actual numeric computation plays a minor role in this factor. Quantitative reasoning is strongly related to fluid intelligence. The demands of precise description and transformation afforded by mathematical representations complement the more descriptive and associational features of language, and the holistic analog properties of spatial representations. Together, these three constitute the major categories of representational forms on which intelligence operates.

Memory

The third facet of cognitive abilities directly concerns the operational efficiency of memory. Critical parameters in the system are the processing capacity of working memory and the efficiency of moving information into and out of long-term memory. In the case of *working memory*, the robust relationship between *g* and working memory capacity has already been noted. Intelligence is at least partly characterized by the ability to welcome and manage complexity in working memory (Halford, 1993; Kyllonen & Christal, 1990). Efficiency parameters for the storage and retrieval of information from long-term memory are also vital to the cognitive system. A person's ability to store information in long-term memory, and to retrieve it on demand, has great importance in the intelligence repertoire.

Pertinent here is an association made by many theorists, which is that intelligence and the ability to learn are closely related. Learning is, in cognitive terms, the transfer of information from working memory to long-term memory. Carroll (1993) described associative memory as one of the more prominent factors in the psychometric tradition. This factor, which I have called *learning memory*, is manifest in tests of paired-associate learning, which involve the ability to form linkages between two entities (typically numbers, pictures, or words), and to retrieve one given the other. The ability to form associations between arbitrary stimuli seems a far cry from meaningful verbal learning, but associative learning probably depends on finding or creating meaningful connections between initially arbitrary stimuli and knowledge already held in long-term memory. Clearly, the ability to record information in long-term memory efficiently and effectively— "engramming" capacity—contributes directly to the accumulation of crystallized intelligence. And indeed, experts seem to be particularly good at recording domain-relevant experience to long-term memory (Ericsson, 1996).

Finally, memory usage entails cueing and retrieving information from long-term memory. A corresponding third memory factor, complementary to learning memory, is what I have called *retrieval memory*. This is a composite of ideational fluency, measured as the ability to retrieve a quantity of ideas that meet a particular criterion, and originality/creativity, which is the ability to produce "remotely associated, clever, or uncommon responses" (Carroll, 1993, p. 395). Both factors are strongly related to the Stratum II factor called *broad retrieval ability* and, to some extent, creative thinking (Jensen, 1996).

Because the cognitive factors described in this model are substantially derived from Carroll's (1993) theory, their linkages to psychometric intelligence are demonstrable. These factors, which I assert constitute key efficiency parameters of the cognitive system, are theoretically and empirically connected to the construct of intelligence, psychometrically defined. More exactly, they are empirically linked to the theoretically important but incomplete construct of analytical intelligence, which is associated with tests of cognitive ability and, to a lesser degree, with the content of formal schooling.

THE EVALUATIVE QUALITY OF INTELLIGENCE

Common sense tells us that intelligent thought and action are impossible without an underlying knowledge base. Rich, accurate, and articulated knowledge is the kind that is most likely to support skillful cognitive performance. From a psychometric viewpoint, the existence of the robust higher-order factor of crystallized intelligence reinforces the idea that a strong knowledge base is one manifestation of intelligence. Cognitivists and artificial intelligence theorists also have come to recognize that general process models of cognition are inadequate because of the strong contribution of rich and elaborate knowledge to expert performance.

In this third facet of my 3E model, the one that is most speculative, I propose that intelligence derives largely from the ability and propensity to evaluate and improve the quality of knowledge in the forms of schemas. By schemas, I refer to knowledge that is organized into coherent networks. Schema knowledge includes both knowing *that* and knowing *how* (Ryle, 1949); that is, schematic representations can be declarative or procedural. As coherent and often complex knowledge structures, schemas are composed of multiple representations and representational forms. Because all human knowledge is schematic (i.e., not corresponding point by point to external reality or even sense perception), schematic knowledge is *the* medium of mental life (Martinez, 1999).

Schema Types

I propose four types of schemas: descriptive, imaginative, evaluative, and transformative. Together, these four types of schemas support intelligent thought and behavior within a problem space, and their individual and collective quality determine the degree to which thought and action are intelligent.

Descriptive schemas are knowledge structures about what is true or meaningful about the world or oneself. They connect strongly to the construct of declarative knowledge (Ryle, 1949). Descriptive schemas include all self-knowledge concerning what one knows and can do, as well as theories and models of the larger world. Descriptive schemas also refer to that subset of knowledge that describes the current situation one faces and the competencies needed in that situation. Componential studies of psychometric task performance have shown that good reasoners tend to be careful and thorough in encoding relevant aspects of whatever problem they face (Carroll, 1980). Before acting, they build a high-quality schema of *what is*. Descriptive schemas can vary in the degree of confidence that is placed in them and in their degree of development (i.e., completeness, elaboration). In a highly developed state, we could say that schemas constitute or permit *understanding*.

Descriptive schemas are the cognitive structures we most often refer to as *knowledge* (i.e., declarative knowledge). The knowledge constituent to descriptive schemas is in no way static, but instead transforms as different and perhaps better knowledge states supersede old ones. The transformation of knowledge can be seen as taking place within a problem space where the driving goal is to understand. The process of acquiring understanding may be guided by a heuristic of successive approximations, such as "hill climbing," in which schemas transform incrementally toward great elaboration, coherence, comprehensiveness, and parsimony. I propose that such transformations—toward greater quality—are a fundamental mechanism of intelligent thought.

Imaginative schemas reflect possible future states that might arise from the transformative effects of thought and action on the environment or on descriptive schemas. Possible future states can become goals and lead to plans if they are sufficiently consistent with one's own purposes and capabilities, real or perceived. Much of cognition is purposeful, directed toward transforming aspects of the internal environment of representations and the external environment of people and things. Belmont (1989) characterized thinking as essentially "goal-directed strategic activity," highlighting its problem-oriented and purposeful nature (p. 142). Goal-directed behavior is therefore an essential component of any complete model of problem solving or intelligence (Belmont et al., 1982). Consistent with this claim is Binet's description of intelligence as "the tendency to take and maintain a definite direction" (translation by Terman, 1916, p. 45).

The "lookahead" feature of human thought is vital to any purpose- and problem-oriented account of thought and action, and therefore for understanding intelligence (Holland, 1995). As expressed by Ohlsson (1993), "Mature minds think about that which is not present in experience because it has not yet happened; the future, the envisioned, the hoped-for" (p. 52). Intelligent minds frequently shift to a "lookahead" mode. Ochse (1990) reported that a considerable amount of conscious thought is devoted to imagining and rehearsing possible future scenarios. These imagined states might project the very near future, medium-range possibilities, or long-term scenarios and strategic planning. The temporal depth dimension is likely to be important in organizing resources effectively, and in integrating short- and long-range goals.

According to Newell's (1990; Hunt, 1995) SOAR model, which was proposed as a grand unified theory of cognition, *thought itself* is always motivated by an attempt to reach a goal. Goals, and the subgoals necessary to reach them, involve the production of states that "do not preexist as data structures within the problem solver" (Laird et al., 1987, p. 6). Even the behavior of rats in mazes is most readily interpretable as "purposive" and goal directed (Tolman, 1932). In the human being, and to a degree in the intelligent machine, intelligence requires the exercise of imagination to generate and consider possible future states. Production systems, a means of modeling human thought as a concatenation of if-then rules, always assume a goal. What is the origin of such goals? In the present account, goal states are conceptualized as schemas of imagined states that constitute desired, or possibly desirable, futures.

Evaluative schemas embody standards by which the current situation and possible future states are evaluated. These standards include all considerations that impel behavior, including sensory pleasure and pain, morals, values, ethics, commitments, ideals, felt needs, likes and dislikes, fears and fascinations. This category subsumes all possible (and possibly conflicting) factors that channel behavior, whether impetuous or strategic, hedonic or altruistic. In machine intelligence, evaluative representations clearly do not take the form of abstract morals, values, or ethics, but instead are exemplified by goals and test procedures, specified by a programmer (e.g., the capture of a king in chess) that might be satisfied by any one of a large number of specific states.

Motivators are complex. At one time, motivation theorists posited that human behavior is driven by attempts to reduce physiological deficits through consummatory acts (Harlow, 1953; White, 1959). Thus, even complex behavior was thought to be traceable, ultimately, to attempts to satisfy needs for food, water, sex, sleep, and the like. Drive theories, however, were unable to explain the gamut of human and animal behavior, especially the tendency to explore. Exploratory behavior, psychologists found, is not always in the service of "tissue needs." Furthermore, exploratory behavior is often self-reinforcing, meaning that it can lead to *increases* in arousal, not its reduction (White, 1959). Evaluative schemas can therefore subsume physiological drives, but must include much more.

Evaluative schemas supply the motivation to change current situations and the criteria needed to select future situations as goals, or to pose new problems. Evaluations of any real or possible situation can be complex, involving multiple standards or motivators that may conflict, leading to indecision or ambivalence, and to satisficing (Simon, 1969).[4] Some evaluative standards are more conducive to intelligent thought and action than are others. Baron (1987), for example, cited the importance of wanting to be correct, to make the best possible decision, or to be prudent in the service of long-term interests rather than immediate satisfaction. This led Baron (1987) to the insight that "the teaching of intelligence is in part the teaching of character" (p. 66).

Finally, *transformative* schemas are those that bridge the gap between the current situation and possible future states selected as goals. Positing transformative schemas recognizes the dynamic quality of human thought, and links the discussion of schema quality to the idea that intelligence operates within a problem space. Transformative schemas organize goals into subgoals, manage multiple and competing goals, elicit the competencies and knowledge structures required to carry out plans to move toward desired states, and evaluate progress toward goals and subgoals, switching strategies if necessary. Included in this repertoire is subgoal management, a competency that has been linked directly to performance on IQ tests. Performance on Raven's Progressive Matrices, for example, was found to be related largely to individual differences in subgoal management (Carpenter,

Just, & Shell, 1990). Low-g participants were able to manage only about two subgoals, and high-g subjects could manage three or four. It is possible that even a modest upward shift in the complexity of problem structures one is able to manage would have a large effect on the range of problems that are within reach.

Enhancing Schema Quality

According to the 3E model, effective thought and action—the way intelligence is manifested—derive from the quality of schemas supporting the pursuit of goals. Schema quality can be evaluated within each of the four schema structures; each can be of poor or high quality. For example, a *descriptive* schema might construe the current situation poorly by neglecting or misrepresenting key features, thus leading to maladaptive action. *Imaginative* schemas might be inadequate if they are based only on short-term goals or are insufficiently productive in generating multiple goal options or goal paths. *Evaluative* schemas could fall short by involving only a limited range of motivating standards, such as short-term pleasure, or by failing to consider the evaluative complexity (costs and benefits) of a possible goal. *Transformative* schemas might not take into account the efficiency of a particular goal path, or might fail to use available competencies, tools, or other environmental supports, such as other people.

The quality of each component schema is important individually, but effective thought and action also depend on the harmony among schemas. For example, intelligent action depends on having a considered evaluation of one's current state and possible future states using the appropriate evaluational schema. Possible future states must be compared with an understanding of transformational representations that could plausibly lead to those future states. Therefore, effective thought and action depend on both the internal quality of schemas and their combined quality expressed as coherence, consistency, and composition.

The pursuit of quality in schemas might depend on a general tendency to search for relations within and between schemas. In Baron's theory, rationality is at the heart of intelligence, and the breakdown of rationality is a consequence of premature termination of *search*. In the language of the 3E model, intelligent thought fails when not enough thinking has occurred to ensure high-quality schemas. The emphasis on schema quality implies that possession of important competencies (the intelligence repertoire) is necessary, but not enough. Those functions must be orchestrated so that thought and action begin to acquire a "quality of behavior" that is purposeful, considered, reflective, and strategic (Anastasi, 1986, p. 19). This holistic quality of intelligence conforms with Cronbach's (1977) proposal that " 'intelligence' is not a thing, it is a style of work" (p. 272), akin to efficiency. Building and deploying high-quality schemas might depend on the availability and tendency to use certain concepts, which become test procedures or internalized standards against which knowledge and plans can be evaluated.

Concepts for evaluating descriptive transformations might include, for example, *clarity* and *evidence*. The availability and tendency to use of such concepts have been referred to as *dispositions* by Perkins (Tishman & Perkins, 1997) and Baron (1987). If intelligent thought depends on the quality and coordination of schemas, then dispositions serve to test and transform schemas to improve their quality. Evaluational concepts can describe poor qualities of schemas, such as *unclear* or *inefficient*, and point to qualities of good schemas, such as *coherent* and *effective*. Tishman and Perkins (1997) noted that the English language has many words that pertain specifically to kinds and qualities of thinking. Costa (1991) identified much the same effect, giving the name *cogitare* to describe this "language of thinking." Tishman and Perkins (1997) also distinguished epistemic status terms such as *suggest, speculate*, and *confirm*—which demonstrate that knowledge can be calibrated along continua of completeness and certainty. The ability to use such terms correctly requires the metaknowledge to make this appraisal. Once that appraisal is made, the concept's epistemic status can activate other dispositions to improve schema quality.[5]

Search moves to a second order when it extends into testing the quality of one kind of schema. A schematic of sample second-order evaluations is illustrated in Fig. 5.1. The bold diamond at the center depicts four basic types of schemas: descriptive, imaginative, evaluative, and transformative. Each schema type can be unpacked to reveal an *internal* four-part structure (indicated by the four diamonds at the periphery), which can then be subject to quality test procedures. For example, an evaluative schema can have descriptive elements (What standards control my behavior?), imaginative elements (What new standards might I adopt?), evaluative elements (Are there good reasons to change my guiding standards?), and transformative elements (How can I change the standards, beliefs, and goals that guide my behavior?). A similar unpacking process can be described for each schema type, and the kind of reflective activity that moves search to this second order of evaluation is hypothesized to be intimately associated with intelligent effectiveness.

Quality test procedures are hypothesized to be guided by internal language. According to Tishman and Perkins (1997), language that describes the quality of thought not only permits communication to others, but can be used more instrumentally to guide one's own internal thought processes. The importance of internal language to thought has long been recognized. For example, Tishman and Perkins (1997) invoked Socrates, who called thinking "a discourse the mind carries on with itself." The Russian psychologists Vygotsky (1986/1934) and Luria elaborated a theory of cognitive development that relied largely on the internalization of linguistic patterns experienced first in the social milieu. Others, including Meichenbaum (1977), have developed the idea and tested it empirically, confirming its importance to self-regulation.[6] Still more recently, neural evidence for the importance of verbal mediation in problem solving has also been found.

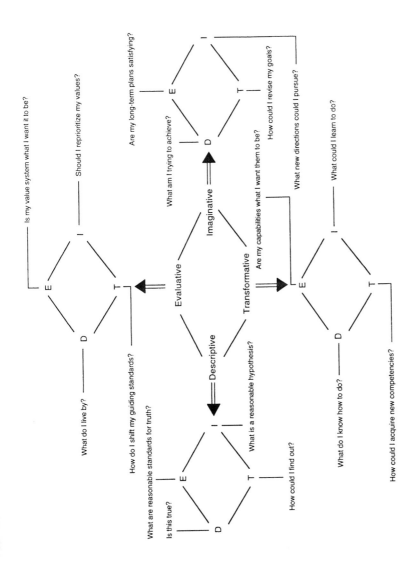

FIG. 5.1. The evaluative aspect of intelligence: reflective unpacking and quality test procedures.

When Haier et al. (1988) used PET scans to study glucose uptake during performance on Raven's Progressive Matrices, a nonverbal test, they found involvement of the temporal lobe, which is strongly associated with language processing.

CONCLUSION

In presenting the 3E model, three aspects of intelligence were identified. The first is an assertion about the nature of intelligent thought and action—that problem solving and problem finding can serve as a general model for intelligence. The second aspect is the means by which intelligent thought and action are accomplished, namely the set of cognitive functions that permit the construction, transformation, storage, and retrieval of schemas. These functions correspond to what cognitivists and psychometrists call *cognitive abilities*. The third aspect pertains to the knowledge base itself, and in particular to four kinds of schemas that support goal-oriented behavior within a problem space, and also to test procedures needed to evaluate and improve the quality of those schemas.

In building more powerful theories of intelligence, the conceptual expansion and elaboration of intelligence must continue. Writing on the topic of cross-cultural differences in the meaning of intelligence, Berry (1974) observed that the full meaning of intelligence will never be understood until "psychologists engage in a thorough exploration of all cognitive behavior which is valued and exhibited in a wide variety of cultural systems" (p. 227). The same could be said about our understanding of intelligence *within* cultures. In the 3E model, theoretical consolidation may be achieved through the proposal that intelligence is fundamentally problem-solving behavior. The effectiveness of problem solving is, in turn, a function of an effective information-processing system, whose key parameters are associated with prominent psychometric factors. Finally, intelligent problem solving relies on high schema quality, and the ability to reflect on and improve schema quality.

NOTES

1. A large body of psychological research shows that transfer is, at best, not easily achieved (Detterman, 1993). Knowledge is often bound to the particular tasks and contexts in which it was acquired. This does not mean that transfer never occurs—that it must occur is obvious when we consider that each day we face situations that are not identical to those we have previously encountered. The application of existing knowledge to situations that are analogous to, but not identical with, previous situations requires transfer. But even if we possess the knowledge to think or act effectively in a new situation, we may fail to see how our knowledge applies, or even that it is

relevant. Because transfer sometimes happens and sometimes does not, one pertinent question is: Under what conditions does transfer occur? Perkins and Salomon (1987) described two categories of conditions that facilitate transfer, which they call *high-road transfer* and *low-road transfer*. In low-road transfer, the schema to be transferred is so practiced and familiar that it applies to new situations with little or no hesitation. Low-road transfer describes expert behavior: The expert's sheer volume of experience can produce such flexible knowledge that new problems are fitted into existing schemas with little difficulty. In the case of high-road transfer, the schema to be applied is new and relatively unpracticed, but it is learned with an awareness of its relevance so that a higher-level understanding of the pertinent schema substitutes for a lack of practice (cf., Judd, 1908; Gick & Holyoak, 1980, Experiment 4). That is, a metacognitive understanding about rules or conditions of applicability makes transfer possible.

2. In their seminal study on the problem-finding behavior of student artists, Getzels and Czikszentmihalyi (1976) discerned that the more creative student artists were distinguished from less creative peers in two ways. First, the exceptionally creative artists spent more time exploring alternative approaches to solving their particular artistic problem. Second, they were willing to change strategies as problem solving progressed. Students who engaged in problem finding exhibited an active and flexible approach to their work and recognized that finding the right problem to solve is the key to significant creative accomplishment.

3. In Arlin's (1989a) model, problem finding also requires the ability to coordinate two or more systems of thought, which in turn depends on the prior consolidation of the constituent formal schemas (cf. Case, 1991). There are, however, competing accounts about the nature of cognitive development in adulthood (Alexander, Druker, & Langer, 1990).

4. Simon (1969) coined the word *satisficing* (as opposed to optimizing) to refer to decision processes that result in "good enough" solutions.

5. Tishman and Perkins (1997) allowed that dispositional concepts, and their associated operations, are laced with affect and emotion. They described, for example, the pain of a new idea, as well as noted William James' (1896/1956, p. 63) observation that the transition from perplexity to understanding is "full of lively relief and pleasure."

6. Not to deny its power, the idea of language regulating thought does have limitations. It cannot explain all intelligent thought. It is clear, for example, that creative and complex thought is sometimes nonverbal. Thus, language used in thinking is not the same as the thinking itself—the two are not equivalent (Tishman & Perkins, 1997).

Part III

Can Intelligence Be Learned?

6
Genetics and the Plasticity of Intelligence

The assumption of fixed intelligence so pervades our culture that, like freeway noise, it recedes from conscious attention to form a life-drama backdrop that is seldom noticed, let alone scrutinized (Hunt, 1961). To test that assumption requires that attention be directed to evidence bearing on the plasticity of intelligence—to whether intelligence can and does change. We will see that intelligence is indeed plastic; even so, genetics is not irrelevant. On the contrary, genetic heritability makes a "significant and substantial" contribution to intelligence (Pederson, Plomin, Nesselroade, & McClearn, 1992, p. 346). The finding is robust and acknowledged by virtually all who have read the relevant research; some call it "indisputable" (Bouchard & McGue, 1981, p. 1058). A more debatable question is: How much of a contribution does heredity make? That is, what is the *heritability* of intelligence? A follow-up question, and one that bears more directly on the polemic of this volume, is whether a genetic contribution to intelligence places a cap on the level of intelligence attainable by an individual.

HERITABILITY AND ITS LIMITATIONS

Heritability, denoted h^2, is defined as the proportion of variance of any trait that can be accounted for by variation in the degree to which genes are shared (Gustafsson & Undheim, 1996; Neisser, 1998). Although the precise value of h^2 for IQ varies from study to study, central tendencies of heritability estimates are around 0.50, with as much error as 0.2 in either direction (see also Bouchard & McGue, 1981). This means that roughly 50% of the variance in measured IQ is associated with genetic variation. This also happens to be the approximate genetic contribution to psychological traits in general (Harris, 1995), including personality traits (Bouchard, 1994), narrower cognitive factors such as verbal and spatial ability (Plomin & DeFries, 1998), and psychopathology (Scarr, 1992). Heritability values are about the same magnitude in accounting for variation in academic achievement (Plomin & DeFries, 1998).

Genetic influences on intelligence are polygenic, involving the expression of many genes in the DNA sequences composing individual genotypes. Empirical data relating IQ to different kinds and degrees of familial relationships are consistent with a polygenic model; that is, the coincidence of heritability values and familial distance is largely a function of the percentage of shared genes.

Recently, geneticists have forayed into exploring the molecular correlates of intelligence. The first single gene associated with high cognitive ability, known as IGF2R (located on the long arm of Chromosome 6), has been identified (Chorney et al., 1998). One particular version of that gene, Allele 5, is about twice as common in high-IQ children as in children of average ability. However, because genetic influences on IQ are strongly polygenic, allele variation in IGF2R can account for only about 2% of the variance in IQ, or about 4 IQ points, in contrasts of high and average IQ samples. The biochemical pathway by which IGF2R exerts its effect on IQ is, at this point, a mystery.

The real workhorses of behavioral geneticists, however, have been studies of twins ("experiments of nature") and adopted children ("experiments of society"; Plomin & DeFries, 1998). Both have shown that the contribution of genotype to variation in IQ is real and substantial (Loehlin, Horn, & Willerman, 1997). Between identical, or monozygotic, twins, the percentage of shared genes is 100%. Across studies, the median IQ correlation for monozygotic (MZ) twins reared together is 0.86; for MZ twins reared apart IQ is correlated 0.76 (Scarr, 1997; see also Bouchard & McGue, 1981). The difference between the two heritability values shows that environmental influences exert an effect, but the still substantial IQ correlation for MZ twins reared apart also speaks to the importance of genetic influences. High heritability values for MZ twins reared apart—in the region of 0.76—are sometimes taken to be evidence for strong genetic determination of IQ. Interpreting this correlation warrants caution, however. It would be a mistake to assume that a heritability value of 0.76 is strictly attributable to heritability. This would be true only if there were a zero correlation between the environments of identical twins reared apart *and* if shared experience prior to separation were irrelevant to IQ. Neither condition is met.

Scientifically, it would be ideal if adoption agencies placed babies at random with families representing the full range of socioeconomic standing. In reality, placement is never random and adopting families tend not to be representative of the population as a whole. Adopted children are more commonly placed with families of higher socioeconomic status (SES), and families with higher SES and IQ are more likely to participate in the types of social science research that document the effects of adoption on cognitive development (Scarr & Weinberg, 1978, 1983). The resulting restriction of range would reduce estimates of environmental (i.e., family) effects, and would therefore magnify the apparent effects of heritability (Neisser et al., 1996).[1] To complicate matters, there are mild associations between natural and adoptive parents in both socioeconomic status and IQ, which has the effect of inflating the correlations of adopted children's IQs with adoptive parents (spuriously supporting environmental effects) and with biological parents (spuriously supporting genetic effects; Scarr & Weinberg, 1983).

Even when twins are separated at birth, they still share some experience, namely the 40 weeks or so that they cohabitate their mother's uterus.[2] Because twins have similar exposure to protein and micronutrients, as well as toxins, those demonstrably potent environmental factors might later be mistakenly attributed to shared genotype. Even identical twins can differ in their share of placenta-supplied nourishment, which is manifest most obviously in birthweight discrepancies. In fact, in-utero "maternal effects," which are shared by MZ twins reared apart, can account for about 20% of the IQ variance otherwise mistakenly attributed to genes (Devlin, Daniels, & Roeder, 1997). Factoring in these maternal effects reduces the heritability estimate for MZ twins reared apart to around 0.5, which is consistent with other behavior-genetic data. Thus, "nature," although generous to scientists on many counts (e.g., by controlling genotype among "identicals"), does not cooperate fully in providing strictly rigorous "experiments of nature." To completely eliminate genetic/environmental confounds would require not separation at birth, but separation at conception.

Implicative Limitations

The problems of interpreting data from twin and adoption studies do not nullify the important finding that population variation in IQ can be linked to genetic sources. Nonetheless, genetics is not destiny. Even if we take the rough estimate of 50% heritability at face value, the equivalent conclusion is that 50% of IQ variance is attributable to nongenetic influences (Rose, Harris, Christian, & Nance, 1979). Thompson and Plomin (1993) remarked that, in this sense, "genetic research provides solid evidence for the importance of nongenetic factors" (p. 104). Likewise, Scarr and Weinberg (1983) noted that "the major contribution of behavioral genetic studies is to clarify the impact of environmental differences on human development" (p. 266). Counterintuitively, behavioral genetics provides empirical support for the importance of nongenetic factors in shaping intelligence, and has additional theoretical and pragmatic value because it can point to features of the environment that promote the development of intelligence. In the experience of one behavioral geneticist, presenting his data "to public groups outside academia often moves them toward a less hereditarian position" (Goldsmith, 1993, p. 336).

Other data from behavioral genetics supports the importance of experience in shaping intelligence. Consider that the IQs of fraternal (dizygotic) twins are more strongly correlated (0.58) than that of nontwin siblings (0.45), even though their genetic relatedness is the same (Bouchard & McGue, 1981). The cumulative experience of fraternal twins is apparently much more alike than that of nontwin siblings, and this shared experience is reflected in the higher correlation of their IQ scores. Environment effects are also evident in families in which some members are not genetically related, as in the case of adoption. For example, significant IQ correlations are found between siblings who are *not* biologically related (approximately 0.30), and also between parents and adopted children who are unrelated (about 0.20; Bouchard & McGue, 1981; Thompson & Plomin, 1993). A strictly hereditarian model would of course predict zero correlations for each. Differing family experiences also have effects in reducing IQ correlations among relatives. For example, the IQs of siblings raised apart are correlated about 0.24, which is considerably *less* than the expected value of 0.50 that an extreme hereditarian model would predict.

Even if some consensus is achieved about the relative contributions of genes and the environment to intelligence, the theoretical limitations of these estimates must be recognized. Most important, the relative contributions of genes and the environment to intelligence should *not* be regarded as parameter estimates for the human species for all time. For all its redolence of scientific-sounding precision, h^2 is not like Planck's constant or the speed of light, which are taken to be universal and eternal. Instead, heritability estimates are *descriptive* statistics (Thompson & Plomin, 1993) that characterize a particular sample of people who have definable genetic variability and who reside in definable environments. Given a different distribution of genes (compare the United States and Japan) or environments (compare Switzerland and the Philippines), heritability estimates would shift. For example, if environmental variation increases (imagine a society that becomes more polarized by wealth and educational opportunity), the measured genetic contribution to IQ, that is h^2, would fall (cf., Plomin & DeFries, 1998).

Another limitation of heritability estimates is that they cannot be extrapolated to account for between-group differences (Lewontin, 1970). Group differences in mean IQ, including differences between racial/ethnic groups, certainly exist, but heritability estimates for IQ are immaterial to explaining those differences. As Lewontin (1970) put it, "Between two populations, the concept of heredity of their differences is meaningless" (p. 7). To illustrate, Lewontin asked the reader to imagine taking two handfuls of seed corn (containing plenty of genetic variation) from the same sack, and planting that seed in two types of soil (See Fig. 6.1). The first soil mixture is rich, containing optimal concentrations of all nutrients needed by the corn; the second soil mixture is deficient, containing only half the concentration of nitrates and insufficient zinc. Predictably, the corn in the rich soil mixture will thrive, grow tall, and yield an abundant harvest, but the corn in the impoverished soil will wither. Yet within each soil type, there will be some variation among individual plants in height and other characteristics.

What is the explanation? Because the soil mixtures are strictly controlled, 100% of *within*-group differences must be attributable to genetics. That is, within each soil mixture, heritability is 1.0. What about differences between groups? Genetically, the two handfuls of seed corn do not differ in quality, therefore 100% of *between*-group differences in plant height (and all other characteristics defining health and productivity) are caused by differing environments. If the same corn were planted in a field, genetic variability in the corn and local variation in soil quality might produce a heritability value around 0.5. Yet, we see that it would be a mistake to apply a heritability value of 0.5 to the two experimental conditions in which there are known differences in soil quality. More important, we would be in error to infer that differences in the quality of the corn crop between the two experimental conditions arose from the genetic inferiority of one handful and the superiority of the other.

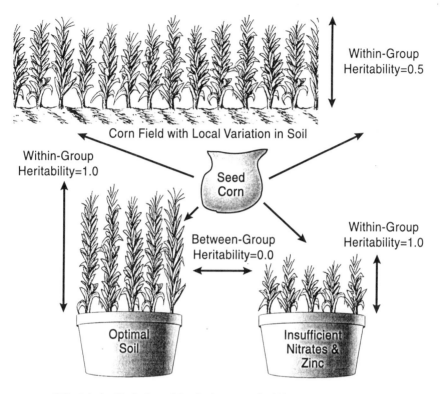

FIG. 6.1. An illustration of the irrelevance of within-group heritability to between-group differences when groups have differing environments.

In *The Bell Curve*, Herrnstein and Murray (1994) co-opted Lewontin's metaphor but planted one hypothetical handful of seed corn in Iowa and the other in the Mojave desert. However, the outcome and the message are the same: The flourishing and the withering "will have nothing to do with genetic differences" (p. 298). To Kaus (1995), "The comeback is obvious: plant the next generation of corn in Iowa. Or water the Mojave" (p. 137). The metaphor applies immediately to the question of why there are large differences in mean IQ between African Americans and Whites, an issue to which the next chapter is devoted. For now, Kamin's (1974) summation removes ambiguity: "To attribute racial differences to genetic factors, granted the overwhelming evidence of cultural-environmental differences between races, is to compound folly with malice" (p. 177).

Merely recognizing the joint influence of genes and the environment on intelligence is not sufficient because this recognition risks the conceptual error of thinking that a heritability of about 0.5 places limitations on how much intelligence can increase. No such limitations exist, at least not by the "fact" of h^2 = approximately 0.5. In fact, even if the heritability of intelligence were 100%, there is no reason why intelligence could not be modified through environmental factors. Heritability and improvability are logically independent. The point is made vividly in the case of intergenerational increases in height. Angoff (1988) noted that "height has been consistently regarded as an example of a trait with an extremely high heritability index—close to 1.0" (p. 714), and yet in many countries average height has changed dramatically from one generation to the next. In Japan between 1946 and 1982, the heights of young adult males increased on average about 4 inches. The average heights of Europeans and Americans have been increasing at a rate of about 3 centimeters per generation since the mid-1800s; the heights of East Asians have been increasing, since World War II, even faster (Bock & Moore, 1986). These gains are logically independent of the heritability coefficient for height because the coefficient is maintained so long as taller parents continue to have taller children. This is so because, in the computation of correlations, all information on group means and standard deviations is lost; the correlation itself simply reports the degree of correspondence between variables. Even if our descendants were 10-foot-tall giants, the heritability index for height could remain unchanged from current values. For that matter, it could increase—the point is, heritability values are not sensitive to changes in the absolute magnitude of any trait.

The implicit principle—that heritability and modifiability operate independently—applies with equal force to intelligence as to stature. Referring to height, Angoff (1988) concluded that "if a trait with this degree of heritability is so changeable, then other traits, like intelligence, which are acknowledged to have lower heritability coefficients, may also be changeable" (p. 714). Angoff's point, although crucial, has been lost even on some specialists in the field. For example, Herrnstein and Murray (1994) spoke of "the limits that heritability puts on the ability to manipulate intelligence" (p. 109). Recognizing that misconceptions about intelligence are widespread, Scarr noted that "the most common misunderstanding of the concept of heritability relates to the myth of fixed intelligence" (1981b, p. 73), and lamented that "the myth of heritability limiting malleability seems to die hard" (1981a, p. 53). Other behavioral geneticists have likewise decried the mistaken idea that if a trait has a genetic component it cannot be influenced by the environment (Thompson & Plomin, 1993). Binet (1909) himself spoke against the "brutal pessimism" of seeing intelligence as a prescribed and intractable quantity (p. 54). We now know that the idea is not only pessimistic, it is unscientific.

We are correct, of course, to regard genes as setting limits on the range of phenotypic variation. Paul Bunyan cannot exist because biomechanical considerations would make such a design unworkable, and more realistic ranges for height are encoded by DNA gene frequencies and combinations. Phenotypic limitations exist, but who knows for sure what those limitations are? What were once dictatorial holds of DNA on phenotype have been abrogated through technologies. Even the expression of monogenic traits, as for phenylketonuria

(PKU), can be modified by environmental intervention (Lewontin, 1970; Plomin & DeFries, 1998). In the case of PKU, exposure to the amino acid phenylalanine can be deadly, but with an appropriate diet the affected person can lead a normal life. Therefore, although genes impose theoretical limits on phenotype, including, presumably, upper bounds on intelligence (Hebb, 1949), it is impossible to know a priori what those limits are (Hunt, 1961). As geneticists have long recognized, knowing the "range of potentialities of a human genotype" would require that a genotype be exposed not only to all existing environments, but to "all the lives possible to human beings" (Sinnott, Dunn, & Dobzhansky, 1958, p. 24). Because this condition has never been met, nor can be, no one can foresee the limits of human intelligence (Lewontin, 1970). It is possible that the human race can become far more intelligent than it is at present (Perkins, 1995).

Conceptual Limitations

Influences on cognitive development do not cleave into genetic and environmental factors as neatly as we might suppose (Keating, 1996). Even when genes play a role in behavior, the actualization of that role might depend completely on experience. For example, a child's rate of vocabulary acquisition has a genetic component, even though every word is learned through experience (Neisser et al., 1996). This illustrates a general principle well known to biologists, which is that the environment affects gene expression. The reverse is also true: Genes can shape the environment. Genetic factors can lead to qualities of behavior to which the environment responds, producing *reactive* (or evocative) covariance between genes and the environment (Scarr, 1992; Wachs, 1996). Physical, mental, and psychological characteristics, some of which have a genetic origin, can shape the psychosocial and physical environment, which then echoes back to shape internal characteristics (Joffe, 1982). The net effect is a reverberating codetermination of genetic and environmental influences. Think of how sensitive parents respond to a precocious child. Competent parents calibrate interactions with their child according to that child's needs and abilities, and parents' responsiveness can have reciprocal effects in advancing the development of the child (Ho, 1987). Such processes can form either positive feedback loops, which reinforce and extend interindividual differences, or negative feedback loops, which reduce differences (Harris, 1995).

    Gene-environment covariance can also be *active*, as when a person's genotype leads to the pursuit of certain qualities of experience through the selection or construction of environments (Greenough & Black, 1992; Wachs, 1996). That is, genes can cause children to "create their own environments" (Bouchard, 1994, p. 1701; Scarr, 1992). The importance of idiosyncratic experience pathways is suggested by the fact that, for many traits, most of the variance attributable to the environment is actually associated with *nonshared* aspects of experience, whose effect is to make members of the same family different from one another (Scarr,

1992). This mechanism might also explain why the genetic contribution to intelligence appears to *increase* through the life span. A growing genetic contribution is consistent with the idea that children have relatively little say in the structure of their day-to-day experience, whereas older adolescents and adults are "freer to seek their own niches" (Scarr & Weinberg, 1983, p. 260). Presumably, genes have more freedom for expression because adolescents and adults have options that are not available to young children.[3]

However, the volition of even young children can result in the construction of specialized experience. Winner (1996) cited the case of 4-year-old Jacob who, upon hearing heavy metal music for the first time, begged his parents to let him play an electric guitar. After listening to Jacob's incessant pleading for 2 years, his parents relented, bought him a guitar, and found a music teacher. Winner (1996) recounted what followed:

> At his first lesson, scheduled for 30-minutes, Jacob refused to leave. Whereas most children are relieved that a lesson is over, Jacob did not want it to end. After his second lesson, his teacher was certain that Jacob was a prodigy. He would play back just about anything by ear, he could master complex music seemingly without effort, and he could improvise in a musical manner. Once while on an outing with his father, Jacob passed a group of street musicians. He asked to try their electric guitar and astonished bystanders, who were heard joking that he must be the reincarnation of Jimi Hendrix. (p. 285)

We do not know for sure whether Jacob's obsession with heavy metal guitar music was genetic in origin, but given his parents' reluctance to pursue this path (they felt that this was not a "childlike kind of music"; Winner, 1996, p. 285), a "nurture" explanation is hard to accept.[4] The example of Jacob illustrates how active gene-environment covariance might operate—by genes producing experience through the person's own agency. It also injects a dose of skepticism into claims that the environment is prepotent.

How are the effects of active gene-environment covariance parceled into nature and nurture? The answer is, not easily (Neisser, 1998). Active covariance between genes and environment is not clearly nature *or* nurture, but is more accurately described as an example of reciprocal determinism in which each can affect the other, and in which the relative influence of genes and experience varies depending on the trait, behavior, and situation (Bandura, 1986). The importance of active choices and niche building might extend far beyond their intrusion into gene-environment covariation. Fine-textured, idiosyncratic microexperience might be responsible for that much larger "bucket" of individual variation that cannot be accounted for by either genotype or commonalities of experience between persons (i.e., that troublesome slice of the variance pie that statisticians like to call "error").

Active covariation finds a parallel in Hayes's (1962) drive theory of intelligence. Hayes (1962) proposed that "intelligence is acquired by learning, and [that] inherited motivational makeup influences the kind and amount of learning that occurs" (p. 302). According to Hayes, experience-producing drives originate from genotype but are actualized only through experience. This hybrid mechanism represents an annoying exception to tidy dichotomous models that segregate genetic and environmental effects. By Hayes' account, genes can lead to differences in experience that are mediated by the learner's own experience-seeking behavior. So what is causal? In one sense it is genetics, because genes produce differences in experience-seeking behavior. But intelligence is enriched *only* by means of consequent experience, and must also be limited by the range of experiences that are available. The complicating element inserted by Hayes is that the individual can select and shape experience. Environments don't just "happen" (Wachs, 1996; see also Sternberg, 1985a).

It gets more complicated. Not only can genes affect the environment, but the environment can also affect gene activity. Genes depend on appropriate environments, or rather a hierarchy of environments, for their normal expression, but they also respond to specific events and experiences to produce idiosyncratic development (Greenough & Black, 1992). At a molecular level, the immediate environment of each DNA strand determines which of tens of thousands of genes turn on within a cell nucleus. The nucleus is, in turn, enveloped by cytoplasm, and the cytoplasm by a cell membrane (Figure 6.2). Each cell is affected by the paracrine hormones secreted by adjacent cells, and by the endocrine environment of the organism as a whole. Beyond the skin interface is the "outside," which is itself composed of concentric shells of physical and social contexts. Each hierarchically nested environment can exert effects on adjacent environments, and these effects can cascade through several levels (Weiss, 1959). More to the point, the experience of the organism can regulate the intensity of gene expression, such as when exposure to light induces protein synthesis in the visual system (Greenough & Black, 1992).[5] In neuroscience research, the level and location of mRNA expression by the gene *c-fos* is used to map which brain structures are activated by different types of learning (Gall, Hess, & Lynch, 1998). When gene expression is understood in these terms, we might see the genotype itself as expressing behavior—some of which is dependent on experience, some of which is not. Does that raise the nature-nurture question for the behavior of genes?

Multicausality, reciprocal causality, and unresolved conundrums reinforce the message that the nature-nurture question, so glibly posed—"as if the conjunction were 'or'" (Scarr & Weinberg, 1983, p. 260)—is actually the wrong question because it tacitly accepts simple-minded and misleading assumptions. Some geneticists have even called the nature-nurture question "meaningless" (Sinnott et al., 1958, p. 19). To ask, "Is it nature or nurture?" or even "How much of each?" glosses complexity by smoothing over intricate and powerful interactions of causal forces that cannot be dismissed as mere hair-splitting technicalities.

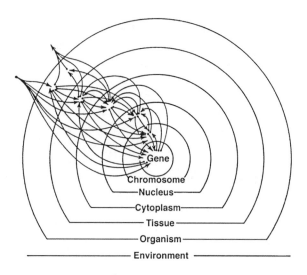

FIG. 6.2. The interparticipation and mutual regulation of multiple levels of biological, cognitive, and sociocultural systems in the developing person. From "Cellular Dynamics," by Paul Weiss, 1959, *Reviews of Modern Physics, 11*(1), p. 18. Copyright 1959 by the American Physical Society. Reprinted with permission.

INTRA-INDIVIDUAL PLASTICITY

The idea that cognitive abilities are products of experience was probably articulated best by Ferguson (1954). Ferguson argued that abilities represent overlearned skills that reach asymptotic limits, and that those asymptotes will vary from culture to culture. This is so because cultures differ in their demand for and valuation of various cognitive abilities, as well as in the provisions they afford for their development. One vivid example is Gladwin's (1970) account of the rigorous training and high regard given to open-ocean navigators in the Micronesian atoll of Puluwat. Similarly, Hungarians have historically maintained a deep commitment to the universal development of musical proficiency. Within cultures, the developed abilities of an individual should be regarded not as *limitations*, but as stable plateaus whose elevation is a function of environmental demands and opportunities (Kohn & Schooler, 1973). This view of cognitive abilities, as learned skills that are shaped by culture, applies equally to intelligence as to any other psychometrically defined ability. The same principle, expressed by Lohman (1993), is that "intelligence tests, like achievement tests, measure *developed* abilities, not innate capacity and potential" (p. 13). Humphreys (1989) likewise declared that "general intelligence is itself a developed ability" (p. 198). Cognitive abilities, including intelligence, are plastic.

The plasticity of intelligence is not a mere theoretical possibility, but is an established fact. This is clearest in the case of absolute levels of intelligence. As perhaps obvious proof, consider (as Piaget did) the average differences in cognitive ability among children at ages 2, 7, and 12. In all normal children, cognitive ability rises rapidly with maturation and enculturation (Boring, 1923; Carroll, 1997; Sternberg, 1990a), a trend long appreciated by developmental psychologists and sometimes described by *stages* (Inhelder & Piaget, 1958), and indexed by psychometrists as *mental age* (Cronbach, 1984). The steep rise in absolute levels of intelligence, measurable as raw scores on ability tests, necessitates the calibration of norms to age levels. Typically, mental age climbs steadily through early adulthood at least, and one way of interpreting IQ is the steepness of this curve (Carroll, 1997).

Norm-based measures of intelligence, indexed by IQ scores, also change over time. For example, IQ drift is common during childhood and adolescence (Hunt, 1961). Within-person correlations of IQ scores drop steadily from age 2 to age 15 (Humphreys, 1989). This instability, according to Humphreys (1989), "is a monotonic function of the amount of time between the original score and the score at retest" (p. 200). As the period of time between tests increases, the relationship between successive IQ scores becomes weaker. Yet, paradoxically, the heritability of IQ seems to increase as a function of age (Pederson et al., 1992). This does not necessarily reduce the importance of the environment, however, because the apparent increase in heritability with age may be driven by genetically influenced tendencies to seek certain kinds of experience; and, as one grows older, there is typically greater discretion to choose among life paths that vary in their experiential quality. The opportunity to pursue high-quality experience then becomes crucial.

IQ "instability" has been observed not only from year to year, but also from hour to hour. There is evidence, for example, that crystallized, fluid, and other abilities exhibit diurnal fluctuations with characteristic patterns (Cattell, 1987). Studies of circadian and sleep-wake rhythms have revealed that cognitive performance oscillates according to the time of day, although the form of that oscillation depends on the specific type of cognitive performance measured (Folkard & Monk, 1985). For example, many simple reasoning tasks yield performance curves that parallel the inverted-U pattern of general physiological "arousal," as indexed by body temperature. Performance on low-demand tasks peaks at midday, but as tasks increase in working memory load, optimal performance shifts to earlier in the day. For tasks highest in working memory demand, the curve turns upside down—performance is highest in the early morning hours, drops off by midday, and surges again in the evening hours (Folkard & Monk, 1985). These fluctuations appear to reflect both external events, such as food consumption, as well as endogenous biochemical cycles (Horn, 1967). In psychometric models, these temporal fluctuations are embedded in the estimated unreliability of mental tests; in reality, they exhibit regularities that are at least partially understood.

Although IQ scores can change from year to year, they tend to show appreciable stability. However, the interpretation of that stability is unclear. Initial IQ differences may lead to separate experiential paths that reinforce or even magnify the initial cognitive differences. This is so because environments can be responsive to differences in ability between people—consider, again, the sensitive parent or the talented teacher. IQ stability might therefore reflect, in part, the effects of a responsive environment that preserves the initial rank orders of IQ and therefore limits IQ mobility (Lewontin, 1970). To the degree that such effects come into play, IQ stability should not be taken as evidence for the controlling influence of genes over experience. In other words, the inference from stability to unchangeability is logically flawed. As Lewontin (1970) expresses this point: "To say that children do not change their IQ is not the same as saying they cannot" (p. 4).

The plasticity of intelligence is lifelong. Cognitive development continues into adulthood and extends through the life span (Alexander & Langer, 1990). Separating the age trends of crystallized and fluid intelligence leads to a more precise picture of how intelligence changes over time (Dittmann-Kohli & Baltes, 1990; see Figure 6.3). Crystallized intelligence (CI) continues to grow to at least the age of 50, and perhaps longer. Fluid intelligence (FI), however, usually reaches a plateau between the ages of 16 and 30, and then declines thereafter at a rate of about 0.04 standard deviations per year (Cattell, 1987; Hunt, 1995). Horn (1967, p. 30) cheerily described this trade-off as the substitution of "wisdom for brilliance." A composite intelligence represented by the FI + CI curve presents a hopeful picture about the way cognitive power ebbs and flows over the life span.

What is unclear, and controversial, is whether the decline of fluid intelligence is inevitable. The explanation for a decline in fluid ability may rest simply with the notion that there is less need for adaptation to new situations as one ages. On the other hand, the explanation may be biological—the loss of cognitive powers may be a consequence of accumulated neuron loss or degeneration, attributable in part to injury or exposure to toxins. Cattell (1987) noted that brain mass typically declines by about 10% between the ages of 30 and 90. A loss of fluid ability may not be debilitating, however, if an older person can exploit his or her accumulated experience in the form of knowledge, just as in an expert-novice transition the relative importance of cognitive resources shifts toward a greater reliance on domain knowledge. Researchers who study the question of why fluid ability declines, regardless of their position, *do* agree on one thing, however: Neither fluid nor crystallized intelligence is fixed, but each can (and does) shift up or down over the life course, contingent largely on individual interests, allocation of time, and opportunity (Baltes & Schaie, 1976; Cattell, 1987; Horn, 1967; Sternberg, 1990a; Vernon, 1948). As life experience varies from over time, IQ can rise or fall, sometimes radically (Dittmann-Kohli & Baltes, 1990; Hunt, 1961).

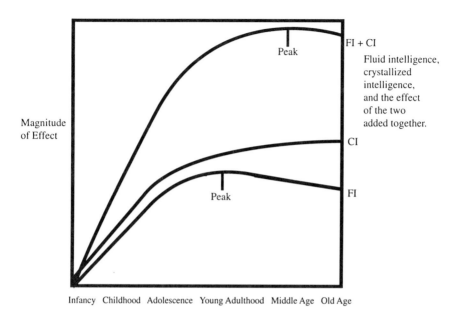

FIG. 6.3. Change trends for fluid and crystallized intelligence, and their combination, over the life span. From "Intelligence—Why It Grows, Why It Declines, " by J. L. Horn, 1967, *Trans-Action, 5*, November, p. 31. Reprinted by permission of Transaction Publishers. Copyright ©1967 by Transaction Publishers; all rights reserved.

Early in the 21st century, the American workforce will experience a significant shift in age distribution: Older workers will have much greater representation in the workforce than they do at present. Given this age redistribution, Hunt (1995) worried that the life-span trendlines for fluid and crystallized intelligence do not bode well for American economic competitiveness. Age-related trends for fluid and crystallized intelligence imply that the distribution of cognitive abilities in the American workforce will shift such that crystallized intelligence (i.e., knowledge and expertise) will be amply supplied, but that the flexible problem-solving ability denoted by fluid intelligence may, per capita worker, be less available (Hunt, 1995). To be sure, any absolute changes in fluid and crystallized intelligence would be small, but the fact that they would apply widely across the workforce means that their summed effect could be substantial. According to Hunt (1995), an age-related shift in the composition of cognitive abilities could not come at a worse time because the global economy and the technologies that drive it make greater demands than ever on the ability to solve new problems and grasp new ideas.

INTERGENERATIONAL PLASTICITY

The Flynn Effect

Another form of IQ instability is its plasticity between generations. Intergenerational plasticity is strikingly demonstrated in the worldwide, decades-long trend of rising IQs, sometimes known as the *Flynn effect* (Flynn, 1987, 1998). This phenomenon recognizes that IQs have been rising for most of the 20th century in every country for which pertinent data are available. So robust is the trend that James Flynn (1998) referred to the trans-national secular IQ gains, his namesake, as a "brute phenomenon" (p. 25). "Somewhere out there," said Flynn (1998, p. 53), "environmental variables of enormous potency are creating IQ differences." Figure 6.4 illustrates the effect as gains in Wechsler-Binet IQ for the U.S. White population during the period 1918 to 1995.

Flynn (1987) has estimated that during the 20th century there was an IQ gain per generation (30 years) of about 15 points—a full standard deviation. In a later paper, Flynn (1996) contended that an intergenerational IQ gain of about a standard deviation has been found, without exception, in the 20 industrialized nations for which he had obtained data. In Britain, these IQ gains have been accumulating for at least a century, and the trend's starting point seems to coincide approximately with the advent of industrialization (Flynn, 1998). A recent restandardization of the Wechsler tests show a further gain in mean IQ since 1978 (Jencks & Phillips, 1998c). There is no indication that the trend is leveling off; in some countries, such as the Netherlands, the *rate* of IQ gain has been increasing (Flynn, 1998).

Rising IQ trends are not mere artifacts of greater familiarity with tests and test taking (Lynn, 1990; Teasdale & Owen, 1987). For one thing, the intergenerational

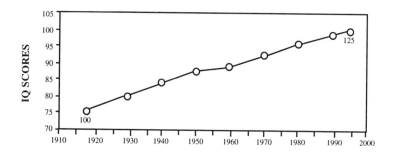

FIG. 6.4. An example of the Flynn effect: Gains in Wechsler-Binet IQ for the U.S. White population. From "Get Smart, Take a Test," by J. Horgan, 1995, *Scientific American, 273*(5), p. 14. Copyright 1995 by Dimitry Schildlovsky. Adapted with permission.

escalation of IQ actually pre-dates the widespread use of cognitive tests and has persisted into an era when IQ testing has become less common. Also, the gains are simply too large to be attributed to test sophistication. Repeated exposure to IQ tests can produce gains of about 5 or 6 points, but nothing like the IQ gains in Britain, which are on the order of 30 points (Flynn, 1998). Indeed, intergenerational IQ gains are so massive that they are unlikely to be explained by any single factor.

The Flynn effect is demonstrable across a broad spectrum of cognitive abilities. Lynn (1990) pointed out that "increases have been found in all major components of intelligence, including reasoning, verbal comprehension, and visuo-spatial abilities" (p. 280). However, the magnitude of IQ gains depends substantially on the cognitive ability factor assessed. A broad distinction can be made here between gains in fluid intelligence and gains in crystallized intelligence. IQ gains have been greater on tests of decontextualized problem solving (or fluid intelligence), such as measured by Raven's Matrices, than on tests corresponding more closely to school subjects (or crystallized intelligence). In the Netherlands, Raven-based IQ has leaped about 21 points in 30 years, far higher than gains on tests that tap domain knowledge (Neisser, 1997). Broad measures of IQ, including the Stanford-Binet and Wechsler Adult Intelligence Scale (WAIS) batteries, have evinced smaller although equally consistent effects on the order of about 3 points per decade (Neisser, 1998). Because intergenerational IQ gains are more pronounced on measures of fluid intelligence than of crystallized intelligence, the Flynn effect cannot be explained by saying that later generations simply possess more knowledge than their forebears.

One consequence of rising IQ is that tests of cognitive ability been "recentered" periodically to reestablish their means at 100. The periodic renorming has tended to conceal the upward trend in raw test scores, producing a fictitious constancy of meaning of IQ across time (Sowell, 1995). Therefore, although IQ = 100 has been reasserted and redefined with each new generation—what *was* average now is not. IQs have increased—that much is known. A wide-scale increase in measured IQ in the 20th century is now beyond dispute (Neisser, 1997, 1998). But has *intelligence* also increased? Flynn (1987) proposed that "those who wish to identify the problem-solving ability IQ tests measure with intelligence must argue that the current generation is radically more intelligent than the last" (pp. 184-185).

Flynn himself, however, did not believe this. The problem for Flynn was what a large rise in intelligence *implies.* Flynn considered differences between U.S. populations in 1918 and 1995, which are separated not only by time but also by an IQ gap of 25 points. An average person (IQ = 100) in 1918, if transported to 1995, would be very much below average (IQ = 75); in fact, that person would be borderline retarded. Flynn (1998) asked, "Does that mean that during World War I about half of White Americans lacked the capacity to understand the basic rules of baseball?" (p. 36). To Flynn, the suggestion is absurd, and thus a large IQ gain cannot really indicate an increase in intelligence. But is a substantial gain in intelligence really so farfetched? Although we do not have data on WWI soldiers' understanding of baseball, Humphreys (1989) argued that there were discernible differences between WWI soldiers and WWII soldiers in the speed with which they were able to master their duties, namely that the latter soldiers learned much more quickly. In chess competition, the average age of world-class players dropped steadily in the 20th century, a trend that Howard (1999) took as "real-world" evidence that intelligence was rising. At the same time, daily life became more complex (Schooler, 1984, 1998). Granat and Granat (1978) demonstrated that people with low IQ scores found social adjustment increasingly problematic. Some who would not have been called retarded in the past exhibited functional deficits that justified the label. More to the point: It was not genetics that differentiated the 1995 adult from his or her 1918 counterpart, but that each lived in different ecologies with different demands and opportunities (Greenfield, 1998).

Flynn also considered the reverse situation. If a typical person (IQ = 100) were transported to 1918, that person would be considerably above average (IQ = 125). The inference is that if intelligence really has increased, the world holds a lot more smart people now than it did back then. So, asked Flynn, where's all this brilliance? If today's average person is so bright by 1918 standards, do we see evidence for this? Flynn did not think so. As contrary evidence, he pointed to the fact that in the Netherlands there are fewer patents issued now than in the past. This particular example, however, is patently flawed. It is obvious that patent filing is a competitive enterprise, and the nature of the competition changes over time. During the 20th century, invention moved from the shed to the laboratory, where welding was more typically done with a laser than with a torch. The inventor of today competes with a population that is more highly trained and technologically equipped. Patent laws have changed in the interim. Schooler (1998) pointed out that unless all these potentially relevant factors are held constant, which is probably impossible, a change in the number of patents issued is not a good index of intellectual productivity. Even without such controls, is it really so unreasonable to believe that rising levels of intelligence have been manifest as escalations of creative productivity? The incessant proliferation of technologies, ideas, and art forms of all kinds suggests that the world is rife with intelligence and creative production, and of course knowledge itself has mushroomed.

No doubt the meaning of the Flynn effect will continue to be debated. However, the *cause* of rising IQs is also at issue. As noted earlier, explanations based on shifting gene frequencies can be quickly discounted because there has not been enough time for natural selection to produce such a large effect and, thankfully, the "eugenic" agenda of selective reproduction has for the most part been relegated to dystopian fiction.[6] Moreover, population studies have actually confirmed the negative correlations between IQ and fertility so dreaded by eugenicists, but without the feared IQ decline.[7] The explanation for the Flynn effect is not genetic, but environmental. Referring to the secular gains in IQ, Neisser (1998, p. 15) remarked that "however one may choose to interpret it, . . . the environment matters!" But which aspects of the environment are responsible? Several hypotheses have been advanced, including improvements in nutrition, increases in cognitive stimulation, urbanization, proliferation of information technologies, and the eradication or reduction of childhood diseases.

It is likely that the Flynn effect has arisen not from a single cause, but from a combination of influences. Indeed, IQ gains in different countries may have different patterns of underlying causes (Flynn, 1998). Lynn (1990) favored a nutritional explanation, and showed that in prior decades there has been widespread suboptimal nutrition, manifest as deficiencies in vitamins, minerals, essential fatty acids, and protein, and that improved nutrition has been experimentally linked to increases in IQ (however, see Flynn, 1998, for counterevidence). Widespread nutritional improvement may have had effects on IQ, brain weight, and body size; Lynn demonstrated that the magnitude of IQ gains over the past 50 years corresponds roughly to increases in average height and head circumference—all are on the order of one standard deviation (Miller & Corsellis, 1977). Moreover, better nutrition has been shown to have stronger effects on visuospatial abilities than on verbal educational abilities, a pattern that coincides with the Flynn effect pattern of larger gains on tests of nonverbal than verbal ability (Benton & Roberts, 1988).

Although improved nutrition may have contributed to rising IQs, nutrition alone is unlikely to account for the phenomenon. The jump in cognitive power indexed by rising IQs can be thought of as a response to the demands and opportunities of living in a complex world—that is, "complexity of life" has produced "complexity of mind" (Neisser et al., 1996, p. 90; Schooler, 1998). Environmental complexity has been associated with enhanced cognitive capabilities across the life span, and in non-human species enriched environments are known to produce more complex brain structures (Schooler, 1984). In human societies, environmental complexity is multidimensional. Greenfield (1998) argued cogently that rising IQ scores are the product of four interlocking factors of societal transformation: technology, urbanization, formal education, and nutrition. All four can be seen as reflecting the demands and affordances of the cultural change that some call modernization, whose onset and pace varies between countries and by locale within countries.

To illustrate, Greenfield cited Wheeler's (1970/1942) study of Tennessee mountain children, and in particular his documentation of the upward trend of IQ scores during the period 1930 to 1940. During that 10-year span, children living in rural eastern Tennessee displayed an 11-point increase in IQ. Also during that decade, the region experienced a number of social changes that correspond to Greenfield's interlocking factors of modernization. Most important, perhaps, were improvements to the local road system, because this renewed infrastructure had secondary, cascade effects. Better roads, for example, permitted visits by a circulating library of 14,000 volumes. There were also fewer one-room schoolhouses as students were provided with transportation to larger consolidated schools that were better equipped and better supplied with textbooks. Hot lunches were introduced in the larger schools, ostensibly improving the dependability of good nutrition. School enrollment increased by 17%, and school attendance increased by 32%, partly as a result of new incentives for student attendance. During the same decade, teacher training requirements were raised to a minimum of 4 years of college education. Finally, because of improvements to the road system, many residents had easier access to industrial employment and so could supplement or replace their agricultural livelihoods.

Presumably as a combined product of these improvements, the characteristics of the typical student in each grade changed substantially (Fig. 6.5). In 1930 (dotted lines), chronological age (C.A.) and mental age (M.A.) were quite discrepant. By 1940 (solid lines), C.A. and M.A. had converged substantially, with mental age increasing by 9 months, and chronological age decreasing by 8 months, on average, at each grade level. The convergence meant that the difference between M.A. and

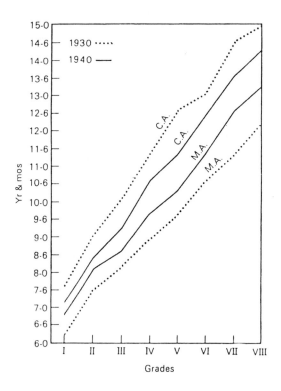

FIG. 6.5. Convergence of mental age and chronological age among Tennessee mountain children. From "A Comparative Study of the Intelligence of East Tennessee Mountain Children," by L. R. Wheeler, May 1942, *The Journal of Educational Psychology, 33*(5), p. 326. Public domain.

C.A. had shrunk by two thirds and IQs were therefore higher. This translated to an increase in median IQ from 82 (classified "dull") to 93 ("normal"). To Wheeler (1970/1942) these findings demonstrated that "intelligence, as measured by these tests, may be improved with an improvement in educational and general environmental conditions" (p. 132).

A more contemporary aspect of modernization highlighted by Greenfield (1998) is the massive exposure to electronic technologies that involve visuospatial displays of information. Visual media—including television, video, film, and computer graphics—are plausible agents of the wide-scale cognitive enhancement of nonverbal abilities identified with the Flynn effect. Visual media may be more complex than in the past (Neisser, 1997); many require the viewer to adapt rapidly to shifting spatial perspectives, exercising the viewer's ability to hold and transform three-dimensional representations. Also, computer-based instructional technologies sometimes present externalized representations, including mental model analogs, that can be internalized and manipulated by the learner (Greenfield, 1998; White, 1993).

Yet another possible explanation for the rightward shift of IQ is the greater availability and intensity of formal education—the "schooling effect" hypothesis (Cahan & Cohen, 1989). There now exists a large accumulation of data, reviewed in the next chapter, showing that schooling does have an effect on IQ. This effect is supported indirectly by the best-documented instance in which *no* increases in IQ were found over roughly a generation. Virtually no differences in IQ were detected among Scottish 11-year-olds between 1932 and 1947, a constancy that the investigators attributed to similar levels and quality of education between the two cohorts (Loehlin, Lindzey, & Spuhler, 1975). However, these same authors also found that, in other times and locations, improvements and expansions of education were associated with a rise in IQ of as much as 15 points. Other nonschool factors also come into play. In the Netherlands, for example, schooling effects accounted for only a small fraction of variance associated with IQ gains (Flynn, 1998), and thus schooling should be considered only part of the explanation for rising IQs.

Although the rising IQ trend is a worldwide phenomenon, it is possible that there are substantial differences among nations in the slope of that trend. There are small-sample data showing, for example, that the rate of IQ gain among Japanese schoolchildren may be double that of their White American counterparts. Hunt (1995) already broached the possibility that the gentrification of the American workforce may result in an insufficient "supply" of fluid intelligence—a small shift statistically, but possibly one with large economic consequences. International variation in IQ growth rates might alter the vocabulary of national debates on the interlocking factors of education, human capital, economic competitiveness, and national security. In one form or another, these factors have fueled debate or shaped policy for some time—at least since 1957, when the launch of Sputnik triggered a massive federal investment in revitalizing education, or the comparable jolt of 1973 when the OPEC oil embargo announced the death of American economic self-sufficiency.

Intergenerational IQ Shifts Among Immigrants

The worldwide, intergenerational rise in IQ known as the Flynn effect is remarkable in its own right. Whatever its causes, its existence is proof that absolute levels of intelligence are not genetically prescribed (Neisser, 1998; Sowell, 1995). However, in certain subgroups, intergenerational changes in IQ have been observed before the Flynn effect was discovered. Sowell (1995) cited, for example, the case of Jewish immigrants to the U.S. following World War I. Their mental test scores were so low as to prompt Carl Brigham, creator of the Scholastic Aptitude Test, to remark that the results "disprove the belief that the Jew is highly intelligent" (Sowell, 1995, p. 74). However, within a decade, Sowell noted, Jews in the United States were scoring above the national average. Similar trends over generations and immigrant status can be cited for other ethnic groups, including Hungarians, Italians, Russians, and Poles (Gould, 1981; Sowell, 1995). Unfortunately, American immigration policy has at times been influenced by bigotry and propaganda surrounding the alleged preponderance of "defectives" among certain ethnic groups. Enactment of the Immigration Restriction Act of 1924 imposed severe quotas on immigration from nations of "inferior stock," largely southern and eastern Europeans (Gould, 1981, p. 232). Such dark moments in U.S. history should make us hesitate before pronouncing judgment on the intellectual qualities or capabilities of any group. The following chapter returns to this theme.

CONCLUSION

This chapter rests on two arguments. First, although genetics plays a role in the development of intelligence, its constraints on intelligence are far less than is typically believed. Second, the plasticity of intelligence is readily demonstrable, both within individuals and across generations. These two principles converge in the Flynn effect—the phenomenon of global IQ gains during the 20th century. Rising IQs around the world demonstrate that the heritability of IQ imposes no logical constraints on the actual values of IQ. The Flynn effect is vivid evidence of the principle that heritability does not limit malleability. Intelligence is plastic not only between generations, but also within individuals over time—both in absolute terms (as mental age) and in comparative terms (as IQ, fluid, and crystallized intelligence). Although genetics must ultimately place phenotypic limits on organisms in intelligence as in all other traits, no one yet knows what those limits are.

NOTES

1. Problems of representativeness are characteristic of behavior-genetic studies generally, not just studies involving adoption. Samples have been predominantly White (raising questions about generalizability) and restricted in SES range (reducing estimates of environmental effects; Waldman, 1997).

2. It is possible to estimate the effects of "correlated environments" that include shared prenatal experience, independently of "shared rearing environments" (Pederson et al., 1992). However, these effects are usually estimated only after variance attributed to genetics is removed—variation that might be confounded with prenatal experience (e.g., in the IQ correlation of MZ twins reared apart). In any case, estimates of the effects of correlated environments (excluding shared family experience) are rarely computed.

3. In a theory of gene-to-environment effects, Scarr (1992) recognized a third type of genetic influence on experience. *Passive* effects are those that are obtained by the fact that biological parents provide genes and also structure the home environment, ensuring that the two are positively correlated.

4. In fact, one could ask if *nurture* is even the right word to use, because nurture implies the intentionality of others but dismisses the agency of the subject (Bidell & Fischer, 1997).

5. Another example is the adaptation of eye shape to visual experience. Myopia, or nearsightedness, is much more common in literate than in nonliterate populations (Wallman, 1994). For example, incidence of myopia among students in Hong Kong and Taiwan was found to be between 70% and 80%, compared to 20% to 30% in rural areas of China. Among Greenland Inuits, the incidence of myopia increased tenfold in 32 years. Myopia is caused by eyes that are structurally too long to focus distant images. Eye length, in turn, is influenced by physiological events that are at least partly governed by gene activity. These genetic events appear to be responsive to how frequently the eyes are focused at the distance of a page (among readers) or at infinity (among those whose activities are largely outdoors).

6. One notorious exception was the Nazi breeding campaign called the Lebensborn ("Fountain of Life") project (Hammer, 2000). Under the direction of SS chief Heinrich Himmler, the project urged blond, blue-eyed women to mate with tall, fit SS officers to produce a "master race." Between 1935 and 1945, 11,000 children were born under the auspices of the Lebensborn project (Williams, 2000).

7. Shockley's (1972, pp. 307-306) fear of "down-breeding" among low-IQ Americans led him to make the outrageous proposal of providing incentives for voluntary sterilization, with a $1000 "bonus" delivered for each IQ point below 100.

7

The Race Question

Unequal achievement among population groups is a source of unrelenting frustration to all who care about education and social equity. Historically, Black-White differences have dominated the discussion of unequal achievement and opportunity in the United States. For many generations, African Americans have lagged behind Whites in every available measure of cognitive ability and achievement (Loury, 1998). A difference in mean IQ between Blacks and Whites of about one standard deviation (15 points) has been amply documented (Jencks, 1972; Scarr & Weinberg, 1976). At the tails of distributions, moderate differences in means translate to gross differences in representation. When group means differ by 15 points, only 16% of the lower-scoring group exceeds the mean of the higher-scoring group (Gustafsson & Undheim, 1996). Although a gap of this magnitude is well established in Black-White comparisons, a similar lag can be found for Hispanic Americans (Rodriguez, 1992).

Differences in achievement across ethnic groups are not peculiar to the United States. Strikingly similar patterns of discrepant achievement among ethnic groups can be found in many other nations around the world. Japan is a good, although perhaps surprising, example. In Japan, the pariah-caste Barakumin have been subjected to prejudice for centuries, confined to ghettos, limited largely to butcher and tanner trades, and prohibited from marrying outside their group. They exhibit much lower academic achievement and career attainment than do mainstream Japanese and, notably, their mean IQ is about one standard deviation below that of the non-Baraku majority (De Vos & Wagatsuma, 1966). However, unlike Black and White Americans, there is no race difference between the Barakumin and the Japanese majority. To some observers, parallel gaps in achievement in Japan and the United States both reflect "early damage to self identity and self-respect vis-a-vis cultural expectations held toward the traditionally disparaged group" (De Vos & Wagatsuma, 1966, p. 262).

THEORIES OF INEQUALITY

The roots of racial inequality are complex, and several competing theories have been advanced to explain race differences in cognitive and social outcomes (Ogbu, 1978; Steele, 1999). One prominent theory, which was largely responsible for the social programs associated with the Great Society movement, is the doctrine of *cultural deprivation*. This is the idea that Black children are often poorly equipped by their families with the cognitive skills and motivations necessary for success in mainstream society. A competing model, the *cultural conflict* theory, holds that Black children are not culturally deficient, but merely different, and are in fact prepared for life in a culture that differs from that of the dominant culture. According to this view, schools are often at fault for failing to capitalize on the cognitive strengths that Black children bring with them into the classroom. *Institutional inequality* theory holds that institutional structures established by the larger society preserve inequality. This theory places blame on the lower expectations held for black children, on inferior resources allocated for their education, and on policies that bar them from success-bound tracks.

By Ogbu's account, none of these explanations is quite right. Rather, racial inequality arises most fundamentally from the ascription of African Americans to caste status, in which *caste* refers to a socially reinforced system of stratification based on lower status ascribed at birth. If Ogbu is right, then African Americans have something in common with the Barakumin of Japan and the Harijan, or "untouchable," infracaste of India. By virtue of assignment to a caste, only certain social roles and attainments are permitted, and socialization experiences are geared to the prescribed possibilities. It is the caste status of African Americans, said Ogbu, that drives all social mechanisms that reinforce inequality. In mixed-race settings, the constant pressure to disprove cultural stereotypes can lead to "disidentification," or rejection of academic competition, which really amounts to a refusal to be complicit in a "game" in which African American students are not allowed to win (Steele, 1999).

Within the theoretical matrix sketched earlier, the position I have taken is closest to the cultural differences theory. Here, the concept of *aptitude* is relevant. Intelligence is a very general aptitude, but like all aptitudes it describes readiness to succeed within a context (Snow, 1996). When the context changes, different competencies become adaptive. The intelligence repertoire consists of a *limited* subset of capabilities that permit effectiveness, in which *effectiveness* will be defined somewhat differently across cultures and between individuals. The exact composition of the intelligence repertoire is acknowledged, therefore, to be sensitive to variations in the demands and affordances of cultures or subcultures, although many elements of the repertoire are likely to transcend cultures. The Black-White gap in IQ and achievement is partly an expression of differences in enculturation in the repertoire sampled by IQ tests. Yet, with respect to Ogbu's (1978) theory, the IQ gap should not be seen as simply reflecting cultural differences, but as traceable also to deeply entrenched prejudices and social structures that reinforce race-based inequality. This means that the educative experiences I refer to as the *cultivation of intelligence* cannot, in themselves, lift society from the quagmire of repression and social injustice that has been oozing for centuries. Any hopeful attempt to cure society of deep-rooted problems associated with race must face the complexity and moment of its underlying causes.

Nonetheless, to understand unequal opportunities and outcomes associated with race, one must take seriously differences between population groups in the acquired and culture-laced cognitive set that I identify as intelligence. The acquisition of that repertoire is estimated, albeit imperfectly, by IQ. This makes IQ truly important without being all-important. Some observers have suggested that differences in IQ test performance may reflect differing task motivation (Nisbett, 1995). However, the IQ gap is unlikely to be purely an artifact of differing motivation. Simply ascribing the gap to motivational differences is contradicted by the finding that the Black-White discrepancy on any cognitive test is a direct function of that test's *g* loading, an association that Jensen (1992a) referred to as the *Spearman hypothesis* (Spearman, 1927). However, as I argued in the previous chapter, saying that differences in IQ reflect real differences in the intelligence repertoire is *not* to say these differences are genetically prescribed.

The very idea that racial differences in IQ might be rooted in genetics is a source of unrelenting public interest, triggering vituperative outrage in some and quiet acceptance in others (Sowell, 1995). Scholars who study race and IQ have sometimes been accused of bigotry and even outright fraud (Wade, 1976).[1] Herrnstein and Murray, authors of the incendiary *Bell Curve*, may have been correct in claiming that although the topic of race differences in intelligence is taboo, people are privately fascinated by it. Murray even referred to writings on the subject as "social science pornography," a provocatively ambiguous comparison (DeParle, 1994, p. 50). In writing this book, I had no great desire to address the subject of race differences in IQ, and yet the social importance of the subject is too great to ignore. In the end, I found the message to be hopeful.

INDIRECT EVIDENCE

Is genetics responsible for race differences in IQ? The answer is unknown (Jensen, 1998). Genetic influences must be acknowledged as a *possibility*, but *only* a possibility, and one that does not have much evidence in its favor, let alone proof (Gustafsson & Undheim, 1996). In the last chapter, we saw that the practice of applying within-group heritability estimates to between-group data is mistaken (cf. Jensen, 1998). The point was made vividly in Lewontin's (1970) metaphor of seed corn. That model can be applied hypothetically to human beings. Imagine that in some dark future every human being has a clone who is relegated to low-caste status, subject to prejudice and squalid living conditions, restricted to menial labor, and provided with only poor-quality education. Social scientists then move in and discover that the IQ distributions of the two populations differ by one standard deviation in the expected direction. The social scientists also find that genetic factors explain a substantial fraction of the IQ variance in both privileged and subjugated populations, and in the combined population. Imagine that a heritability value for IQ is calculated at 0.5. It might then be tempting for social scientists to apply the 0.5 heritability value to explain IQ differences between the two groups. However, that would be a fallacy because the two populations, like the seed corn, would be genetically indistinguishable.

Of course, Black and White populations are *not* genetically indistinguishable. But genetic differences, per se, are not germane. The pertinent question—whose answer is unknown at this point—is whether Black and White populations differ in the frequencies of genes that are functionally instrumental to (not merely correlated with) cognitive performance. What is known is that there are large between-race differences in modal *experience*; or, returning to the seed corn metaphor, "Blacks and whites do not grow up, on average, in the same kind of pot" (Tavris, 1995, p. 63).

Race differences in modal experience begin before birth. For reasons that remain mysterious, infant mortality is about twice as common in African American than in White populations (Jensen, 1998). Low birthweight among urban African Americans has been found to be two to three times that of Whites and more affluent city dwellers (Rush, Stein, & Susser, 1980). As of 1994, incidence of low birthweight (<2,500 grams) among African American newborns (13.3%) was more than double that of White newborns (6.2%; U.S. Department of Commerce, 1997). Massive between-race differences in newborn health can be found historically. In a study of race and SES associations with pregnancy complications conducted in Baltimore hospitals in the 1950s, only 5% of high-SES mothers suffered pregnancy complications; this contrasted with 15% of low-SES White mothers, and 51% of non-White mothers (Pasamanick, Knobloch, & Lilienfeld, 1956). Perinatal complications have, in turn, been associated with much higher incidences of behavior problems, mental health disorders, learning impairments, and mental retardation (Joffe, 1982). Of course, many other experiential factors can be hypothesized to contribute to differences in Black-White IQ distributions. For example, the proposal that nutritional deficiencies contribute to Black-White IQ differences is, in Jensen's (1998, p. 508) words, a "promising hypothesis [that] . . . is well worth studying."

When there are systematic differences in environments, whether of differing soil types for corn or of differing experiential histories for people, heritability coefficients cannot be applied to explain between-group differences (Tavris, 1995). What is needed are data sources other than heritability coefficients, which are actually descriptive statistics that are sensitive to variation in experience and in gene frequencies. As data accumulate, the Black-White IQ gap seems more believably accounted for by differences in modal experience. Relevant here is the worldwide trend of rising IQs known as the *Flynn effect*, described earlier. These IQ shifts are too rapid to allow genetic explanations. The fact of rising IQ contributes viability to the idea that the Black-White IQ gap is environmental in origin (Flynn, 1998). After all, the magnitude of IQ gains is of the same order as the historical Black-White gap. To be specific, Black-White IQ differences have historically been calibrated at around 15 points, or one standard deviation, from the 1930s to the 1980s. Yet, between 1930 and 1980, *both* curves shifted rightward about one standard deviation. In other words, the IQ distributions of 1980s Blacks is congruent with that of 1930s Whites; the identity of those two curves is separated only by time and attendant societal changes. By implication, a gap of 15 points "can easily result from environmental differences" (Neisser, 1998, p. 18).

DIRECT EVIDENCE

The Flynn effect supplies evidence that intergenerational differences in IQ on the order of one standard deviation, or greater, can be accounted for by nongenetic mechanisms. This constitutes *indirect* evidence that group differences in IQ of the same magnitude can also be explained by differences in typical experience. However, there is also *direct* evidence that Black-White IQ gap is environmental. Nisbett (1995, 1998; also Flynn, 1980) cited a set of studies that bear more directly on whether genes contribute to Black-White differences in average IQ.

The Minnesota Transracial Adoption Study

Of the research cited by Nisbett, only the Minnesota study on adoption provides any support for Herrnstein and Murray's claim that the Black-White IQ gap is genetic in origin. In this study, White ($n = 25$) and Black or mixed-race (Black-White) ($n = 130$) children were adopted into White families (Scarr & Weinberg, 1976, 1983). When the subjects were older adolescents (mean age of 18.5 years), the adopted White children had the highest IQs (mean IQ = 111.5), followed by mixed-race children (mean IQ = 109.0), and then children of two Black parents (mean IQ = 96.8). At first blush, it seems that this study supports the genetic doctrine. However, when the data are limited to Black children who were adopted before the age of 12 months, a different picture emerges. The average IQ of the Black early adoptees was 110, which was 20 points higher than the IQ of comparable children raised in the Black community, and 10 points higher than the population mean. For Black children placed before the age of 12 months, IQ correlations with adopted siblings were "embarrassingly similar" to those between natural siblings (Scarr & Weinberg, 1983, p. 264). It is true that the IQs of adopted Black children averaged 6 points below that of their White adoptive siblings, but this gap is small enough to be accounted for by differences in pre- and postnatal experiences prior to adoption. (IQ differences of 6 points or so are not unusual even among identical twins.) The same study showed that the IQs of adopted children were more strongly correlated with their biological mothers ($r = 0.34$) than with their adoptive mothers ($r = 0.21$), reinforcing the belief that genetic forces are not to be dismissed; but these correlations are both rather weak, accounting for, at most, 10% of the variance in IQ. More important, these correlations mask the *upward shift* in IQ enjoyed by the adopted children compared to their nonadopted peers. Again, we are confronted with the statistical independence of measures of association (i.e., correlations and heritability coefficients) and the actual levels of measured ability (i.e., IQ and mental age). Thus, quite in contrast to the inferences drawn by Herrnstein and Murray (1984) in *The Bell Curve*, the original investigators concluded that "genetic racial differences do *not* account for a major portion of the IQ performance differences between racial groups" (Scarr & Weinberg, 1983, p. 261, emphasis added).

Residential Schools

What about the other direct evidence cited by Nisbett? One study contrasted the cognitive ability of Black or mixed-race (West Indian) children with White (English) children in a residential preschool (Tizard, Cooperman, Joseph, & Tizard, 1972). Although the IQs of the parents were not known, the study had the advantage of controlling, roughly, for the quality of environmental enrichment experienced by children. Moreover, all children had been healthy, full-term babies, thus reducing the possible influence of large discrepancies in prenatal care. Children were tested between the ages of 2 and 5 years. Their measured IQs were approximately 103 for White residents and 108 for Black or mixed-race residents, a difference that Nisbett (1995, p. 38) provocatively called "compatible with the assumption of a slight genetic superiority for blacks." Of course, a single study might suggest an overturning of conventional thinking but cannot accomplish it; at least, however, the findings cast doubt on the doctrine of Black genetic inferiority.

Blood Group Studies

Two studies have capitalized on the fact that the African American population as a whole has a substantial degree of European ancestry (about 25%, on average), but which varies considerably between individuals (Jensen, 1998). According to Shockley's (1972) hypothesis, if Europeans are superior to Africans in IQ, then the IQs of African Americans ought to be a function of their degree of European-African admixture. In one test of this hypothesis, researchers estimated the association of European genotypes with various blood group genes, and then computed "odds coefficients" to rank-order Black subjects according to their probabilistic genetic similarities to African ancestors ("ancestral odds"), and to a local Caucasian reference group ("sample odds"; Scarr, Pakstis, Katz, & Barker, 1977). None of the correlations between the two indexes and five measures of cognitive ability differed significantly from zero. Correlations between the first principal component of cognitive measures, estimating g, and "White blood-genes" were -.03 for ancestral odds and -.05 for sample odds. Both values were trivial and statistically insignificant.

In a similar study, 16 blood group genes were ordered according to their representations in Black and White populations (Loehlin, Vandenberg, & Osborne,

1973). The blood group gene that most differentiated between the two populations was labeled Fy^a, and was present in 80% of Whites and 22% of Blacks. The rank-order correlation between the ordered list of genotypes (which indexed the "Europeanness" of blood type) and the associated IQ of Black adolescent subjects was -.38, with higher IQ values associated with *non-European* genotypes. Although this correlation was not statistically significant, perhaps owing to the small sample size ($n = 42$), the direction of the association is provocative, to say the least. In fact, the blood group gene Fy^a, which was most characteristic of the White subjects, was *negatively* correlated with IQ in both White subjects ($r = -.21$) and Black subjects ($r = -.35$), although again these correlations were not statistically significant. In another sample studied by the same investigators, the correlation between Black subjects' IQ and "White blood-genes" was a trivial +.01 (again statistically insignificant). Point-biserial correlations between individual blood genes and IQ were also trivial, ranging from +.03 to -.09 in the White sample.

Blood group studies have been criticized for their lack of power to detect gene-IQ associations. One weakness of the methodology is that the independent assortment of genes across generations is certain to dissociate blood genes from those that are hypothetically associated with cognitive ability. Given Jensen's (1998) claim that European genes were introduced primarily during the period of American slavery, the fact of many subsequent generations has made the independent segregation of gene alleles a serious problem. One exception cited by Jensen is the blood gene Fy, which (as noted previously) most discriminates between Black and White populations but has not been shown to correlate with IQ. For now, Shockley's (1972) hypothesis that the degree of racial admixture can predict g has found zero support, but whether the blood group studies had the statistical power to test the hypothesis adequately is not clear.

Gifted Black Children

Another, older study followed a logic similar to that of the blood group studies—namely, that the degree of Black-White admixture ought to predict cognitive ability if the genetic hypothesis of race differences is correct. Investigators examined two groups of high-IQ children in suburban Chicago, one with IQs of 125 and above (labeled "superior"), and the other with IQs of 140 and above (labeled "gifted"; Witty & Jenkins, 1934, 1936). The idea was that if race differences in IQ were genetically based, a high degree of Caucasian ancestry should be more typi-cal of high-IQ Black children than of the Black population generally. Parents of participating children were asked to identify their child's racial mixture, in six-teenths, and on the basis of these self-reports the children were classified into one of four groups based on degree of European background. Witty and Jenkins found that children in both high-IQ groups were slightly *less* likely to have substantial European ancestry than the U.S. Black population as a whole (distributional differences were not statistically significant, however). In both high-IQ groups, the highest scores were obtained by students with *no* reported Caucasian ancestry. In summarizing these findings, the investigators placed their study in the context of similar research, which on the whole showed that "superior intelligence test ability is *not* exhibited by those Negroes having the largest amount of white ancestry" (Witty & Jenkins, 1936, p. 187, emphasis in original).

Mixed-Race Children

A fascinating study by Eyferth (1961) focused on the offspring of American fathers (Black and White GIs) and German mothers conceived during the Allied occupation of Germany following World War II (Eyferth, 1961).[2] Eyferth matched triads of two "Black" (i.e., mixed-race) children and one White child (Ns = 181 Black and 83 White) for age, gender, number of siblings, school experience, locale of residence, and the socioeconomic background of the custodial parents (natural mothers or foster parents). Flynn (1980) scrupulously evaluated Eyferth's data for the possibility that African American troops were either unrepresentative of the U.S. Black population, or that sexual contact between GIs and German women was uneven across military ranks (and therefore possibly IQ). Flynn concluded, however, that neither factor undermined Eyferth's data: African American soldiers in the occupation forces were representative of the U.S. Black population within about 3 IQ points,[3] and American-German sexual liaisons were not only common but as characteristic of high-ranking officers as of privates. Eyferth's major finding was that there was essentially no difference in IQ between the offspring of Black GIs (mean IQ = 96.5) and White GIs (mean IQ = 97.2). The conclusion drawn by Flynn (1980, p. 95), and shared by Eyferth (1961), was that "whatever IQ gap existed between black and white fathers was absent in the offspring and was therefore environmental."

A final study cited by Nisbett (1995) focused on the mixed-raced children of one White parent and one Black parent (Willerman, Naylor, & Myrianthopoulos, 1974). The question was whether there was any relationship between the parents' gender/race configuration and their child's IQ. In other words, if a child has one Black parent and one White parent and the goal is to predict cognitive outcomes, does it matter which parent is Black and which is White? Participating Black and White mothers were similar on pertinent background variables, including SES and income, and their children were similar on perinatal variables, such as gestation length and birthweight. However, the investigators found that the children of White mothers (and Black fathers) had nearly a 10-point IQ advantage over the children of Black mothers (and White fathers). When the data were adjusted for small group differences in maternal education, the IQ gap reduced to about 7 points. Most of that gap was accounted for by the depressed IQ scores of male children of Black mothers. Because participating children were genetically comparable in terms of race (half Black/half White), and because mothers have tended to be "the primary agent of socialization in the early years," the most straightforward interpretation of the 7- to 10-point IQ difference is that it arose from different socialization experiences (Willerman et al., 1974, p. 84). Although the content of differential experience was not investigated, genetic explanations for the gap appear to be implausible.

As Nisbett (1995) recognized, none of the studies cited is beyond critique. One design weakness involves the possibility of parents' self-selection in the case of mixed-race offspring—Black parents might have higher IQs or White parents lower IQs than in the general population. Nisbett (1995) countered, however, that the magnitude of the demonstrated effects would require a degree of self-selection that is "implausibly great" (p. 41). Also, because similar conclusions were reached in studies conducted in different circumstances, times, and locales, the artifact-of-selection argument is weakened. And, despite design weaknesses of the studies cited by Nisbett, they are arguably more representative of the research literature than is the "highly selective" subset cited by Herrnstein and Murray, that ostensibly supports (but in fact does not) a hereditarian position (Nisbett, 1995, p. 42). A more thorough examination of the research literature leads to a rather different conclusion. Nisbett (1995) summarized: "So what do we have? There are a total of seven studies providing direct evidence on the question of a genetic basis for the B/W IQ gap. Six of them are consistent with a zero genetic contribution to the gap (or with very slight African superiority) based just on the raw IQ numbers" (p. 41).

Others concur. On reviewing the literature on Black-White differences in measured intelligence, Brody (1992, p. 309) concluded that "there is no convincing direct or indirect evidence in favor of a genetic hypothesis of racial differences in IQ." Even Herrnstein and Murray equivocated. Although they maintained that it is "highly likely" that genetics contributes to race differences in IQ, they refused to say just how much (Herrnstein & Murray, 1994, p. 311). Kaus (1995, p. 134) retorted: "In other words, the genetic contribution could be 50 percent, it could be 1 percent, or .001 percent for all they know. Or (though it is not 'likely') it could be zero." Indeed, after decades of research on the question of race and IQ, the hypothesis of *zero* genetic contribution to race differences remains both plausible and defensible.

THE GAP CLOSES

The hopeful news is that the race-defined gap associated with IQ and academic achievement is shrinking (Herrnstein & Murray, 1994; Neisser, 1998; Nisbett, 1995; Sternberg, 1996b). A shrinking cognitive gap has theoretical importance but also, possibly, profound social consequences. This is because, more than ever, social opportunity is mediated by cognitive ability, and (as we will see) this is true both within and across racial-ethnic groupings.

The once intractable Black-White IQ gap of one standard deviation (15 points) is starting to close. In 1991, Vincent used data from norming studies of major IQ tests to show that Black-White IQ discrepancies have shrunk in the post-Civil Rights era. The key year is 1980. Studies conducted after 1980 show a Black-White difference of 7 to 12 IQ points among children. When SES is controlled, these differences are even smaller, 1 to 9 IQ points. Humphreys (1988) obtained similar data supporting a somewhat more moderate gap shrinkage. The closing IQ gap is exemplified in Raven's Standard Progressive Matrices, which before 1980 registered a Black-White difference of 16 points among adults, but after 1980 a gap of only 7 points, or about one half standard deviation, among 12-year-old children. What is causing these IQ shifts? No one knows for sure, but a likely candidate is the complex of societal transformations spurred by policy, legal, and judicial decisions launched in the Civil Rights era, which resulted in a more open society. Vincent's (1991, p. 269) interpretation of these changes was that "Black/White IQ differences are in a very real sense a barometer of educational and economic opportunity," and that "the quarter-century push toward equal opportunity in the United States is finally beginning to show results."

Black-White differences in academic achievement have also shrunk (Hunt, 1995). Grissmer and colleagues documented a rapid rise in academic achievement between 1970 and 1990, during which the verbal and mathematics ability of Black students increased in the range of 0.4 to 0.8 standard deviations (Grissmer, Williamson, Kirby, & Berends, 1998). This jump in achievement among millions of children is "rare and perhaps unprecedented" (p. 252). Between 1971 and 1996, the Black-White gap in reading ability shrank by almost one half (from 1.25 to 0.69 standard deviations), and the Black-White gap in mathematics achievement closed by about a third (from 1.33 to 0.89 standard deviations; Jencks & Phillips, 1998a, 1988c). A narrowing of the Black-White achievement gap can be found in nearly every subject and every grade assessed in the National Assessment of Educational Progress (NAEP) since its founding in the late 1960s. The escalating trend lines for reading and mathematics achievement among black students is illustrated in Fig. 7.1.

Trend data on IQ and academic achievement tell the same story. The cognitive gap separating the means of Black and White students is shrinking approximately 2.5 IQ points per decade, stabilizing at about 10 points in 1990. The gap may have continued to shrink in the 1990s: More recent data indicated a Black-White IQ gap of between seven and ten points (Nisbett, 1995). As suggested graphically in Fig. 7.1, the narrowing of the gap is explained not by falling White scores, but instead by rising Black scores, a pattern that Herrnstein and Murray (1994, p. 291) called "an encouraging picture." Although the pace of the gap shrinkage may have slowed in the past few years, the convergence of IQ and achievement curves makes two points quite forcefully: Cognitive ability, as estimated by IQ and manifest in achievement, is not an unalterable fixture; and it is neither nonsensical nor contrary to data to think that the Black-White IQ gap can close completely (Jencks & Phillips, 1998c).

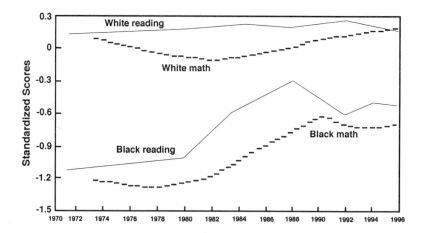

FIG. 7.1. U.S. Reading and mathematics scores for Black and White 17-year-olds. Tests score means for all years are presented in a common metric based on a 1996 mean of zero and a 1996 standard deviation of one. From "The Black-White Test Score Gap: An Introduction," by C. Jencks and M. Phillips, in *The Black-White Test Score Gap* (p. 4), by C. Jencks and M. Phillips (Eds.), 1998, Washington, DC: The Brookings Institutution Press. Data Source: National Assessment of Educational Progress. Copyright 1998 by the Brookings Institution. Reprinted with permission.

Vincent (1991) suggested that the closing of the cognitive gap is a reflection of more equitable educational and economic opportunity. Grissmer et al. (1998) tested this idea analytically by modeling the relationships between family and demographic characteristics and student achievement for the U.S. school population as a whole. In doing so, they used the nationally representative data sets of the National Longitudinal Survey of Youth (NLSY) and the National Education Longitudinal Survey (NELS). They found that the most powerful predictor of reading and mathematics achievement was parents' education, which had an independent effect of about 0.5 standard deviations when other variables were controlled. This effect was much larger than that of the next most important predictor, family income, which had an independent effect of between 0.1 and 0.2 standard deviations. Once these predictive equations were generated, the investigators plugged in values for the changing demographic characteristics of minority families between 1970 and 1990. They then compared the predicted gains in academic achievement to the actual gains reported by the National Assessment of Educational Progress (NAEP). The equations worked fairly well for the White students, but they dramatically *under*predicted achievement gains for Black students and, to a lesser degree, Hispanic students, accounting for only about one third of the achievement gains.

   The underprediction of achievement gains implies that changes in family characteristics alone cannot account for the rise in mathematics and reading scores among Black students. The investigators found, in fact, that regional differences in score gains coincided with changes in public policy and law that impacted regions differently, such as school desegregation in the South (Grissmer et al., 1998). None of this reduces the importance of family-demographic characteristics: The data clearly show that changes in parents' education, family size, and family income have had a positive effect on the academic success of the subsequent generation of Black and Hispanic children. To be specific, between the mid-1970s and 1990, Black families became smaller and parents attained higher education levels. The cognitive gains associated with these changes were offset somewhat by births to younger and single mothers, which had small but detectable negative effects on children's achievement. For Hispanic families, increases in parental education were smaller, as were reductions in family size. In the Hispanic population, these changes and associated academic outcomes were probably complicated by the arrival of immigrants during this period (Grissmer et al. 1998).

Grissmer et al. (1998) portrayed the last few decades of the 20th century as "a major 'experiment' " in American social and educational policy, an experiment marked by intense investment in disadvantaged children and families. This investment has resulted in rising incomes and improvements to education, health care, nutrition, and housing (p. 254). Public spending on programs devoted to children more than doubled (in constant dollars) from 1960 to 1988, and these funds were spent disproportionally to the benefit of low-income and minority children. During the past 4 decades, Black families have made large socioeconomic gains. From 1959 to 1995, the percentage of Black workers who held low-skilled jobs dropped steeply, whereas the percentage of those holding "good" and "elite" jobs grew (Carnevale & Rose, 1998). The facts of rising representation of African Americans among the middle class and the affluent, and of concomitant reductions in the cognitive gap, argue that the sustained public commitment to creating a more equitable society (with peaks and valleys duly acknowledged) has not been in vain.

Interestingly, the social changes concomitant with the rise in minority test scores, especially those of Black students, are not unlike those transformations that accompany more gradual cognitive gains in Western countries. The parallels suggest that there may be a larger pattern of causal forces underlying both the closing of the Black-White gap in the United States and the global Flynn effect. In fact, the rapid rise in the cognitive proficiencies among American Black students might be viewed as "mini" Flynn effect—smaller in scope, but more vigorous in execution (Grissmer et al., 1998). Neither is connected with genetic factors; both are fundamentally environmental in origin. The argument that environmental factors are responsible for the upward burst in cognitive outcomes among minority youth is so compelling that the hereditarians Herrnstein and Murray (1994) conceded: "In a period as short as twenty years, environmental changes are likely to provide the main reason for the narrowing racial gap in scores" (p. 292). In response, Kaus (1995) chided the authors: "Sounds like the environment may ultimately explain everything!" (p. 133).

SOCIAL PROSPECTS

The one-two punch of rising IQs and closing IQ gaps has radically reshaped the terms of discussion about race, intelligence, the environment, and social evolution. The new data hint at possibilities that were formerly (at least for many) unthinkable. If these trends continue, a narrowing cognitive gap could go a long way toward reaching, at last, the agonizingly elusive dream of racial equality, and fulfilling American precepts that have cruelly tantalized generation after generation. Some observers go so far as to say that the way to reach social equity is through cognitive equity—that cognitive gains and social gains are yoked and move in tandem (Kornhaber, 1998). There is no reason why the process now set in motion shouldn't continue. However, let us be as clear as we can about our goals and the means to achieve them. The explicit adoption of a new driving goal of education—the enhancement of intelligence for all—might foster those powerful cognitive abilities that enable more learners to pursue high academic and career attainment, and higher earnings. What makes this possible is that the cognitive ability/earnings linkage is now (although not formerly) an equitable one, marked by near-parity of earnings by Black and White workers of the same cognitive ability, especially in the high-IQ band (Jencks, 1972; Jencks and Phillips, 1998c). Furthermore, when Black and White 12th-grade students have the same cognitive test scores, it is *Black* students who are more likely to complete college. Greater educational attainment, in turn, is likely to improve employability, earnings, and quality of life. Jencks and Phillips (1998c) made the bold assertion that eliminating the cognitive gap is "probably both necessary and sufficient for substantially reducing racial inequality in educational attainment and earnings" (p. 4).

Obstacles remain. Differences in cognitive ability and achievements derive from several knotty sources, including patterns of parent-child interaction, teacher expectations, and lingering oppression. Black and White children still differ profoundly in modal experience. These include differences in the typical quality of schooling, an inequity that has particularly dire implications for the gifted Black child (Witty & Jenkins, 1934). There is some direct evidence, elaborated in the next chapter, that poor quality of schooling can actually lead to an IQ decline over time, and that differences in quality of schooling might partially account for Black-White differences in IQ (Jensen, 1977). Bigotry and discrimination are still snares. Stereotypes are especially insidious when they are consistent with statistical means—and it may be that "eliminating such stereotypes depends on changing the facts" of differing cognitive ability distributions (Jencks & Phillips, 1998b, p. 71). A renewed optimism, based on data, is building around the idea that cognitive parity is achievable. Ability curves are shifting rightward; eventually, they may coalesce.

CONCLUSION

For many decades, the typical response to evidence or claims of group differences in IQ has been outrage or quiet acceptance. Neither reaction is helpful to scientific or social progress. Group differences can be faced honestly without taking them as destiny. Instead, they are descriptions, report cards on what society has produced. Decades of research support the claim that the Black-White difference in mean IQ is a quantifiable manifestation of deep social inequities, not a Galtonian cause.

More than 50 years ago, Lorge discerned a three-way linkage among intelligence, education, and equity. He wrote, "Society must recognize that the restriction of educational opportunities because of race, color, and economic circumstances may mean the attenuation of its chief human resource—the functioning intelligence of its citizenry" (Lorge, 1945, p. 492). Logically, it follows that greater educational opportunity will result in greater intelligence for all segments of society. However, the relationship is reciprocal: Greater intelligence can also *create* greater opportunity as intellectual and life options expand. This reciprocity is nicely captured in Snow's (1982a) dictum that intelligence is "education's most important product, as well as its most important raw material" (p. 496). Intelligence and education are transactional and mutually reinforcing. Their alignment could lead to a freer and more prosperous world, and to one that conforms more nearly to the ideals of equality, democracy, and opportunity.

NOTES

1. The most infamous example involves data (supporting a high heritability for IQ) reported by Sir Cyril Burt, which at minimum were carelessly handled and, at worst, fabricated (Kamin, 1974; Wade, 1976). In another example, Gould (1981, pp. 160, 168, 172) discovered evidence that the "unsubtle hereditarian," H. H. Goddard, altered photographs of the Kallikak clan (illegitimate descendants of a "feeble-minded tavern wench") to create "an appearance of evil or stupidity."

2. Eyferth's (1961) study also involved "occupation children" of French troops, both White and Black, but Flynn (1980) demonstrated that data from these children do not affect the overall conclusions drawn by both Eyferth and Flynn.

3. Jensen (1998) noted that among prospective Army recruits, 30 percent of Blacks failed the preinduction mental test compared to 3 percent of Whites, raising questions about the representativeness of black soldiers to the Black male population of the U.S. as a whole.

8
Intelligence and Experience

"IQ, *g*, and school achievement are all massively affected by environmental factors"—so concluded Ulric Neisser (1998, p. 21) after summarizing a bounty of recent data bearing on the topic. The data show that preconceptions about the fixedness of intelligence are unwarranted; rather, intelligence is plastic. It can shift in form and degree both within persons and across generations. This chapter explores the plasticity of intelligence by considering what *kinds* of experience are known to stimulate or stunt its development.

For convenience, experiences that bear on intelligence development are divided into seven categories: prenatal experience, family experience, school experience, university experience, job experience, experience in old age, and a seventh category, nutrients and toxins, which spans the life stages. Experiences at each stage are not independent, but instead function as contingent sieves that limit or expand readiness to profit from experience at subsequent stages. Operative all along the developmental continuum is a law of cumulative advantage in which the cognitively rich become richer still. Aptitudes, including intelligence, always represent both finished work and foundation, product and raw material, an achieved "quality or power that makes possible the development . . . of some further quality or power" (Snow, 1991, p. 250).

Because the educative quality of experience is cumulative and contingent, education itself can be redefined to consist of all those varied experiences that enrich a person's ability to benefit from future experience. Dewey (1938) defined educative experience as having a certain quality that he called *continuity*. By this, he meant the ability of an experience to live on fruitfully in the future, and insisted that all experiences worthy of the term *education* must satisfy this criterion. Quality of experience is everything, and experiences all along the life sequence can vary in educative quality. If intelligence is defined to consist of those functions that permit future effectiveness, then an alignment obtains between the intelligence repertoire and Dewey's criterion of continuity. The cultivation of intelligence then becomes possible only through those experiences that are most justifiably called *education*.

PRENATAL EXPERIENCE

At the conclusion of a 40-week pregnancy, newborns differ in the degree to which they have experienced nutritive environments and been spared exposure to toxic

112

ones. These experiential differences have long-term consequences for development, including cognitive development. Thus, experience can be educative or noneducative, even from the moment of conception.[1] In behavior genetics research, prenatal effects are often assumed to be negligible (Devlin, Daniels, & Roeder, 1997). However, the contribution of prenatal experience to IQ can be estimated in behavior-genetic models by introducing a term for maternal effects, including the environment in utero. The magnitude of these effects has been estimated at $h^2 = 0.2$ for twins, or about 40% of all nongenetic effects on IQ (Devlin et al., 1997). This estimate underscores the tremendous importance of the prenatal environment for optimizing the cognitive development of children, and has direct implications for how intelligence might be enhanced on a large scale (Devlin et al., 1997).

Toxins and Trauma

Prenatal exposure to neurotoxins, teratogens, and mechanical injury can find later expression in the health and functioning of the child. Known deleterious agents include alcohol, cigarette smoke, pesticides, radiation, and drugs (including obstetric medications). Maternal exposure to the sedative phenobarbital, for example, has been linked to depressed IQ scores in adults. After controlling for background variables, exposure to phenobarbital during pregnancy can produce a negative effect of at least 0.5 SD, or 7 IQ points (Reinisch, Sanders, Mortensen, & Rubin, 1995). Environmental contaminants also have documented negative effects. Through biomagnification at higher levels in the food chain, the environmental toxins methylmercury and polychlorinated biphenyls (PCBs) are found in high concentrations in the fatty tissues of contaminated fish. If large amounts of contaminated fish are consumed during pregnancy, these toxins can disrupt prenatal neural development and, in the case of PCBs, may result in depressed IQ scores when children reach school age (Jacobson & Jacobson, 1996; Joffe, 1982; Marsh et al., 1995). Even maternal stress can threaten neurological development. In rhesus monkeys, pregnant females exposed to chronic stress have offspring that suffer permanent neurological impairment (Nelson, 1999). In humans, moderate-to-severe maternal stress (presumably mediated by stress hormones, e.g., glucocorticoids) has been linked to neurological "nonoptimality" and smaller head circumference—a coarse measure of brain size—in newborns (Lou et al., 1994). Birth trauma, including anoxia, can also have harmful effects on the CNS, perhaps contributing to learning disabilities or cerebral palsy.

Prenatal exposure to alcohol is notorious for its vitiating effects on cognitive and physical development. Fetal alcohol syndrome is identified with facial abnormalities, growth deficiency, and dysfunction of the central nervous system. Mean IQs for children with fetal alcohol syndrome are typically in the range of 65 to 75, and as much 35 points below the mean IQ of matched controls (Mattson, Riley, Gramling, Delis, & Jones, 1997). Fetal alcohol syndrome is widespread, affecting more than 8,000 newborns every year. However, the number of children chronically exposed to alcohol in utero is much higher, roughly 12 times that number, or about 100,000 births each year. Most alcohol-exposed children display none of the physical characteristics associated with fetal alcohol syndrome, and yet they too have significantly depressed IQ scores. In one study, alcohol-exposed but structurally normal children had a mean IQ of 84, which was 25 points below that of matched control children (Mattson et al., 1997).

Adverse environmental effects are not limited to maternal exposure (Joffe, 1982). In animal studies, male exposure to lead, morphine, methadone, alcohol, and other agents has been linked to deleterious effects on progeny, including low birthweight, increased mortality, and decreased learning ability. In men, exposure to lead, anesthetic gases, cigarettes, and caffeine have all been associated with negative effects on offspring, including a higher incidence of low birthweight and spontaneous abortions. Smoking, for example, has been associated with depressed maternal weight gain during pregnancy and with low birthweight (Rush, Stein, & Susser, 1980). In turn, small-for-date newborns (i.e., those whose birthweights are lower than expected, given the gestational age) are at greater risk for impaired development (Joffe, 1982).

Infection

Prenatal exposure to infectious agents also contributes to the risk of impaired cognitive development. For example, infection by the cytomegalovirus (CMV), which is found in about 1% of all live births, has been linked to IQ decrements and other impairments (Scheiner, Hanshaw, Simeonsson, & Scheiner, 1977). Most infants with congenital CMV infections are born to young, disadvantaged mothers, who are least likely to provide the rich home environments that could compensate for their child's compromised health status. CMV and other intrauterine infections "may contribute significantly to the incidence of developmental retardation" among the poor and, by implication, to cognitive differences among racial/ethnic groups statistically associated with poverty (Breitmayer & Ramey, 1986, p. 1152).

Placental Blood Supply

Evidence that in utero experience can have significant consequences for cognitive development has been found in studies of identical twins. There is a mild IQ disadvantage associated with twins generally, an effect linked to higher incidences of prematurity and low birthweight, and to the necessity of sharing intra-uterine resources. Differences in midpoint birthweights between pairs of twins can account for between-pair IQ differences as large as one standard deviation. In Storfer's (1990) analysis, twins that were relatively heavy at birth had IQs in the range of 105 (for weights > 6 pounds) to 113.1 (for weights > 7 pounds), whereas lighter twins (weights < 4 pounds) had an average IQ of 96.2.

Monozygotic (MZ) twins, although genetically identical, can also differ phenotypically, even at birth. For example, they often exhibit substantial *within-pair* differences in birthweight (averaging about 300 grams, or 10% of birthweight) and IQ (averaging 6 points; Storfer, 1990). The heavier twin typically enjoys an IQ advantage, and that advantage becomes larger as within-pair weight discrepancies increase and as birthweights decrease. When one or both twins weighs less than 6.5 pounds, the cognitive advantage associated with the heavier twin is about 9 IQ points, suggesting that IQ effects appear below some prenatal nutritional threshold. Storfer found effects on the order of 6 IQ points for low-birthweight twins, excluding from his analysis data on seven pairs of Black twins because their birthweights were "extremely low and their IQ scores averaged only 72" (1990, p. 13).

Other investigators have found that whether monozygotic (MZ) fetuses share a chorion (outermost) sac, or each has a separate chorion, also has an effect on IQ variation during childhood (Rose, Harris, Christian, & Nance, 1979). When monozygotic twins share a chorion, they also share a placenta and have a common blood supply. In dichorionic MZ twins, each has a separate chorion and (at least initially) an independent placenta and blood supply (placentas merge in 40% of cases). Differences in the quality and efficiency of placentas may contribute to within-pair IQ variation. IQ variation is greater in dichorionic twins than in monochorionic twins, a finding that reinforces the "rather considerable influence of the prenatal environment on . . . intelligence" (Melnick, Myrianthopoulos, & Christian, 1978, p. 428).

Vitamin and Protein Supplementation

The ingestion by women of vitamin supplements during pregnancy can have a positive effect on their children's IQ scores. In Harrell's classic study conducted in Norfolk, Virginia, poor pregnant women, 80% of whom were Black, were given daily vitamin/mineral supplements (Harrell, Woodyard, & Gates, 1955). The Stanford-Binet Form M was administered to their children at the ages of 3 and 4 years. Children whose mothers had received supplementation during pregnancy had an IQ advantage on the order of 4 to 8 points over children whose mothers had received a placebo.

A similar study carried out by Rush and colleagues involved protein and vitamin/mineral supplementation in the diets of expectant Black women (Rush et al., 1980). The effects of protein supplementation were not entirely as predicted or hoped: There was, unfortunately, a higher incidence of fetal demise in the experimental group—with no ready explanation. At 1 year of age, however, children in the experimental group displayed faster stimulus habituation and had longer play episodes (but not higher IQ scores), outcomes that are regarded as signs of cognitive development. The investigators concluded that nutrient supplementation during pregnancy probably exerts cognitive effects, but only in cases where prenatal malnutrition is likely to be severe.

Breastfeeding and DHA

Both the practice and duration of breastfeeding have been statistically associated with cognitive development. In a longitudinal study conducted in New Zealand, Horwood and Fergusson (1998) found that the duration of voluntary breastfeeding was mildly but positively predictive of WISC IQ (at ages 8 and 9), reading and mathematics achievement (at ages 10 and 12), and high school examination scores (at age 18). When the effects of confounding influences (e.g., SES and smoking) were removed through regression analysis, a "small but detectable" effect remained for breastfeeding (Horwood & Fergusson, 1998, p. 6). Children who had been breastfed for at least 8 months had an IQ advantage of about 4 points over those who had not been breastfed at all. Although this result is consistent with other research findings, a causal link between breastfeeding and higher IQ cannot be established with certainty because the correlation may ultimately be explained by other, as-yet unidentified confounding factors (Krugman & Law, 1999).

Some investigators, including Horwood and Fergusson (1998), suspect that any cognitive advantage conferred by breastfeeding might be traced to the presence in breast milk of the long-chain fatty acid known as *docosahexaenoic acid* (DHA). DHA is a structural component of neural tissue, including brain tissue, but it cannot be synthesized by the human body and thus must be obtained in the diet. At the time of writing, DHA is not an ingredient in infant formula produced in the United States, although it is used in Europe and Asia. The question of whether DHA ought to be added to infant formula is a contentious issue on both scientific and political grounds (bottle feeding is much more common among poor mothers; Kaufman, 1999). DHA supplementation has been associated with superior visual acuity in infants, and there is some evidence for its ability to enhance infants' performance on problem-solving tasks (Birch, Hoffman, Uauy, Birch, & Prestidge, 1998; Willatts, Forsyth, DiModugno, Varma, & Colvin, 1998).

As the launching point for all further human development, prenatal experience matters. The relevance of prenatal experience to all subsequent experience is a point that is sometimes missed or ignored when behavior geneticists parcel effects into genetic and socialization causes. For example, when adopted children resemble their biological parents, some of that covariation may be related to differences in prenatal experience. Typically, that variance is neatly co-opted into the genetics bucket (Scarr, 1997), even though for the fetus it is experiential (genetic factors may also be involved, of course). Pertinent, here, are the well-known modal differences in health status between Black and White newborns. Variation in prenatal experience may help explain group IQ differences. If so, redressing group differences in prenatal experience could contribute to greater equity of cognitive experience and, therefore, cognitive outcomes. Jensen (1998) acknowledged, for example, that Black-White IQ differences might be partly "attributable to the combined effects of LBW [low birthweight] and a low frequency of breastfeeding" (p. 507). Other investigators have suggested that "interventions aimed at improving the prenatal environment could lead to a significant increase in the population's IQ" (Devlin et al., 1997, p. 470).

FAMILY EXPERIENCE

By any criterion, the family is a potent medium for cognitive growth. For better or worse, parents are their children's educators and the home is a "classroom" that can impede or advance the development of each child (Sigel, Stinson, & Kim, 1993). Discerning the interactions between school and family effects on learning, Heyns (1978) concluded that "the role of families in the achievement process is ubiquitous; few educational outcomes can be unequivocally dissociated from parental influences" (p. 185). However, does family experience influence the development of intelligence as such? Several streams of evidence, including behavioral genetics, now answer this question in the affirmative (Thomson & Plomin, 1993). Such data highlight vast differences in the home experiences of children, differences that are related to socioeconomic class and that are manifest in the linguistic, literary, emotional, and sensory qualities of daily life.

Home Environment

Independent of SES, the quality of the home environment impacts children's cognitive development. In a multisite study, a consortium of researchers used the Home Observation for Measurement of the Environment—the HOME inventory— to identify which features of the home environment are most strongly associated with cognitive growth (Bradley et al., 1989). Table 8.1 displays some of the correlations found among the cognitive and emotional richness of the home (as measured by the HOME inventory), maternal education, children's cognitive development (MDI—Mental Development Index) at 24 months, and IQ at 36 months. MDI and IQ scores correlated approximately 0.50 with measures of cognitive simulation, especially the availability of play materials, the interaction of the primary caregiver with the child, and the variety of experiences presented to the developing child. Correlations of about 0.50 were also found between maternal education and aspects of the home environment related to cognitive stimulation; somewhat lower correlations were found between maternal education and emotional support.

Although SES was moderately correlated with HOME scores (again, approximately 0.50), the quality of parental care varied considerably *within* socioeconomic groups. Regression analysis supported the assertion that the home environment is more potent than SES in shaping a child's cognitive development. When two variable sets—SES and HOME—were entered into regression equations in alternate orders, HOME scores accounted for much more residual variance in

TABLE 8.1
Qualities of Home Environment and Children's Cognitive Development

Age/HOME Subscales	Maternal Education	MDI (24 months)	IQ (36 months)
24 months			
Responsivity	.28	.40	.47
Acceptance	.25	.33	.39
Organization	.20	.22	.31
Play materials	.50	.53	.52
Involvement	.49	.55	.54
Variety	.34	.42	.45
Total	.50	.58	.62
36 months			
Learning stimulation	.40	.47	.49
Pride and affection	.09	.28	.34
Total	.38	.50	.54

Note. HOME = Home Observation for Measurement of the Environment; MDI = Mental Development Index. From "Home Environment and Cognitive Development in the First 3 Years of Life: A Collaborative Study Involving Six Sites and Three Ethnic Groups in North America," by R. H. Bradley et al., 1989, Developmental Psychology, 25, p. 222. Copyright © 1989 by the American Psychological Association. Adapted with permission.

cognitive outcomes than did SES. Stronger relations between HOME variables and cognitive scores were found for middle-class families than for either lower-middle-class or lower-class families.

Because the data reported in this study are correlational, it is possible that the cognitive richness of the home does not produce differences in cognitive development, but instead reflects them. One could imagine, for example, that some parents will actively seek ways to stimulate a child who shows above-average cognitive ability early in life. There is actually some evidence for this effect: Positive (but low) lag correlations were found between MDI scores and HOME scores obtained 1 year later. However, lag correlations were much more robust in the other direction: HOME scores more strongly predicted MDI scores a year later. On the basis of this difference, Bradley et al. (1989) concluded that "the primary direction of effect was from environment to development" (p. 231). It is also possible that qualities of the home environment are confounded with genetics— that is, some parents might be more inclined than others, genetically, to provide home environments that are cognitively rich. However, even if this were true, it is unlikely that experientially proximal variables, such as the quality of parent-child interactions, are epiphenomenal. Moreover, there is no obvious reason why intelligence-promoting parenting strategies cannot be taught and learned, a fact that has been recognized in many intervention projects.

Among Black families, correlations between home environment variables and cognitive development were rather weak, and even smaller correlations were found among Mexican American families. Bradley et al. (1989) acknowledged that the weak correlations might be artifacts of the research design. Alternatively, the weak correlations might be related to the confounding of race/ethnicity with SES, and to the consequent restriction of range on the HOME inventory for these subsamples. Within these groups, however, the availability of stimulating play materials was moderately related to cognitive development. Also, among Black children, "pride and affection" were moderately correlated ($r = 0.53$) with IQ at 36 months.

Other studies have also demonstrated positive relationships between the quality of the home environment and early cognitive development (e.g., Brooks-Gunn, Klebanov, Liaw, & Spiker, 1993). Ho (1987) found that the relationship between a mother's interaction with her child and the child's cognitive development is not adequately described by main effects. Maternal responsivity at age 12 months interacted with children's cognitive status, and did so in an interesting way. At 24 months, the slope of the regression line was *negative,* indicating that the lower-ability children benefited relatively more from maternal responsivity. By the age of 48 months, the regression slope had reversed and become *positive*, meaning that higher-ability children became even more capable given high-quality interaction with their mothers. Thus, high-quality mother-child interaction seemed to have a compensatory function early on, but later had a cumulative advantage function, serving to make initial differences even greater. These findings were not simply an epiphenomenal product of shared mother-child genotype because they were detected in both biological and adopted children.

Research by Sigel and his colleagues likewise demonstrated a connection between patterns of parent-child interaction and cognitive development (Sigel et al., 1993). When parents adopt high-level distancing strategies—sociolinguistic patterns that encourage open-ended thinking and transcendence of immediate experience—their children typically have higher levels of cognitive ability and academic achievement. By initiating *distancing acts*, parents foster cognitive competence in their children, including the ability to see differing symbolic structures as pointing to the same physical referent, or what Sigel called *representational competence* (Sigel, 1993; Sigel, Anderson, & Shapiro, 1966). Cognitive distancing, symbol-referent identity, and the equivalence of symbols are much the substance of formal education, and all likely to be central elements of the developing intelligence repertoire.[2]

Socioeconomic Status

Socioeconomic status (SES) is a powerful construct for understanding differences in social behavior, social standing, and social mobility. It is also a powerful predictor of life paths. It is well known, for example, that family socioeconomic background exerts long-term effects on measures of adult success, including educational and career attainments (Bowles & Nelson, 1974). Positive correlations between socioeconomic status (SES) and cognitive outcomes have long been recognized (Joffe, 1982; Stoddard & Wellman, 1940). Values, expectations, childrearing practices, and other qualities of family life associated with SES may impact cognitive outcomes directly. In fact, Davis and Havighurst (1946) construed SES *in terms of* its cognitive implications: "The pivotal meaning of social class to students of human development is that it defines and systematizes different learning environments for children of different classes" (p. 699). Spaeth's (1976) path-analytic model likewise accounts for the effects of parents' SES on children's IQ entirely in terms of cognitive socialization, manifest as environmental complexity, within the family.

As a global variable, SES summarizes a collection of more functionally active variables, such as parents' education level and occupation, and family income. It is these more proximal variables that are potentially causal in growing and shaping a child's cognitive repertoire. Parents' education level especially is a potent differentiator of high- and low-achieving children. In nationally representative data sets, both mothers' and fathers' education levels constituted the strongest family-demographic predictors of a children's academic achievement (Grissmer, Williamson, Kirby, & Berends, 1998). The effect of a parent's college education versus noncompletion of high school amounted to more than one standard deviation in children's mathematics scores, or about one half standard deviation when controlling for other factors such as income. Parents' education is *not* a mere proxy for genetic characteristics shared across generations. Adopted children whose biological mothers had less than a high school education were sensitive to the educational level attained by their adoptive mother. Differences in the educational attainment of the adoptive mother can account for about one half standard deviation in the IQs of adopted children (Scarr & Weinberg, 1983).

Again, effects associated with SES or parents' education must be exercised through variables that are more proximal to the child's experience. Patterns of language use are especially notable, because language shapes what aspects of the environment and internal thoughts and emotions are worth attending to (Bernstein, 1961). Sentence syntax can constrain or liberate a child's capacity to combine ideas flexibly. Patterns of language use have their origin in the style of communication between parents and children. Mothers with no formal education tend not to ask "known-answer" questions (a basic convention of mental tests and schooling) of their children, whereas mothers who have even minimal exposure to schooling can mimic teacher behavior by asking such questions (Greenfield, 1998). Parents also differ in the quality of answers they provide to their children's questions: High-SES parents tend to supply more elaborate responses to questions asked by their children (Sternberg, 1994a), and in general have richer verbal interactions with them (Hart & Risley, 1995). High SES parents also tend to be less directive of their children's behavior, are more likely to see their children as being independently motivated, and are more likely to communicate with their children in a positive affective tone (Jennings & Connors, 1989).

SES-related patterns of parent-child interaction are associated with children's cognitive development. Hart and Risley (1995) found that children's verbal abilities and measured IQ were strongly related to patterns of verbal interaction between parents and children, even when variance associated with SES was removed. Positive affective tone (e.g., praise, encouragement) has repeatedly been found to mediate SES and children's verbal ability, presumably because it establishes a safe and inviting environment for children to experiment with verbalizing their thoughts and questions (Jennings & Connors, 1989). Low-SES mothers tend instead to be directive in their children's play, a pattern negatively associated with nonverbal (or fluid) competency, even when SES is partialled out. High directiveness is probably a general parenting style and not just reactive to children's need for assistance; this style of parental control is asserted soon after tasks are presented and is exhibited even in open-ended play (Jennings & Connors, 1989).

Middle-class home life tends to be flexibly structured, adopting a middling path between the extremes of weak structure in which activities lack regularity, and rigid structure in which behavior patterns are strictly enforced. A flexibly structured home exhibits regularities (such as a default "bedtime"), but allows for exceptions given certain contingencies (like a weekend). Tension between the familiar and perturbation of the familiar has been hypothesized to elicit the Piagetian mechanisms of disequilibrium followed by equilibration through the formation of new schemes, and therefore to cognitive advancement. Statistically, flexible home structures have been associated with higher-level Piagetian task performance and with higher levels of academic achievement (Ogilvy, 1990). Like other parenting variables described earlier, home structure is also associated with SES, but its instrumental utility is evident in that it predicts cognitive outcomes even when variance from SES is controlled (Ogilvy, 1990).

Adoption studies constitute another stream of evidence showing that environmental factors associated with SES are instrumental in cognitive development (Locurto, 1990). Children who are adopted into high-SES families tend to have higher IQs than do similar children reared by their birth mothers (Neisser et al., 1996; Scarr & Weinberg, 1983), although their IQs are usually not as high as those of their nonadopted siblings (Locurto, 1990). The reactivity of IQ to SES is most clearly demonstrated in adoption studies that feature highly contrasting environments, in which the SES of the biological and adopting families differ markedly. Locurto's (1990) rather conservative analysis of cross-SES adoption effects led to the conclusion that the average IQ of adopted children was around 106, which was about 10 to 12 points higher than it would have been had those same children not been adopted.

One of the better-known studies of cross-SES adoption is the French Adoption Study (Dumaret, 1985). In this study, children of low-SES mothers were adopted into "privileged" families before the age of 7 months. Dumaret contrasted these children with their full- and half-siblings who where raised by their biological mothers or by close relatives, and with siblings who were raised in foster or group homes. The three groups were compared on measures of IQ, school achievement, and social adjustment. The groups differed markedly, with higher IQs and academic achievement associated with children adopted into high-SES homes. On the full Wechsler Intelligence Scale for Children (WISC), the mean IQ for the adopted children was 109.2, whereas siblings raised by biological relatives had a mean IQ of 93.0, and foster/group home children had a mean IQ of 80.8 (all differences, p < .002). The three groups also differed in academic success: Adopted children had very few instances of grade repeats or of leaving school, and were more often rated as "gifted" by their teachers. Among children in the other two groups, academic failure and behavior problems were common. It is notable that comparison siblings who were raised in emotionally stable biological families— that is, in homes not characterized by conflict and disharmony—tended to have fewer behavior difficulties and higher IQs than comparison siblings raised in dysfunctional homes.

A more recent investigation, the French Cross-Fostering study, is unique in its four-group design, formed by crossing high- and low-SES biological families with high- and low-SES adoptive families (Capron & Duyme, 1989). This design permits examination of the adoption effects of moving *up* in SES, and of moving *down*. Although the sample size was smallish (total N = 38), the study had the technical advantage of equating children on possible confounding factors, such as birthweight, age at adoption, and the prevalence of perinatal complications. In this study, there was no evidence of selective placement or influence of attrition. IQ testing using the WISC-R was performed by psychologists who were uninformed as to the nature of the study.

The main effects of the study are presented in Table 8.2. The table displays independent effects, both of a comparable magnitude, for the SES of biological parents and for the SES of adoptive families. Placement in high-SES adoptive families was associated with a positive effect of 12 IQ points, and this effect held

TABLE 8.2
Cross-SES Adoption and IQ

| | SES of Adoptive Parents | | | | | |
| | High | | | Low | | |
SES of Biological Parents	N	Mean	SD	N	Mean	SD
High	10	119.6	12.25	8	107.5	11.94
Low	10	103.6	12.71	10	92.4	5.41

Note. From "Assessment of Effects of Socio-Economic Status on IQ in a Full Cross-Fostering Study," by C. Capron and M. Duyme, 1989, *Nature, 340,* p 553. Adapted by permission from *Nature.* Copyright 1989 by MacMillan Magazines Ltd.

for children of high-SES and low-SES biological parents. The *detrimental* effects of placing the child of high-SES biological parents into a low-SES family is likewise about 12 points. Nonetheless, the SES of biological parents also had an effect, accounting for about 15 IQ points. The interpretation of this latter effect, however, is not entirely clear. Although the "effect attributable to adoptive parents is clearly environmental," the study was "not equipped to differentiate prenatal from genetic factors" (Capron & Duyme, 1989, p. 553). The effect associated with biological parents could be attributable to either or both factors, or to their interaction.

Not all adoption studies have found comparable effects of SES on the IQs of adopted children. The Texas Adoption Project, for example, demonstrated an effect of only about 1.5 IQ points, which was not significant (Loehlin, Horn, & Willerman, 1997). In this study, however, adopting parents were restricted in range in both SES and IQ, with "high-SES" and "low-SES" groups formed by a median-split procedure, and thus this sample might have underestimated cross-SES adoption effects. Even in studies that do show SES effects, the exact influence of SES remains unclear, primarily because it is difficult to disentangle genetic factors from experiential factors. Resources in the home and parental language patterns are both related to children's IQ, but it is possible that both resources and language patterns are mediated by parents' IQ, which is in turn reflects (to some degree) parental genotype. There is, however, evidence for *independent* effects of home environment on cognitive development, even when maternal IQ is partialled out (Gottfried, 1984).

Despite the importance of the home environment, family influences, over time, tend to be overshadowed by differences in individual life experience—and by genetic factors (Neisser et al., 1996). Peer cultures also play a strong role in development (Harris, 1995), and may be an important channel for the propagation of values and beliefs associated with socioeconomic status. For the adolescent, part of growing up means managing a set of expanding life options, and the resulting unique decision chain weakens the long-range effects exerted by the early childhood environment established by parents. As Scarr (1997) noted, "The everyday world for most people consists of choices about what to listen to and look at, what to ignore, where to be and with whom" (p. 37). At these choice points, genetic differences apparently reassert themselves. Even so, gene-related niche building occurs only through different *experiential* paths, and by any logic these paths must be contingent on the array of available options. Whether genes or experience has primacy is not immediately clear, nor is it clear that attempts to parcel effects into these two sources is meaningful (Bidell & Fischer, 1997).

The relationships between experience and cognitive growth are important, but they are not simple. Functional relationships between such variables as parent-child interactional style and cognitive development vary according to the particular culture in which the child is raised. The complexity of environmental influences on cognitive development is illustrated by the finding that both parent-child interactional patterns and nutrition affect cognitive development, but not additively or independently. For example, the quality of caregiving by adults can be influenced by a child's nutritional status (Chávez & Martínez, 1975; Pollitt, Gorman, Engle, Martorell, & Rivera, 1993; Wachs, 1993). The interactions are also multiplicative, in that the combined effect of poor nutrition and poor caregiving is larger than the sum of the effects of either variable in isolation. This also means that if one variable has a positive valence—if the child receives either good nutrition or competent caregiving—this one variable has buffering effects that attenuate the deleterious consequences of the other. Similarly, a cognitively enriched preschool experience can buffer the effects of "nonoptimal" Apgar status at birth on later cognitive performance (Breitmayer & Ramey, 1986).

These examples demonstrate that the relationship between a child's experience and cognitive development is not always reducible to a nomothetic, stable, and transportable pattern, but is often mediated by cultural, subcultural, and sociodemographic contextual variables (Wachs, 1996). Thus, the complexity that laces social phenomena generally applies to cognitive development. Straightforward laws connecting experiential input and cognitive output are elusive. Instead, undercomplicated main effects give way to the disorienting reality of complex interactions—Cronbach's (1975, p. 119) "hall of mirrors that extends to infinity"—in which the relationship between two variables depends on a third variable, and that three-way pattern depends in turn on a fourth variable, a fifth, and so on.

SCHOOL EXPERIENCE

The association between IQ and amount of formal education is impressive—correlations range from about 0.50 to 0.90 (Ceci & Williams, 1997). Perhaps the most ready interpretation of this association is that schooling provides incentives for those who have more native cognitive ability to pursue higher levels of education. By this account, intelligence is the driving force leading to higher levels of educational attainment, better jobs, and higher pay. However, there is another possibility—that education actually promotes the growth of intelligence (Ceci & Williams, 1997). These explanations are not necessarily contradictory: Causal influence may be bidirectional. But because the hypothetical role of education on the cultivation of intelligence is much less appreciated or even recognized as a possibility, evidence for effects in the education-to-intelligence direction are presented in this section.

Contrasts of WWI and WWII American Soldiers

Although Flynn (1987, 1998) is credited with compiling and synthesizing evidence pointing to a rather abrupt, large-scale, and perhaps global rise in IQ, he was not the first to discover data of this kind, nor the first to suggest the possibility (e.g.,

Wheeler, 1970/1942). In 1948, Tuddenham documented increases in IQ among American soldiers between WWI and WWII. Tuddenham showed that between 1917 and 1942 the mean IQ of men who enlisted or were drafted into the U.S. Army rose about one standard deviation. The increase had observable effects. According to Humphreys (1989), the jump in IQ was manifest functionally in that "the average 18-year-old in 1942 was able to learn general military and specialty skills more quickly than his counterpart in 1917" (p. 198). Humphreys attributed the intergenerational IQ gain to an increase in the average number of years of schooling during the intervening period. Between the wars, the mean duration of schooling for American males rose from about 9 years to about 12 years. These 3 additional years of schooling in later adolescence might have afforded WWII soldiers a greater opportunity to study material that was more abstract, complex, and demanding than was possible at younger ages (cf. findings by Husén, 1951).[3]

English Canal Boat Children

Several studies converge to support the causal association between amount of formal education and IQ (e.g., Loehlin, Lindzey, & Spuhler, 1975; Teasdale & Owen, 1987; Vernon, 1948). One example is Gordon's (1970/1923) study of the intellectual characteristics of English canal boat children. Gordon's original report, published as a government pamphlet in 1923, described canal boat families as spending most of their lives ferrying cargo along the waterways of Great Britain. Their itinerant lifestyle meant that children in these families had little exposure to formal education. Even though the government had established special schools for canal boat children, their families were so transient that the children attended school fewer than 10 days each year, on average. Canal boat children were in general healthy, clean, well clothed, and well mannered, and yet their average Stanford-Binet IQ and "EQ" (educational quotient, based on achievement in reading and arithmetic) were both approximately 70 (and correlated 0.72, N = 36), which by traditional criteria would put them in the borderline retarded range.

More telling than average IQ was the tendency of IQ scores to decline with age. The steady downward trend is depicted in Fig. 8.1. The graph displays data from the subset of Gordon's sample of families that had at least two school-age children, a reduced sample that provides some measure of control over possible environmental and genetic confounds. The graph shows that although the youngest children had IQs that were near normal, the mean IQ for firstborn children was around 60 (N = 76). So strong was the downward trend that the age-IQ correlation was robustly negative ($r = -0.76$). Gordon noted that cognitive development tended to rise during the preschool years and then flattened out, such that school-age siblings, regardless of age, typically had a mental age of about 6 or 7 years.[4] From these observations, Gordon concluded that the retardation of canal boat children was "not due to heredity, seeing that the youngest children test more or less

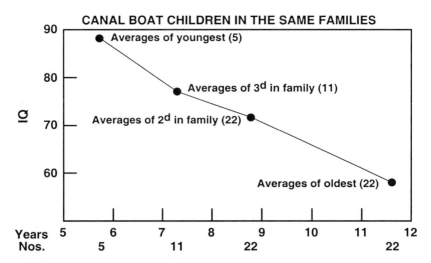

FIG. 8.1. Decline of IQ with age among canal boat children. From "The Intelligence of English Canal Boat Children," by H. Gordon, 1970. In Cross Cultural Studies of Behavior (p. 117) by I. Al-Issa and W. Dennis (Eds.). New York: Holt, Rinehart and Winston, Inc. Originally appearing in Mental and Scholastic Tests Among Retarded Children, Educational Pamphlet, No. 44. London: Board of Education. Copyright 1923 by Her Brittanic Majesty's Stationery Office. Reprinted with permission.

normally," and inferred "with some reasonableness that the lack of schooling has affected both 'mental' and scholastic attainments to the same extent" (Gordon, 1970, p. 119).

IQ and Amount of Schooling: United States

Binet's original IQ test was designed to predict school attainment; however, the relationship also works in the reverse—school attainment can predict IQ. Working with adult subjects, Lorge (1945) compared intelligence test scores for 130 men at ages 14 and 34. Across the sample, correlations between IQ scores at age 14 and age 34 were 0.64 for the Otis and 0.62 for the Thorndike scales. The more impressive finding is that when subjects were blocked according to their IQ at age 14, IQ scores on the later-administered Otis and Thorndike scales rose as a function of the highest grade completed. The association of IQ with education is again evident when the data are examined another way. The correlation of IQ at age 14 with the amount of formal education eventually completed is 0.36, showing that adolescent IQ can predict later academic achievement, but only modestly. However, the correlations between education and IQ at age 34 were much larger—0.67 for the Otis and 0.68 for the Thorndike—even though the later IQ scores were more distal in time from schooling and obtained *after* formal education was completed (cf. Husén and Tuijnman, 1991, for a corroborative finding).

When the two sets of correlations are squared to reflect variance accounted for, the plausible effects of schooling on IQ are clearer still. IQ measured at age 14 accounts for about 13% of later variation in educational achievement, but educational achievement can account for about 45% of the variation in adult IQ. In other words, IQ does predict educational attainment, but educational attainment predicts subsequent IQ even more. This implies is that the relationship between intelligence in education is one version of the chicken-and-egg problem. Snow (1982a, 1982b) described intelligence as both a raw material for education and a product of education. Which has primacy? Most take for granted the idea of intelligence as raw material. Lorge's data hint that the characterization of *intelligence* as *product* is also to be taken seriously. His conclusion was unequivocal: "Schooling, therefore, makes a difference in the intelligence score that an adult will obtain" (Lorge, 1945, p. 489).

IQ and Amount of Schooling: Sweden

Lorge's findings were corroborated by Husén's (1951) study of schooling and IQ change. Husén's subjects were 722 boys born in 1928 in Malmö, Sweden. IQ scores were obtained when the cohort was 10 years old and again at age 20. During the intervening 10 years, subjects' educational paths diverged, their attainment ranging from completion of primary school (Grade 7) to matriculation from senior secondary school (Grade 12 or 13). Table 8.3 summarizes Husén's findings. IQ gains increased monotonically as the level of schooling rose, with gains for three highest-attaining groups deviating significantly from zero. The increase is not linear, but accelerates at the higher grades of secondary school—an effect Husén associated with the more theoretical character of subjects in the higher grades. Because the three highest groupings did not differ significantly in initial IQ, their divergence in IQ gains cannot be attributed to different starting points.

TABLE 8.3
Effects of Schooling on IQ Change—Malmö, Sweden

Level of Schooling Completed	N	Grades Completed	Mean IQ Change	Percentage of Subjects With Increased Scores
Primary School	431	7	-1.18	46.2
Junior Secondary (no cert.)	28	7-10	2.07	53.6
Junior Secondary (cert.)	73	9-10	2.99	63.0
Senior Secondary (no cert.)	66	11-13	7.23	77.3
Matriculation	15	12-13	11.03	86.7

Note. From "The Influence of Schooling Upon IQ," by T. Husén, 1951, *Theoria, 17*, p. 71. The Copyright 1951 by the Swedish Council for Humanistic and Social Science Research. Adapted with permission. Abbreviations *cert.* and *no cert.* refer, respectively, to the attainment of a school leaving certificate or not.

When Husén's (1951) subjects were blocked by initial IQ, educational attainment was found to be related to subsequent IQ, just as in Lorge's (1945) study. Within IQ blocks, Husén found that IQ gains associated with a junior secondary school certificate (Grade 10) were 6 to 14 points higher than the IQ gains of those who completed primary school only (Grade 7). Moreover, Husén found that the effects of social variables, including family income, were much smaller (about 3 IQ points for the highest income groups) than schooling effects on adult IQ. On the basis of this analysis, Husén (1951) concluded that schooling "has incomparably the greatest significance for the systematic changes in IQ between 10 and 20 years of age" (p. 71). Härnqvist (1959, cited in Härnqvist, 1968) later reanalyzed Husén's data by regressing follow-up scores on original scores, rather than simply computing gains, and found somewhat smaller IQ gains associated with schooling. Decades later, Husén and Tuijnman (1991) analyzed the Malmö data once again, this time using multivariate path analysis procedures. The analysis confirmed a direct effect of educational attainment on adult IQ, independent of home background and IQ at age 10.

Härnqvist (1968) conducted a comparable study of the effects of education on IQ, also in Sweden. Subjects constituted roughly 10% of the Swedish population of boys born in 1948. IQ was assessed in 1961, when subjects were 13 years old, and again in 1966 at age 18 (N = 4,616). Regression analyses showed that IQ drift over the intertest period was a function of the level of education attained. Those who had received more formal education experienced an upward IQ increment corresponding to an effect size of +0.34, and those who received less education experienced a downward drift of -0.21. The "distance" between the higher group and the lower group corresponded to an effect size of 0.55, or about 8 IQ points, which is somewhat lower than that found by Husén but still appreciable.

Härnqvist found a slightly larger effect when he contrasted groups that were more extreme in educational experience. When students were separated into those who completed only compulsory school (up to Grade 8) and those who received some education in the *gymnasium* (a university preparatory school), IQ drift distance amounted to 10 IQ points. Härnqvist explored the possible contribution of home environment to IQ shift, and found that such factors as parents' education and occupation, as well as municipality of residence, contributed somewhat to the magnitude and direction of IQ drift. The schooling effect was only slightly diminished in magnitude when home environment was "controlled" by comparing educational effects within five strata of home "background level." However, when students were compared within the five strata of educational experience, the prediction of IQ change from home background was weak.

Härnqvist's study was replicated and expanded by Balke-Aurell (1982), who examined yet another Swedish cohort, born in 1952. Again in this study, extent of education predicted shifts in IQ between the ages of 13 and 18. The magnitude of the shifts, over the spectrum of educational experience, was slightly greater than one half of the pooled standard deviation of IQ. Beyond this main effect, Balke-

Aurell found that subjects' *profiles* of cognitive abilities were sensitive to educational and occupational experience. In particular, technical (including scientific and mechanical) education and job experience enhanced spatial/technical abilities, whereas verbally oriented education and job experience enhanced verbal abilities. Initial verbal-spatial ability profiles also predicted the choice of field of study. These data therefore show that cognitive ability profiles *influence* and are *influenced* by subsequent experience, much as general intelligence predicts educational experience and is also shaped by it.

Wartime Disruption of Schooling

De Groot studied how the disruption of schooling in Holland during World War II affected the cognitive abilities of children (de Groot, 1948, 1951). Between 1941 and 1944, Eindhoven, Holland, was occupied by the German army and was later garrisoned as a Nazi military center. Residents of Eindhoven suffered severe disruption of their lives during that period as they faced air attacks, a lack of transport and fuel supplies, and the commandeering of their schools and other facilities. Also during that time, many adult males, including teachers, went into hiding, and schools were closed intermittently. Even when schools were in session, truancy was a serious problem. The situation grew worse: In September 1944, Eindhoven was at the front lines of battle, and even after its liberation the disruption continued as Eindhoven became a transit center for Allied troops. De Groot calculated that partial or complete school closures put school-age children in arrears by about a year and a half.

De Groot wanted to know if the disruption of schooling affected local children's IQ. To find out, he examined test scores for applicants to the Philips Industrial Training School in Eindhoven. The applicants were boys whose average age was approximately 13 years, 6 months. The Philips entry test battery included a Dutch translation of the American National Intelligence Tests. De Groot found that during the prewar period from 1938 to 1943, applicants' test scores hovered close to 100— the expected mean. Between 1944 and 1948, near the climax of the war and its aftermath, the mean IQ dropped 4 to 5 points. Later, in 1949 and 1950, scores returned to their prewar levels. Both downward and upward shifts were statistically significant. The data suggest, but do not prove, the instrumentality of formal education in inculcating the cognitive skills measured by IQ tests. Other factors could have contributed to the effect: Notably, the co-occurrence of war and the disruption of schooling complicates the interpretation of IQ changes over time. At the very least, according to de Groot, the Eindhoven data show that intelligence should not be regarded as an innate and immutable entity, but as a product of experience.

Public School Closure in Virginia

In the United States, the effect of schooling disruption on IQ was demonstrated during a study of school shutdowns in the Civil Rights Era. The shutdowns were not precipitated by war per se, but by the desegregation of schooling mandated in *Brown v. Board of Education* (1954). Following *Brown*, the   Board of Supervisors of Prince Edward County of Virginia resisted integration and eventually closed all public schools in the county between the spring of 1959 and the fall of 1963 (Green, Hofmann, Morse, Hayes, & Morgan, 1964). During that period, the education of White students was maintained through the establishment of the Prince Edward School Corporation, which opened all-White private schools in September 1959. These actions left 1,700 Black children without any formal provision for their educational needs for 4 years.

In response to this dire situation, leaders in the Black community arranged for short-term educational experiences, such as summer "crash" programs, to help compensate for lost time in classrooms. Those students who participated in the compensatory programs received, on average, the equivalent of 1.5 to 2 years of schooling during the 4-year period. In a study of the shutdown effects, these students were collectively called the EDUCATION group (N = 150); those who received no compensatory experience were labeled the NO EDUCATION group (N = 138). Cross-sectional analysis of subsequent Stanford-Binet scores show that mean IQs in both groups dropped about 15 points during the years of school closure, although the data show higher overall IQs for the EDUCATION group. The results are somewhat complicated by the fact that the EDUCATION and NO EDUCATION groups were probably not strictly comparable in initial IQ and family background, and the sample sizes at each grade level were small, generally less than 20 students. Nonetheless, the dramatic fall of IQ in both groups during this period reinforces the proposal that depriving children of educational opportunity can have deleterious effects on their general cognitive growth.

Grade Acceleration and Delay

In the school-age population, children within each grade are approximately the same age, but of course not exactly. Cahan and Cohen (1989) took advantage of this fact when they compared the educational achievement of students whose school experience differed as a consequence of the arbitrary cutoff dates for school entrance. The research design permitted comparisons between students of similar chronological ages, but who differed experientially by 1 year of schooling. The study involved approximately 10,000 fourth-, fifth-, and sixth-grade students in Jerusalem schools. Using a between-grades regression analysis, the investigators assessed the independent contributions of maturation (chronological age) and schooling to performance on 12 tests of cognitive ability. They addressed the possible confounds of grade acceleration (with giftedness) and delay (with learning problems) by eliminating from their sample students born in November and December (the months nearest the cutoff date).

The most impressive finding was that the effects of schooling were more powerful than the effects of chronological age on all tests of cognitive ability, and on most tests the schooling effect was about twice that of maturation. According to Cahan and Cohen (1989), the results point to schooling as "the major factor underlying the increase in intelligence tests scores as a function of age" (p. 1245). The effects of schooling differed in magnitude across tests, exerting a stronger influence on tests of crystallized abilities, such as verbal and numerical ability, and a weaker effect on tests of nonverbal fluid abilities, such as figural analogies. Nevertheless, the independent effect of schooling on fluid abilities is significant theoretically, because it challenges the idea that fluid intelligence is developed indirectly (Cronbach, 1984). More generally, the study by Cahan and Cohen (1989) points to the "critical contribution of formal education" to the development of intelligence (p. 1247).

A study conducted in South Africa's Natal province also found substantial correlations between IQ, including fluid intelligence, and variation in years of schooling as a result of delayed entry (Schmidt, 1960). The schooling effects were independent of the chronological age and the SES of students. The research focused on the Indian population, which at the time of the study could not be fully accommodated into schools because of an insufficient number of teachers and classrooms. As a result, Indian children entered school sometime between the ages of 6 and 10, whenever space became available. In a sample of more than 200 13-year-old students, an impressive correlation was obtained between years of schooling and performance on Raven's Progressive Matrices ($r = 0.51$), and the correlation of school experience with verbal ability was even stronger ($r = 0.68$). When data were analyzed across grades, raw scores on Raven's Matrices were almost identical for younger "early starters" and for older "late starters"—that is, fluid intelligence as measured by Raven's seemed to be a function of amount of schooling rather than chronological age. The study's author concluded that schooling is "the decisive factor" in the development of verbal (crystallized) and non-verbal (fluid) intelligence (Schmidt, 1960, p. 429).

Summer Vacation

The suspension of schooling during the summer months (i.e., summer vacation) has been found to impact learning rates, and to do so differentially according to children's economic and racial/ethnic backgrounds. Hayes and Grether (1983) documented this effect from data collected in the mid-1960s. The investigators divided New York City public schools into six groups according to their racial composition (percentage White) and socioeconomic characteristics (percentage of children receiving a free lunch). Employing a cross-sectional design spanning Grades 2 through 6, the authors examined changes in reading achievement and word knowledge on the basis of twice-yearly examinations conducted in early fall and late spring. With these data, they were able to separate the effects of summertime and school-year experience on achievement outcomes. Hayes and Grether (1983) found that, by the end of sixth grade, the gains in reading achievement made by the richer White schools were 2 years greater than the gains made by the poorer minority schools. However, only half of this difference could be accounted for by gains made during the school year; the other half represented differential gains made mostly during the summer months when school was not in session. "Put another way," said the authors (1983, p. 60), "the four summers between the 2nd and 6th grades produce a reading differential almost equal to the effects of five academic years."

The effect of summertime experience on word knowledge was even more dramatic. Very little of the group difference in word knowledge was the product of school experience; most of the differential gain occurred during the summer months. Between the two groups representing the poles of the economic continuum (and, in this sample, groups defined by race), school-year effects were responsible for about a 6-month differential in word knowledge by the end of sixth grade. By contrast, the summer vacation months were associated with a differential gain of a full 2 years. For the poorest children, summer vacation was academically unproductive; gains in reading achievement and word knowledge slowed dramatically, plateaued, or even regressed. Students from wealthier families, however, made substantial achievement gains during the summer. Word knowledge advanced as if nonschool experiences provided much the same cognitive stimulation as did schools, and so maintained a cognitive growth trajectory that was comparable to that achieved during the school year. In other words, for the wealthier children experience of high educative quality was continuous, whereas for the poorer children it was interrupted.

A later study by Heyns (1978) identified some of the nonschool activities that might account for group differences in rates of achievement during the summer months. In findings that paralleled the earlier study by Hayes and Grether, Heyns found that low-SES Black children in Atlanta lost ground in comparison to White students in both relative and absolute levels of academic achievement. In general, high-SES White children had freer access to summer activities that enriched intellectual development. These activities included using the library, going on vacation, and even having a bicycle—all were associated with the larger separation of Black and White learning trajectories during the summer months.

Data demonstrating the educative or noneducative effects of summer experience reinforce the assertion that the term *education* must embrace all forms of experience that have cognitive value, not just the formal apparatus of schooling (Brandwein, 1981). Potent differences in nonschool educational experience certainly extend to the preschool years. However, data on the effects of summer vacation show that, even during the school years, nonschool experiences play a major role in producing and sustaining differential rates of intellectual development. On this point, Hayes and Grether (1983) were direct: "In short, very little of the enormous difference in word knowledge performance of ghetto and relatively rich whites found by the end of 6th grade appears to be attributable to what goes on *in* school; most of it comes from what goes on *out* of school" (p. 64; emphasis in original).

On the basis of their findings, Hayes and Grether (1983) questioned the wisdom of placing hope in the institution of schooling for redressing social inequities. Citing the Coleman Report (Coleman et al., 1966), they reminded the reader that much of the variation in students' academic achievement is a product of nonschool factors, and therefore "not . . . under the direct control of teachers, principals, or school boards" (Hayes & Grether, 1983, p. 66). This is not to say that schools are ineffectual or irrelevant in redressing racial/ethnic and socioeconomic differences in academic achievement. On the contrary, schooling acts as a buffer to reduce differences in the slopes of academic achievement rates (Heyns, 1978). In this sense, schooling is a powerful institution for correcting social inequities. Yet, the potency of nonschool educational experiences makes it clear that it is unrealistic to expect schools to erase all differences between groups in cognitive outcomes. To advance the cause of equity and to promote the fuller realization of potential for all, it is imperative to understand that although schooling is a major instrument for cognitive development, education is accomplished through a far broader array of experiences.

Cross-Cultural Effects of Schooling

Effects of schooling on intelligence have been observed in countries making the transition toward compulsory universal education. Stevenson, Parker, Wilkinson, Bonnevaux, and Gonzalez (1978) examined the effects of schooling on cognitive task performance among selected subpopulations of Peru. The subpopulations were defined by three cultural groups (Mestizo, Quechua Indian, and "upper middle class"), by two locations (urban Lima and jungle Lamas), and by two levels of school experience (first-grade attendance and nonattendance). The investigators found that even a single year of school attendance affected performance on all cognitive tasks they employed, including memory tasks (e.g., serial words, serial numbers, pictorial) and cognitive tasks (e.g., concept learning, categories, seriation). Mean differences in cognitive performance were also found along cultural and location dimensions of comparison, but the effects of schooling were stronger and comparable among all subgroups. Commenting on this study, Greenfield (1978) pointed out that the main effects of schooling are often overlooked by those who expect school experience to reduce group and individual differences. She reminded the reader that "schooling may have a tremendous impact on cognitive performance independent of its capacity to erase group differences" (pp. 84-85).

Quality of Schooling

If differences in exposure to or quantity of schooling influence cognitive development, so might differences in the *quality* of schooling. According to the cumulative deficit hypothesis, when the quality of schooling is very poor, student IQ scores could actually drift downward over time. Jensen (1977) proposed that data supporting the hypothesis would be obtained if, within families, older siblings tended to have lower IQs than younger siblings, and if the younger-older IQ gap widened as age differences between siblings increased.[5] Jensen failed to find support for the cumulative deficit hypothesis in predominantly Black California schools, but later examined data from comparable schools in rural Georgia, where between-race differences in the quality of schooling were much more severe. Jensen reasoned that if evidence for the cumulative deficit hypothesis could not be found in rural Georgia, it probably could not be found anywhere in the United States.

In Georgia, Jensen did indeed find data supporting the cumulative deficit hypothesis. Among Black students between the ages of 6 and 16, cognitive decline amounted to a linear decrement of 1.42 IQ points per year, which is equivalent to a loss of about 15 points, or one standard deviation, over the course of schooling. Jensen tested the possibility that other factors contributed to this effect, but found that birth order was irrelevant to the IQ decrement, and that family size contributed to it only marginally. Jensen speculated that genetic factors might be responsible, in whole or in part, for the IQ decrement by placing limits on the growth curve of *g* among Black students. The data, however, did not support this interpretation because IQ decrements comparable to those found in Georgia were not observed in the less severely deficient schools in California. Jensen (1977) concluded that the contrast between California and Georgia schools "would seem to favor an environmental interpretation of the progressive IQ decrement" (p. 190).

Summary of Schooling Effects

The idea that formal education contributes directly to the formation of intelligence was expressed plainly by Stephenson, who in 1949 "made a passionate plea for recognizing the role of *the school itself* in developing (in a sense even *creating*) the intelligence of the child" (Schmidt, 1960, p. 416). Data bearing on the connection between schooling and the growth of intelligence is primarily correlational, but it is nonetheless convergent. After reviewing eight strands of evidence linking IQ enhancement to schooling, Ceci (1991) concluded that "the most parsimonious account of the correlations that have been reviewed is a direct causal link" (p. 711), an attribution that Carroll (1997, p. 42) called "only too obvious."

Still, the linkage between schooling and intelligence is understood only imperfectly. One problem is that the institutionalized covariation of maturation and schooling in modern societies makes it difficult to separate the independent effects of each. However, with the proper analytic tools they can be disentangled, and in at least one study the effects of schooling on IQ were found to be larger than the effects of maturation (Cahan & Cohen, 1989). This and similar other findings point to a more complex relationship between education and intelligence than is generally recognized. Almost universally, intelligence is thought of as preparatory for education. Intelligence does have that function—as "input"—but it is more. Intelligence is also, in part, an output or product of schooling, but it is so unwittingly. That schooling raises intelligence is, in terms of the stated purposes of schooling, an accident. Intelligence is a by-product. Even if educational institutions have not recognized their role in boosting the intelligence of billions of students in the 20th century, society has come to depend on the intelligence by-product. Society's expectations for and definition of an educated person include the ability to think intensively and flexibly about complex matters in the course of finding and solving significant problems. What schools supply incidentally, society demands insistently and consumes voraciously.

What is incidental can become intentional, and what is by-product can become main product. A recognition of schooling's ability to raise general cognitive preparedness can be used as a basis for restating the function of schooling to embrace the equipping of learners with the most general and powerful of intellectual abilities, intelligence. Of course, schooling is not the only mechanism by which intelligence is grown, and schools are not solely responsible for ensuring the intellectual readiness of future citizens. Schools have never had a monopoly in the business of cognitive development. But in the future schooling can play a critical role in the development of intelligence, just as it has in the past. An explicit adoption of that purpose could lead to even greater effectiveness of schools in making people smarter.

UNIVERSITY EXPERIENCE

For many people, collegiate education is a life phase associated strongly with gains in cognitive abilities, knowledge, and skills. Research synthesized by Pascarella and Terenzini (1991) quantified such gains in formal (abstract) reasoning (effect size approximately 0.33 SD), critical thinking (1.0 SD), ill-structured problem solving (1.0 SD), and the ability to deal with conceptual complexity (1.2 SD). These effects, converted to an IQ scale, suggest that the college experience can produce gains ranging from 5 to 15 points. The research showed that the nature of the cognitive boost is complex: Students improved their ability to weigh evidence and to judge inferences from data, but not necessarily their ability to recognize assumptions or to deduce conclusions from premises. Moreover, the authors were clear that only a portion of the cognitive gains could be directly attributed to the college experience. However, the gains were not illusory: They held up even when possible confounding influences, such as SES and initial intellectual ability, were controlled.

Why should a college education enhance cognitive development? Although the answer is not definitely known, Pascarella and Terenzini (1991) suggested a reasonable explanation: "Of all the experiences a student could have after secondary school, college is the one that most typically provides an overall environment where the potential for intellectual growth is maximized" (p. 156). In the university several potent agents of intellectual enhancement—faculty, students, libraries, and laboratories—are "concentrated in one place" (p. 156). Whatever effects a university education may have on cognition, ancillary effects also result. A university experience can influence the tastes, interests, grammar, and accent of graduates (Herrnstein & Murray, 1994). Many of these acquired characteristics have no direct adaptive value, but instead are signs of privilege and perhaps credentials for further opportunity, a point enlarged on by Hirsh (1987) in his construct of cultural literacy.

College has important short-term effects on students, but the long-term consequences of a college education on subsequent generations may be even more important. Children of college graduates are poised for higher educational attainment, occupational status, and income than are children of parents who did not graduate from college, even when possibly confounding factors (family income, intelligence, aspirations, race, and gender) are controlled (Pascarella & Terenzini, 1991). However, the "confounding" variables are themselves important: The intervening variables of family income and aspirations have instrumental value in the educational and career attainments of children.

Another likely influence pathway is the effect of college on parenting style (Pascarella & Terenzini, 1991). College-educated parents, mothers especially, spend relatively more time with their children on activities that advance cognitive development (e.g., reading, teaching). Even within socioeconomic groups, the level of education attained by a mother is correlated with qualities of the home environment, including cognitive stimulation and emotional support. Home characteristics, in turn, predict children's cognitive development and IQ. Ceci (1996) even found that parents' education is a better predictor of children's IQ than is family income (cf. Grissmer, Flanagan, & Williamson, 1998). Not only will the quality of the intellectual experience be richer (in an important sense) for children of university-educated parents, but family life will often be suffused with the valuing of educational achievement, with expectations concerning reasonable and possible educational goals, and with dispositions that support academic tenacity and a work ethic, especially with regard to the complex and symbol-rich tasks that typify formal education and symbolic-analytic work.

JOB EXPERIENCE

It would be a mistake to think that work experience is unrelated to cognitive development. Work actually constitutes a phase of education, not merely a life stage for which education is preparatory. Of course, jobs—like families and schools—differ in their educative quality. In Reich's (1992) terms, routine production jobs are poor in educative value, but symbolic analyst positions are rich in their potential to expand cognitive capability. This is clear if one considers the educative value of jobs that require only mindless repetition versus those that require a worker to confront and solve new and complex problems on a daily basis. The latter kind of job—that of the symbolic analyst—evokes and exercises the cognitive competencies described by the term *intelligence*. Schooler (1984) showed that jobs demanding initiative, judgment, and independent thought actually increase the intellectual flexibility of workers over time, and encourage a value system that prizes self-direction over conformity.

The best-rewarded and most prestigious jobs have this quality of symbolic analysis. For those who think for a living, work is never business as usual, but rather is defined by the problem du jour. According to Stewart (1997, p. 202), "Instead of jobs, we have projects." To be effective, workers must maintain cognitive flexibility while accessing their own and others' expert knowledge base. Yet the expert's knowledge base is itself shifty, subject to revision and constant expansion. These workers must also be able to interact smoothly with people who carry cognitive repertoires different from their own. In today's workplace, complex projects are commonly posed to groups of people assembled in the hope that their separate cognitive contributions will synergize. The work group takes on a project (i.e., complex problem), solves it, and then disbands so that its members can join yet other ad hoc groups that address other problems.

Job experience may exert intergenerational effects. I have already proposed that university-educated parents will be different *sorts* of parents than those who are not comparably educated. The same might be true of parents who have different job experiences. There are the obvious cognitive advantages associated with high income, and incomes tend to be higher for symbolic-analytic jobs. Family income can affect the experience of the child all along the developmental continuum by contributing to differences in the quality of prenatal experience, preschool experience, schooling, the likelihood of obtaining a college and postgraduate education, and occupational aspirations. More directly, children's social environments, including the values that define the professional class, might be taught at home and reinforced through interaction with other professional-class families, through peer culture, and through the culture of the local school (Harris, 1995). The high valuation of independent thought and self-direction encouraged by parents' intellectually demanding jobs seems likely to be passed on to children, who would then be groomed for their own life careers as symbolic analysts (Schooler, 1984). Such experiences foster in children the tendency, willingness, and ability to engage in problem-finding and problem-solving behavior in complex environments—the bread and butter of their parents by virtue of their membership in the society of the cognitive elite.

EXPERIENCE IN OLD AGE

The trend toward gentrification, especially in affluent and technology saturated nations, is now common knowledge. Gentrification may have economic consequences. We know that as people age, crystallized intelligence tends to grow or at least stabilize, whereas fluid intelligence declines (Stanovich, West, & Harrison, 1995). A case can be made that economic productivity depends increasingly on the exercise of fluid ability because of the constant need to innovate (Hunt, 1995). As life spans stretch, will productivity drop? Not necessarily. The deliberate enhancement of cognitive abilities, especially fluid intelligence, would address Hunt's (1995) concern that the workforce of the future might have insufficient cognitive flexibility to be economically competitive.

The direct training of fluid intelligence has in fact been demonstrated in elderly populations (Willis, Blieszner, & Baltes, 1981). More generally, there is a new optimism that the cognitive system of adults, including older adults, is far more plastic than previously recognized. For example, gains in crystallized intelligence over the life span appear to be largely mediated by exposure to print (Stanovich et al., 1995), an experiential factor that can be controlled by the individual and encouraged by the culture. Evidence is accumulating that certain kinds of experience can lead to reorganization of the adult brain, even late in life (Nelson, 1999). A cognitively interesting and challenging environment, as well as physical exercise, can increase the production of brain molecules known as *neurotrophins*, whose function is to stimulate the growth of neurons and to improve local brain vascularization (Cotman & Neeper, 1996). Neurotrophin levels are higher and cognitive functions are more advanced in physically active men and women than in sedentary peers. The phenomenon of activity-related brain plasticity in the aging population highlights "the fundamental need to maintain and perhaps even increase brain stimulation in aging" (Cotman & Neeper, 1996, p. 293). All such related brain-enhancing and brain-preserving activities can be thought of as broad-sense education.

Equally encouraging is the finding that new brain neurons can be formed in adults, even the elderly. It has long been assumed that the loss of brain cells in adults is irreversible—that new brain cells cannot be developed. The doctrine of the monotonic decline of brain neurons is now known to be false. Newly generated brain neurons have been detected in the hippocampus (a brain structure that plays a crucial role in the formation of long-term memories) in human adults in their 60s and 70s (Eriksson et al., 1998). The investigators who discovered this phenomenon also pointed out that neurogenesis in laboratory animals has been linked to environmental stimulation and to exercise (Hotz, 1999). Connections between specific activities and neurogenesis have not yet been demonstrated in humans, but present a fascinating possibility. The current findings are themselves significant because neurogenesis among older adults suggests that "the human brain retains the potential for self-renewal throughout life" (Eriksson et al., 1998, p. 1315). The maintenance and enhancement of intellectual functioning could yield many benefits, not least of which is a more satisfying life for the elderly.

In the future, "smart drugs" may play a prominent role in maintaining and enhancing cognitive ability in people of all ages, but especially the elderly. There is enormous interest, both theoretical and commercial, in exploring physiological and pharmaceutical pathways that might lead to the enhancement of cognitive performance. The physiology of memory at the level of synapses is leading to the design of pharmaceuticals that enhance memory and, possibly, other cognitive functions. As of 1999, the FDA had approved only two memory-enhancing drugs, Tacrine and Donepezil; both were intended for patients with Alzheimer's disease (Holloway, 1999). These drugs work by inhibiting the breakdown of acetylcholine, a neurotransmitter that appears to be important in memory formation. Some of the drugs now under development target receptors in the hippocampus. These target sites include NMDA receptors and a subclass, AMPA receptors, for which a class of memory-enhancing drugs called *ampakines* is being developed. In early clinical studies, ampakines doubled the recall of elderly subjects (Lynch, 1998). Clearly, as the population gentrifies and life expectancies lengthen, the market for smarts in a bottle will grow.

NUTRIENTS AND TOXINS

Under the very broadest construal of *education,* we might place differences in exposure to nutrients and toxins, and their effects on cognition. Nutrients and toxins are, after all, aspects of the environment that either promote or limit development, and that are controllable. What is not in doubt is that there are important differences among children and adults in their exposure to molecules, "good" and "bad," that are relevant to cognitive performance. Exposure to nutritive and toxic molecules has special importance in the prenatal months, and during childhood. However, because nutrients and toxins have documentable effects all along the life span, this section is organized separately from the previous sections based on life stages.

Nutrition is far more important to the developing mind than is commonly recognized (Eysenck, 1991). Lynn (1990) advanced the idea that worldwide increases in IQ during the past century—the Flynn effect—might be attributed to global improvements in nutrition. To demonstrate that this is plausible, Lynn cited research showing that, in children and animals, suboptimal nutrition is associated with deficiencies in neuronal growth and myelination, and in the formation of synaptic connections. Even if widespread nutritional improvements have supported a general increase in IQ, chronic malnutrition can still be found around the world, including in economically developed countries (Karp, 1993).

Vitamin Supplementation in Britain

There is now a body of research showing that nutritional supplementation in the form of multivitamin tablets can lead to IQ enhancement (Eysenck, 1998). In a double-blind, placebo-controlled study, Benton and Roberts (1988) detected a 9-point rise in nonverbal IQ among British children who received a vitamin supplement over an 8-month period. No such rise was detected in the placebo group. A nutrient analysis of the diet of participants, ages 12 and 13, showed that U.S. RDAs were met for most nutrients prior to the intervention. There was, however, considerable variation around mean nutrient intakes, and for a subset of participants substantial deficiencies were found for vitamin D, folic acid, calcium, iron, and other trace minerals. Benton and Roberts (1988) interpreted their data as showing that gains in nonverbal IQ represent increases in the "more biological" fluid intelligence as a consequence of improved neural functioning. A lack of improvement in nonverbal IQ was interpreted to mean that crystallized intelligence, which is more clearly identified with accumulated experience, would not be expected to rise in a study of such short duration.

Vitamin Supplementation in California

Similar effects were reported by Schoenthaler, Amos, Eysenck, Peritz, and Yudkin (1991) from research conducted among eighth- and tenth-grade California schoolchildren. In a controlled study that varied the level of vitamin supplementation to 50%, 100%, and 200% of RDA, IQ gains associated with supplementation were again more pronounced on tests of nonverbal fluid intelligence than on crystallized intelligence. After only 4 weeks, the 200% RDA supplementation group experienced a significant gain in fluid intelligence as assessed through Raven's Matrices. In the longer term (13 weeks), gains in nonverbal IQ (WISC-R) were larger in the treatment groups than in controls, but the effects were statistically significant only for the 100% RDA group, which demonstrated a gain over controls of 4.4 IQ points. The 100% RDA group also outperformed controls on the reading comprehension and mathematics comprehension subtests of the CTBS achievement battery.

Nutrient deficiencies need not be severe to have cognitive effects; subclinical deficiencies in vitamins and minerals can result in decremented cognitive performance before signs of physical deficiency are observed (Yudkin, 1991). In the theoretical framework employed by Schoenthaler and colleagues (1991), only those students whose diet was nutritionally suboptimal could be expected to benefit significantly from vitamin supplementation. Accordingly, the researchers distinguished between "responders" (those gaining 15 or more IQ points) and "non-responders" (all others). Preliminary analyses of blood samples taken before and after the intervention showed that "responders" were more likely to have lower concentrations of nutrients prior to the intervention, and were also more likely to experience significant changes in blood nutrient levels as a result of supplementation. More detailed blood analyses were reported later (Eysenck & Schoenthaler, 1997). The re-analyses included only those students who initially had low blood concentrations of vitamins. Within this subset of students, the 100% RDA group gained 8.1 IQ points over the placebo control group, and the 200% RDA group gained 5.1 IQ points relative to controls. IQ gains in the 100% RDA and 200% RDA groups were both significantly different from the control group, but not from each other. The recognition that some recipients of vitamin supplements responded dramatically and others did not suggests that vitamin supplementation might have special importance for young learners growing up in conditions of poverty or disadvantage, and in developing countries (Eysenck, 1991).

Dietary Changes in New York City

Improvements to the nutritional quality of diets have been shown to impact school achievement directly (Schoenthaler, Doraz, & Wakefield, 1986). In a study involving approximately one million school children in public schools of New York City, dietary improvements to school-served breakfasts and lunches were phased in over a 3-year period. Those improvements involved the reduction of sucrose, synthetic food colors, and preservatives. In Figure 8.2, diagonally hatched bars display the effects of those dietary improvements on school achievement tests, expressed as national rankings.

The phased-in dietary changes were organized as follows: The first change, implemented in 1979-80, involved the reduction of sucrose levels; the second change, implemented the following year, entailed the elimination of selected food colors. Both changes were associated with rises in percentile rankings. No additional dietary changes were made in the 1981-82 school year, and the percentile rankings remained unchanged. The third dietary change, made during the 1982-83 year, was the elimination of the preservatives BHT and BHA. That change was associated with a further improvement in academic achievement scores. During the 4-year implementation period, the New York City public schools improved their academic performance, expressed as national percentile rankings, from 39.2% to 54.9%—a 15.7% gain.

Subtler effects contribute to the richness of findings and the implications of this study. For example, academic gains were strongest in those schools having the highest percentages of students receiving school meals. Dietary improvements had three times the effect in schools having the most participation in school meals compared to those having the least. Perturbations in national rankings during the 3 control years prior to the study might also be linked to dietary changes. In particular, the 1977-78 school years shows a slight, but statistically significant, improvement in performance compared to the year before. The authors noted that during the 1977-78 "control" school year, the amount of fat in school meals was reduced.

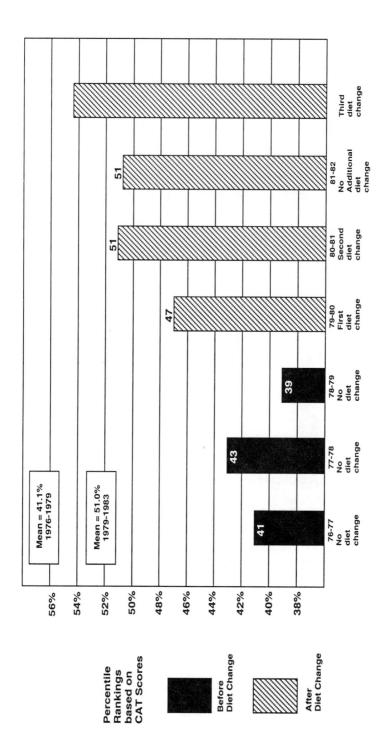

FIG. 8.2. National rankings of 803 New York City public schools before and after dietary changes. The achievement measure, CAT, refers to the California Achievement Test. From "The Impact of a Low Food Additive and Sucrose Diet on Academic Performance in 803 New York City Public Schools," by S. J. Schoenthaler, W. E. Doraz, and J. A. Wakefield, 1986, *International Journal of Biosocial Research, 8*(2), p. 189. Reprinted with Permission.

In interpreting these gains, the authors expressed doubt that academic benefits resulted directly from the elimination of idiopathic effects, such as specific food allergies. A more likely explanation is that the reduction or elimination of sucrose, food colorings, and preservatives resulted in a general improvement in the ratio of nutrients to calories. The dietary reduction of nutritionally poor (e.g., highly processed or empty calorie) foods presumably led to a caloric gap, which students filled by increasing their intake of nutritionally superior foods. This study shows that nutrition is germane to learning outcomes in the United States. Chronic malnutrition is not a phenomenon restricted to Third World countries; American children living in conditions of poverty commonly suffer nutritional deficiencies (Karp, 1993). More generally, nutritionally poor diets are concomitant with poverty and almost certainly contribute to differences in cognitive outcomes among racial-ethnic groups (Sewell, Price, & Karp, 1993).

Protein Supplementation in Guatemala

In developing countries, chronic dietary protein deficiency has long been known to be a major health problem affecting millions of children. The clinical manifestation of protein deficiency is the syndrome known as *kwashiorkor*, identified by hair and skin dyspigmentation, liver hypertrophy, and behavior marked by apathy and listlessness. Protein supplementation can be effective in improving the cognitive performance of children at risk for clinical protein deficiency. In one study conducted in four Guatemalan villages, children in the treatment group were administered a liquid protein supplement twice daily, beginning as early as infancy and extending up to age 7 (Pollitt et al., 1993). For a subset of participants, supplementation was available prenatally through the participation of their mothers.

In comparison to placebo-administered controls, the experimental subjects scored significantly higher in school-related achievement tests, on cognitive reaction time tasks, on IQ as measured by Raven's Progressive Matrices, and on a general cognitive factor. However, the interactions among predictors reveals the true multideterminate nature of cognitive outcomes. In particular, treatment effects were most pronounced in subjects who came from the poorest families. In the treatment group, protein supplementation effectively neutralized the association between family wealth and cognitive outcomes, and so acted as a "social equalizer" (Pollitt et al., 1993, p. 79). Supplementation also interacted with educational experience as measured by maximum grade attained. This latter interaction suggested a synergistic effect of adequate nutrition and educational opportunity such that nutritional factors increase in importance with greater exposure to schooling (Pollitt et al., 1993; Wachs, 1993). Long-term effects were observed in a cross-sectional follow-up study 11 years after supplementation was halted, when subjects were adolescents and young adults. Main effects for protein supplementation were again found on measures of fluid intelligence (i.e., Raven's Matrices), on literacy, and on numeracy. As before, these effects were most pronounced among participants from poorer families.

It is too simple to think that the causal chain linking dietary improvements with cognitive benefits operates exclusively through establishing a more adequate neural substrate for learning. Nutrition probably does have direct effects on the CNS, but an improved diet can also lead to different qualities of behavior in the child and in the caregiver (Ricciuti, 1993; Wachs, 1993). In a supplementation study in Mexico, Chávez and Martínez (1975) found that improved nutrition had large effects on the quality of parent and child behavior. Children who were nutritionally "supplemented," starting at 6 weeks gestation, displayed much more independence, exploratory behavior, and complex play than did "nonsupplemented" control children. Parents of nutritionally "supplemented" children, in turn, were much more responsive: Mother-child speech interaction was twice as frequent, and father-child play was much more common in supplemented children than in controls. Thus, the diet-cognition link may be moderated by the quality of the child's experience, which in turn is affected by the child's own initiative.

Toxins

Along with nutritive molecules, the cognitive effects of environmental toxins must also be considered. High-dose lead exposure, for example, has long been associated with decrements to cognitive and motor performance (Harris, Clark, & Karp, 1993). Low to moderate lead exposure has been found to impair gross and fine motor control in children (Dietrich, Berger, & Succop, 1993). The association between low-dose lead exposure and cognitive decrement has been less clear. Studies of the cognitive effects of lead have sometimes yielded contradictory findings, but pertinent studies have been uneven in data and design quality. Needleman and Gatsonis (1990) conducted a meta-analysis of the effects of lead exposure on IQ, using only studies that had adequate measures of exposure and cognitive outcomes, and measures permitting covariate control over possible nonlead confounds. In 11 of 12 studies, they found a negative effect of low-dose lead exposure on IQ (joint $p < .0001$). Blood serum lead levels between 25 and 40 picograms per deciliter were associated with a 5-point IQ disadvantage, which translates to a magnified incidence of mild mental retardation. On the basis of their analysis, the investigators concluded that "the hypothesis that lead impairs children's IQ at low dose is strongly supported" (p. 673).

Even maternal exposure can have effects on children: Lead is now known to cross the placenta (Dietrich, Berger, & Succop, 1993), and there is a "clear relationship between umbilical cord lead levels and later development at 6 to 24 months" (Needleman & Gatsonis, 1990, p. 677). Maternal lead levels above 10 micrograms per deciliter are known to suppress the cognitive development of children (Harris et al., 1993). Although lead abatement programs have been in place for some time, large numbers of children still suffer from low-level lead exposure, especially from lead-based paint in dilapidated and substandard housing. Even low-level exposure is serious because there is unlikely to be a "safe" threshold below which negative effects can be ruled out. Moreover, it is not clear that chelation therapies are effective; they may, in fact, exacerbate the problem (Harris et al., 1993).

Another class of toxins, insecticides, are a major cause for concern because, as neurotoxicants, they are "deliberately designed to sabotage biological mechanisms," and their widespread use over decades has led to their "total global distribution in human tissues," and indeed the entire biosphere (Weiss, 1997, p. 255). Most research has focused on the potential carcinogenic effects of pesticides, but few studies have examined their possible role as agents of developmental disabilities. Acute poisoning by organophosphorus compounds, such as malathione, has been found to have long-term neurotoxic consequences in adults, including diminished IQ (Weiss, 1997).[6] Organochlorine compounds, which include DDT, are potentially much more dangerous because they biodegrade slowly and accumulate in fat tissues. Organochlorines can also cross the placenta and are passed on through breast milk. As with organophosphates, acute exposure to organochlorines is associated with diminished cognitive functioning in adults and lower IQ in children. Effects of chronic, lower-level exposure (e.g., through residues on food) are less certain. However, even acute pesticide poisonings are common, affecting at least 45,000 people each year in the United States alone.

CONCLUSION

This main theme of this chapter is that a broad range of experiential factors have demonstrable effects on cognitive development, including IQ. Although the experiences of infancy and childhood have special importance in shaping cognitive growth, the experience stream all along the life span—from prenatal life to old age—can boost, nudge, and bend the pattern and pace of cognitive growth or decline. These experiences include, but are not limited to, formal education. Cognitive growth is multidetermined by experiences that vary in educative quality. In light of this, it makes sense to redefine the word *education* to embrace all experiences that enhance the readiness of people to be effective in a complex, problem-centered, and symbol-rich society. Even as IQ scores are rising around the world, we now understand enough about the kinds of experience that enhance intelligence that, collectively, we can cultivate richer cognitive outcomes for everyone.

NOTES

1. Strangely, quality of experience can exercise effects even well *before* conception. In one study, for example, incidences of anencephaly and spina bifida were found to be inversely related to the social class of the child's *maternal grandfather* (Joffe, 1982). That is, these birth defects were more frethe body over time and can cross the placenta (Dietrich et al., 1993).

2. According to the "good enough" parenting hypothesis, parents have little differential impact on children's cognitive development; rather, within a range of "species-normal" home environments, children will seek certain kinds of experience, and this experience-seeking behavior is strongly guided by the child's own genotype (Scarr, 1992). However, the meaning of "species-normal" environments, although perhaps straightforward in nonhuman species, is complicated by the huge variability among human cultures in the existence and relative valuation of symbolic inventions (Gardner, 1983). For example, whether a culture (or a family within a culture) is literate or nonliterate will permit or preclude literacy among children, and this division will cascade to all manner of cognitive outcomes (e.g., crystallized intelligence). Formal education (schooling) is another example of an invention of culture that complicates the meaning of "species-normal." Other inventions, such as computational and information technologies, may ultimately have similar effects on human experience and on the shape of growing minds. Studies of genetic influences on cognitive development within relatively homogenous populations are unlikely to register the effects of large variations in environments that are all "species-normal," perhaps leading to the unwarranted conclusion that these variations do not matter much to the developing child.

3. Other research corroborates the effect: Performance on Raven's Matrices, a test of fluid intelligence, is sensitive to secondary education (Greenfield, 1998).

4. Gordon observed similar patterns in his study of gypsy (Roma) children (Freeman, 1934).

5. Compare with effects observed among English canal boat children (Gordon, 1970/1923), described earlier.

6. On August 2, 1999, the U.S. Environmental Protectional Agency imposed limitations on the use of certain organophoshates (e.g., banning the use of methyl parathion on fruits), recognizing for the first time their potential to disrupt the neurological development of children (Shogren, 1999).

9
Interventions That Enhance Intelligence

We have seen that IQ is sensitive to differing qualities of experience along the life span. The implication is that the enrichment of experience can influence intelligence positively—that intelligence can, in fact, be cultivated. The idea is not new: In 1949, Hebb inquired rhetorically, "Why then should we object to the idea that enriching an inadequate environment will raise the IQ?" (1949, p. 295). Interventions designed to enhance cognitive abilities have also existed for some time. A century ago, Thorndike and Woodworth (1901) tested the improvability and transfer of attention, observation, and discrimination functions; as early as 1925, interventions were designed to counteract the effects of poverty on cognition (Detterman, 1982).

To see intelligence as consisting in a set of learnable cognitive abilities requires overcoming a formidable conceptual barrier. Although the idea has been circulated at least since the time of Binet, it was given further recognition and programmatic importance in the 1960s. In the landmark volume *Intelligence and Experience*, Hunt (1961) defended the view that intelligence is developed through encounters with the environment. Hunt's arguments were a prelude to many early cognitive interventions that aimed to develop general cognitive ability directly. Hunt (1961) wrote:

> Assumptions that intelligence is fixed and that its development is predetermined by the genes are no longer tenable. . . . It is no longer unreasonable to consider that it might be feasible to discover ways to govern the encounters that children have with their environments, especially during the early years of their development, to achieve a substantially faster rate of intellectual development and a substantially higher adult level of capacity. (pp. 362-363)

Hunt's thesis concerning the modifiability of intelligence helped establish an ambitious national agenda in the United States. Impelled by the Civil Rights movement and supportive court decisions, the new federal legislation specified education as a primary vehicle for addressing social inequities. According to Snow (1982b), this new way of thinking led to:

> a decade of educational and psychological research, development, and field development . . . fueled by unprecedented government support. The goal, simply put, was to improve the generalizable intellectual, learning, and problem-solving skills of students all across the public school years. . . . Headstart, Follow Through,

Upward Bound, Sesame Street, and many other attempts at compensatory education aimed frankly at developing intelligence. (pp. 13-14)

In this chapter, we consider a few of the projects that have demonstrated that intelligence can be enhanced through direct intervention. The reviewed projects are organized into three groups according to the age of the participants: infancy (one project), early childhood (six projects), and school age (four projects).

IQ gains are emphasized in the reported studies. This is not to suggest that IQ is equivalent to the profusely rich construct of intelligence, which is only partially revealed through the psychometric and cognitive methodologies. However, neither is IQ to be dismissed. As Neisser (1997) has observed, "No serious scholar claims either that IQ tests measure nothing important, or that they measure everything important" (p. 440). IQ is used because any claim about raising intelligence (as opposed to the more modest claim of improving thinking skills) is more readily defended if gains are observed on what has been, historically, the best recognized index of intelligence, which is IQ. We now turn to a sampling of research that collectively demonstrates that the "hopeful new science" of learnable intelligence is neither a wild fantasy nor an unlikely theoretical possibility, but a demonstrable phenomenon (Perkins, 1995, p. 19).

COGNITIVE STIMULATION DURING INFANCY

Even in the early weeks and months of life, the cognitive experiences of a child, especially one at risk for cognitive delay, are crucial. Scarr-Salapatek and Williams (1973) organized a year-long program of cognitive stimulation for premature and low-birthweight infants born to Black mothers living in urban Philadelphia. The investigators noted that low birthweight and conditions of poverty predispose children to cognitive delays. In response, they organized a program designed to provide enhanced cognitive stimulation during the first year of life. Newborns in the experimental group had "nursery bird" mobiles suspended from their hospital isolettes, and nurses were trained to provide more verbal and physical stimulation than was customary for premature infants. When the newborns were 1 week old, those in the control group evidenced slightly more advanced development on the Brazelton Cambridge Newborn Scales; by 4 weeks, however, the experimental group exhibited superior development and greater weight gain.

After the newborns left the hospital, they and their primary caregivers (e.g., mother, grandmother, foster mother) received weekly home visits by project social workers. The social workers provided rattles and other toys, picture books, and wall posters to the family, as well as an infant seat so that children could more easily observe their environment during waking hours. Project workers trained mothers to interact with their children to encourage "next steps," such as reaching, vocalizing, and self-feeding, in a manner consistent with child development theory.

At 1 year of age, children in the experimental group demonstrated a mean sensorimotor IQ of 95.3 on the Cattell Infant Intelligence Scale, compared to a mean of 85.7 in the control group. Within the experimental group, higher newborn IQs were associated with more intensive mother-child play interactions.

EARLY CHILDHOOD INTERVENTIONS

Iowa Soldiers' Orphans' Home

In 1938 and 1939, Dawe (1942) instituted a program of cognitive enrichment for orphaned preschool children. Like many of the enrichment programs for preschool children in subsequent decades, this intervention focused particularly on the development of language skills. Dawe (1942) believed that, for young children especially, mental ability and language ability were closely related—that "linguistic symbols . . . serve as 'intellectual tools'" (p. 208).

Eleven pairs of preschool and kindergarten children were matched on the basis of age, gender, and Stanford-Binet IQ, and assigned to treatment and control groups. The intellectual experience of the children was somewhat constrained in that, outside of school time, the children had limited interaction with adults. Initial mean IQs were 80.6 for the experimental group and 81.5 for controls.

Dawe's approach was multifaceted: It involved training in understanding words and concepts, discussing pictures, listening to stories and poems, and taking short excursions for enrichment. The experimenter:

> tried to introduce new words and phrases as much as possible and at the same time make them understandable by the liberal use of explanatory phrases. She also attempted to stimulate curiosity, to help the children to think critically, to notice relationships, causes and effects, and to eliminate careless thinking and the careless use of language symbols. (Dawe, 1942, p. 203)

Training was carried out in both group settings (for stories, discussion of pictures, and excursions) and on an individual basis (for vocabulary development). The project consisted of 92 days of intervention, mostly on weekends, over a period of 8 months. During this period, each child received about 50 hours of training.

Posttests showed that the mean Stanford-Binet IQ of the experimental group increased 14.2 points to 94.8, whereas the average IQ of the control group decreased by 2 points. Both groups advanced in vocabulary, science knowledge, and home living information during this period, but in each case gains by experimentals were greater than those of controls (p < .02). Children in the experimental group also made substantial advances in the quality of their verbal interactions with adults. For example, in sessions devoted to understanding pictures, the number of "intellectual" questions asked per hour increased from 2.64 to 10.55 during the training period, and the number of analytical comments per hour (e.g., interpreting, generalizing, contrasting) increased from 4.52 to 10.55. Dawe (1942) also found statistically significant gains by experimentals in mean sentence length and in the number of complex sentences spoken per hour. In attempting to provide children with the knowledge, skills, and attitudes they needed for success, Dawe considered her rather modest intervention a success, and yet felt that the children had not approached the limits of what benefits they might have received from further training.

The Early Training Project

Like many cognitive interventions of the 1960s, the Early Training Project was intended to prevent the intellectual (and therefore academic and social) failure of young children at risk because of poverty. The project was conducted at a preschool serving Black children (Klaus & Gray, 1968). One important goal for the project was to counteract the delay in language development commonly observed in children raised in conditions of poverty. The investigators held the view that poor mothers often speak to children in what Bernstein (1961) called a restricted code, in which much of the mother's meaning is implicit in her tone, facial expressions, and circumstances, rather than finely differentiated in words. Bernstein's restricted code proposal has been controversial, yet differences in linguistic interactions related to poverty have been amply documented, as have associations between parent-child language patterns and cognitive development.

Over the course of 3 summers, 19 children attended 10-week summer sessions for 4 hours each day, 5 days per week (Klaus & Gray, 1968). Even during play periods, instructors tried to foster exactness and complexity in the children's verbal expression. For example, if a child wished to use a tricycle, a project teacher might help the child put the request in the form of a complete sentence, and then ask the child to specify which tricycle by describing it. The teaching of cognitive analysis was also important. When the children played with blocks, instructors taught such concepts as color, number, and position (e.g., behind, beneath, in front of, up, and down). Children were also taught skills in classification, generalization, and the formation of multi-level conceptual hierarchies using familiar objects. The teaching staff attempted to instill cognitively adaptive attitudes and motives, such as persistence, delay of gratification, and interest in books and school materials.

The Early Training Project included weekly home visits by certified elementary teachers during the winter months, when the preschool was not in session. Mothers were taught how to stimulate cognitive and language growth in their children by describing and explaining their actions as they went about their domestic activities. Teachers also brought books to the homes and encouraged mothers to read to their children and to discuss the pictures. During the summer months, mothers were invited to visit the nursery school.

At the end of the 3-year project, the IQ scores of children in the experimental group were 9 points higher than that of matched controls. The progress of participating children was monitored after they completed the program and began elementary school. Even at the fourth grade, the 9-point advantage of the experimental group over controls was maintained, although the mean for both groups had declined. Interestingly, the positive cognitive effects of the program extended to the younger siblings of participants and even to neighborhood children, yet neither group had a direct connection to the project.

The Academic Preschool

The preschool intervention by Bereiter and Engelmann (1966) was based on the understanding that the cognitive abilities of children living in poverty tend to decline with age, relative to peers. This decline, the investigators believed, was caused by deprivation of exposure to a technological-literate culture that fosters such critical thinking skills as inquiry, analysis, explanation, and deduction. According to the investigators, exposure to a technological-literate culture helps children to develop a critical internal dialog that supports such self-questions as "Is this true?"

The Academic Preschool was intended to instill basic patterns of reasoning, such as the ability to construct if-then statements. Instruction consisted largely of intense and highly structured drill, and called for overt responses from children. According to the authors, speedy (and therefore impulsive) responses are often assumed by poor children to be desirable; in the intervention, by contrast, reflective thinking was encouraged. The program was demonstrably effective: In four successive replications, IQ gains of participants averaged 15 points above controls, and IQ values consistently rose from an initial level in the mid-90s to well over 100. One of the four cohorts showed an impressive 25-point gain in IQ over 2 years of preschool (Bereiter, 1969).

Bereiter and Engelmann, like many project directors of that period, did not actually intend to stimulate the growth of intelligence per se. Rather, their goal was the more limited but worthy objective of warding off the cognitive sequelae of poverty. Bereiter and Engelmann, hesitant to claim that the children had actually become more intelligent, at first assumed that they had merely learned more content likely to be sampled by tests of intelligence (cf. Eysenck, 1998). This interpretation received "something of a blow," however, when Bereiter (1969, p. 315) and his colleagues later designed an intervention to teach the content of the Stanford-Binet, and found equivalent increases in IQ on a second administration of the Stanford-Binet and on an IQ test whose content differed markedly. Bereiter (1969) concluded, almost reluctantly, that "there may be more to educationally induced IQ gains than meets the eye" (p. 316).

The Carolina Abecedarian Project

The Carolina Abecedarian Project was designed to break the connection between socioenvironmental retardation and poverty through a cognitively rich day care program for at-risk preschool children (Ramey, MacPhee, & Yeates, 1982). Mothers of participating children had attained, on average, a tenth-grade education and had an average IQ of 85. All but one of the participating children were Black. Children began participating in the program as early as 6 weeks old, and at most 3 months. The program was offered from 7:45 a.m. to 5:30 p.m. every weekday for 50 weeks each year, and extended through the preschool years.

The Abecedarian preschool provided a stimulating environment and a favorable child-teacher ratio of 3:1 for children of age 3 and younger, and 6:1 for 4-year-olds. The project focused on the development of children's communicative competence and adaptive social behavior. Linguistic interaction was rich. Teachers saw conversations with children as opportunities to sharpen the children's communication skills. As teachers evoked and supported effective communicative competence, three dimensions of language use were stressed: pragmatic, representational (involving use of abstraction), and language structure and syntax. Teachers also helped children meet specific objectives in language, motor, social, and cognitive areas.

When the participating children were 12 months old, no IQ difference was found between treatment and control children. However, between the ages of 2 and 5—a period of intense language development—the mean IQ of the control group dropped to around the mid-80s, whereas the mean IQ of the Abecedarian was roughly 10 points higher, and just below the national average. When the participants were 5 years old, the mean IQ of the experimental group was 98 whereas the mean of the control group was about 90. This treatment-control difference would have classificatory and therefore programmatic consequences for children. Using an IQ of 85 as a cutoff below which children can be considered mildly mentally retarded and at risk for school failure, the investigators noted that 39% of the control group fell below the cutoff, whereas only 11% of the treatment group did so.

Program effects were especially strong among children whose mothers were retarded (IQ < 75). Each of these children obtained an IQ score at least 20 points higher than their own mother's IQ, and the mother-child IQ gap averaged 32 points (Ramey & Ramey, 1992). Beneficial effects extended especially to children whose condition at birth was not optimal (i.e., those whose Apgar scores were 8 or lower on a 10-point scale; Breitmayer & Ramey, 1986). The effect of the Abecedarian experience on children with nonoptimal Apgar status was much stronger (about 13.7 IQ points) than it was for children with optimal Apgar scores (about 2.8 IQ points; treatment x Apgar $p = .07$).

Treatment effects were evident not only on psychometric instrumentation but also in the children's thought and behavior patterns. Treatment children, for example, were more socially confident and less fearful than were controls. The daycare children were also superior in attention span and task-oriented behaviors at age 18 months and at 24 months. The authors concluded that the program had improved the ability of participating children to "attend to, comprehend and carry out abstract and complex tasks. Further, the effect appears broad scale rather than specific, leading us to assume that general intelligence or g has been affected" (Ramey et al., 1982, p. 93).

The project was extended into the elementary school years as the original preschool subjects were joined by children who began participating starting at kindergarten. Later, when subjects were 8 years old, the investigators found that cognitive benefit in the form of IQ enhancement was obtained only for those who had participated in the early intervention program (Ramey & Ramey, 1992). When subjects were 12 years old, the preschool participants continued to display much stronger effects on IQ and academic achievement than did those who joined the intervention during the school years. Among the early participants, only 12.8% were classified as "borderline retarded" (IQ ≤ 85), whereas 44.2% of those not participating in the early intervention received that designation.

The Milwaukee Project

Among the intensive early intervention programs designed to forestall the intellectual decline of children raised in poverty, the Milwaukee Project is the best known, most discussed, and the most controversial. In fact, it has achieved something of a "mythic quality" and has been called "the high-water mark of environmentalist accomplishment" (Page & Grandon, 1981, p. 240). Like the Carolina Abecedarian Project, the Milwaukee Project was devised to prevent cultural-familial mental retardation among at-risk young children (Heber, Garber, Harrington, Hoffman, & Falender, 1972). According to the investigators, cultural-familial retardation accounts for about three quarters of those identified as retarded, and has no obvious etiology. The study's participants were 40 mothers from the poorest of Milwaukee's slums, each with an IQ of 75 or less, and their children, who were assigned randomly (either individually or in clusters) to treatment and control groups (Garber & Heber, 1982). The intervention began soon after the newborns were brought home from the hospital and continued until school entry. During the first 3 months of life, a teacher visited the infants in the experimental group for several hours each day. Thereafter, mothers brought their children to the child care center.

The Milwaukee Project curriculum emphasized problem-solving skills, language development, and specific logical concepts. Working with small groups of three or four children, the teaching staff frequently used open-ended questioning to elicit communication from children. Instruction was semistructured and involved dividing the day into "classes," typically 30 minutes in length, that focused on such skill areas as language development, reading, mathematics/problem solving, communication, art, science, and music. Periods of free play were also built into the daily schedule. In addition, mothers were provided with remedial education and training in home management, as well as job training.

Up to the age of about 1 year, cognitive growth in the treatment and control groups was comparable. At around 14 months, however, cognitive development in the experimental group accelerated whereas growth rates in the control group declined in comparison to age-level norms (Garber & Heber, 1982). The divergence continued such that, by the age of 22 months, the mean IQ of the experimental group was 120 whereas the mean for controls was 94. Although the means of both groups declined somewhat thereafter, an experimental/control difference of about 25 IQ points was maintained for the duration of the preschool program through the age of 60 months. Beyond that point, the mean IQ of the control group fluctuated whereas the IQ of the experimental children edged downward. Still, a gap of more than one standard deviation was maintained throughout the follow-up assessments (Fig. 9.1; Garber, 1988).

At age 10, the mean treatment IQ had declined to 104 (range: 93-138), and the mean control IQ dropped to 86 (range: 72-106), a sustained difference of 18 points,

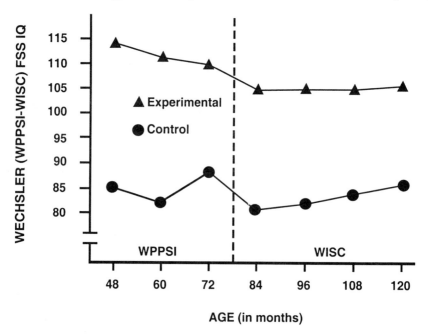

FIG. 9.1. Effects of the Milwaukee Project: IQ means of experimental and control groups from 48 through 120 months. From *The Milwaukee Project: Preventing Mental Retardation in Children at Risk* (p. 228), by H. L. Garber, 1988, Washington, DC: American Association on Mental Retardation. Copyright 1988 by the American Association on Mental Retardation. Reprinted with Permission.

notwithstanding an overall decline by both groups. By the ages of 12 to 14 years, the IQ advantage of the treatment group declined further to 10 points (Garber, 1988). The authors attributed the loss of differential benefit to the often dismal home and school environments faced by the children in both groups.

The Milwaukee Project has not escaped criticism. This criticism deserves attention because of the theoretical importance of the findings if they are valid and the programmatic implications of the effects if they are reproducible. Perhaps prematurely, the Milwaukee Project had a tremendous impact not only in reviving the environmentalist viewpoint during the Great Society era, but also in influencing the allocation of millions of federal dollars to early childhood interventions. Page (1972; Page & Grandon, 1981), the project's most vocal critic, questioned the integrity of the design of the Milwaukee Project, including the equivalence of treatment and control groups, the exact nature of the treatment, and the degree of alignment between the treatment and measured outcomes. Contributing to the skepticism was a lack of detailed information and some contradictory reporting on the design features of the Milwaukee Project. This dearth of information was partly corrected by a technical report published in 1972, in which the Milwaukee Project Staff included nearly 100 pages describing the curriculum (Heber et al., 1972). Meanwhile, the fame of the Milwaukee Project was spreading. By the early 1980s, the project was commonly featured in psychology textbooks, even though it still lacked documentation in the form of a refereed journal article (Sommer & Sommer, 1983).

Are the findings to be believed? Although Page's arguments do engender skepticism, they do not argue effectively that the findings of the Milwaukee Project are to be dismissed outright. On the question of treatment and control group equivalence, Page (1972) made much of the fact that the two groups differed in the standard deviations of infants' length at birth (E = 1.2 in.; C = 1.9 in.), even though their mean lengths were nearly identical (E = 19.4 in.; C = 19.8 in.).[1] Page also questioned whether intervention effects transferred to competencies outside of those specifically taught.[2] Page and Grandon (1981) cited, for example, the well-known reduction of treatment effects following cessation of the intervention, and also the lesser impact of the project on school achievement test scores, especially reading. These criticisms, however, confound the issues of the treatment's generalizability and the maintenance of effects over time. As noted earlier, the dilution of effects over time is well recognized and readily interpretable.

The generalizability of treatment effects might be more legitimately questioned. There is at least some evidence that the intellectual benefits to participants extended to everyday contexts at the time of the intervention. For example, children in the treatment group were distinguished from controls in the approaches they took to intellectual tasks. Experimental children, as a group, employed more sophisticated and flexible strategies in solving problems, and avoided the ineffectual perseverating behavior common among controls. Even in comparison to their own mothers, experimental children "tended to analyze stimulus arrays in a much more thorough manner before responding, and tended to use a strategy behavior in how they attacked the problem" (Garber & Heber, 1983, p. 125). In fact, in the mother-child dyads, experimental children adopted the role of "educational engineer" by taking responsibility for the flow of communication, and soliciting from their mothers information that would be useful in solving the problem at hand.

The intervention effects extended beyond the immediate performance of participants. Even untreated siblings experienced an increment in IQ. The mean IQ for untreated siblings was elevated more than 10 points above the siblings of control children. The Milwaukee Project was not intended to raise intelligence of participants, let alone their siblings (Garber & Hodge, 1996). Nonetheless, the question can be raised: Was the intelligence of participants enhanced? Although not quite answering in the affirmative, the investigators concluded that there had been a "turning of the corner" in their own appreciation of how factors interact to influence cognitive growth (Garber & Heber, 1982, p. 136). Further delineation of these factors, they suggested, could lead to the ability to enhance the intellectual status of all children at all levels.

Project Head Start

Head Start, although similar in mission to some of the "model" projects described in the preceding pages, is really in a category of its own (Haskins, 1989). Like the other projects, Head Start was intended to increase the likelihood of academic and life success for children raised in poverty. However, unlike the small-scale model projects, the intellectual enhancement of preschool children was only one of seven major objectives (Datta, 1976; Zigler, 1979). The quality and characteristics of Head Start programs varied considerably. In one study, the ratio of children to teachers ranged from 3 to 29, and the duration of "full year" programs varied from 3 to 8 months (Smith & Bissell, 1970). Small-scale model projects, by contrast, were typically much more carefully controlled and staffed, and were often carried out under the supervision of university faculty. Expenditures per child in Head Start programs were about half the cost associated with intensive model programs (Zigler, Styfco, & Gilman, 1993). Finally, in terms of scale, Head Start is different: It represents one of the major social interventions ever enacted in the history of the United States, and has served millions of children and their families.

The first commissioned evaluation of Head Start, conducted by the Westinghouse Learning Corporation, cast doubt on the program's effectiveness (Datta, 1976). According to the Westinghouse Report, Head Start children who attended full-year programs were superior to controls in the "total readiness" for school success and "listening" subscore of the Metropolitan Readiness Tests at the start of first grade (Cicirelli, 1969). At Grades 2 and 3, however, Head Start children did not score significantly higher than control children. Reports of the "fade-out" of IQ and school achievement gains during the elementary school years almost led to the dismantling of Project Head Start (Zigler et al., 1993). However, subsequent analyses led to a brighter picture of program effects. Smith and Bissell (1970), for example, reanalyzed the Westinghouse-Ohio data and found that cognitive gains were clearer when control group data were adjusted for background variables. They also found that the effects of Head Start were better appreciated when the data were disaggregated by subgroups. In particular, children who "needed the program most"—those from the southeastern United States, urban children, and especially Black children, were those who enjoyed the greatest benefits (Datta, 1979, p. 418).

Well-designed evaluations confirmed an initial cognitive boost for Head Start children, averaging nine IQ points relative to controls as well as enhanced reading and mathematics achievement. As in the Westinghouse study, however, relative gains dissipated rapidly during the school years (Datta, 1979; Haskins, 1989; Zigler et al., 1993). Across studies, the IQ advantage dropped to almost zero by the end of the first year of schooling (Haskins, 1989). Other benefits, including better health, and less likelihood of special education placement and of grade retention, persisted at least until adolescence. As for the fade-out of cognitive effects, this was unsurprising in retrospect. For many children, participation in the program lasted only a few months, and cognitive goals were only one part of the "total effort" approach espoused by Head Start (Smith & Bissell, 1970, p. 59). To expect radical and permanent redirection of lives is to "ignore the many, many factors . . . that form the total environment" of the child (Zigler et al., 1993, p. 21).

SCHOOL-AGE INTERVENTIONS

Project Intelligence

In the early 1980s, the government of Venezuela adopted the daring goal of enhancing the intelligence of a large number of its schoolchildren. The result was the intervention known as Project Intelligence. The Venezuelan government enlisted the cooperation of Harvard University and Bolt, Beranek, and Newman, Inc., to devise and implement a curriculum designed to raise the intelligence of participating Venezuelan seventh graders, approximately 460 students (Harvard University, 1983; Nickerson, 1986a). Targeted skill areas were observation and classification, deductive and inductive reasoning, the critical use of language, hypothesis generation and testing, problem solving, inventiveness, and decision making (see Table 9.1 for an overview of course units). According to the investigators, these skills could "reasonably be considered to be components of intelligence" and were "sufficiently well defined to lend themselves to explicit instruction" (Herrnstein, Nickerson, de Sanchez, & Swets, 1986, p. 1279).

The Project Intelligence curriculum was implemented for a single year and consisted of 56 lessons. The lessons were conducted three times per week for 45

TABLE 9.1
Curriculum Organization of Project Intelligence

Lesson Series	Unit
Foundations of reasoning	Observation and classification Ordering Hierarchical classification Analogies: discovering relationships Spatial reasoning and strategies
Understanding language	Word Relations The structure of language Reading for meaning
Verbal reasoning	Assertions Arguments
Problem solving	Linear representations Tabular representations Representations by simulation and enactment Systematic trial and error Thinking out the implications
Decision making	Introduction to decision making Gathering and evaluating information to reduce uncertainty Analyzing complex decision situations
Inventive thinking	Design Procedures as designs

Note. Adapted from *Project Intelligence Overview* (p. 4), by Harvard University, 1983. Cambridge, MA: Harvard University. Adapted with permission.

minutes each (Herrnstein, 1987). Pre- and posttests were administered to determine the effects of the project on students' thinking and intelligence. A series of tests targeting the instructional areas showed that the experimental students surpassed control students in gain scores. Experimentals also outperformed controls on tests of intelligence. Some of the pertinent data are presented in Table 9.2; positive values in the *difference* column indicate that experimental students obtained higher scores than did control students. On every measure used, the project was effective in raising students' cognitive abilities relative to controls. When effect sizes are converted to an IQ scale (mean = 100; S.D. = 15), relative gains for experimentals are seen to range up to about 6 IQ points.

In addition to the standardized tests, the investigators administered an open-ended design test to a random sample of 90 experimental students and 90 control students. The task was to design a table that would be functional in a very small room. Students' drawings and written explanations were rated on 14 variables, such as relevant features, clarity of views, and clarity of construction. Experimental

TABLE 9.2
Project Intelligence: Gains on Tests of General Mental Ability

Test	Score Difference	p <	Effect Size	IQ Gain
	Experimental — Control			
Otis-Lennon (80 items)				
Pretest	0.9	.23	0.09	—
Gain	4.1	.001	0.43	6.45
GAT (239 items)				
Pretest	1.4	.6	0.05	—
Gain	10.0	.001	0.35	5.25
Cattell (89 items)				
Pretest	2.1	.02	0.19	—
Gain	1.3	.02	0.11	1.65

Note. Tests listed are the Otis-Lennon School Ability Test, the General Ability Tests (GAT), and the Cattell Culture Fair Intelligence Test. From "Teaching Thinking Skills," by R. J. Herrnstein, R. S. Nickerson, M. de Sánchez, and J. A. Swets, 1986, *American Psychologist, 41*, p. 1283. Copyright ©1986 by the American Psychological Association. Adapted with permission.

and control students differed on all 14 variables; in general, the experimental students provided "more structured, elaborated, explicit, relevant, and functional designs" (Herrnstein et al., 1986, p. 1288). Experimental students likewise outperformed controls on a test involving the construction of an oral argument. Herrnstein (1987, p. 53), later a co-author of the decidedly hereditarian book *The Bell Curve,* commented that "the change in behavior that resulted from this really rather modest intervention . . . was profound and dramatic."[3]

Brown and Campione's Research

Central to Brown and Campione's account of intelligence is that IQ differences are highly associated with the strategic and metacognitive knowledge that facilitate learning and transfer (Brown & Campione, 1986). Among retarded children, for example, even the elementary memory strategy of rehearsal is frequently not exhibited spontaneously, although it can be learned through instruction (Campione & Brown, 1984; Campione, Brown, & Ferrara, 1982). Campione and Brown (1990) demonstrated that deficiencies in metacognitive and strategic thinking—including planning, seeking additional information, and monitoring comprehension—are at the heart of the cognitive difficulties of academically weak students. These functions are central to cognitive conceptualizations of intelligence, and thus the modifiability of metacognitive thought bears directly on the question of the modifiability of intelligence (Belmont, Butterfield, & Ferretti, 1982).

According to Brown and Campione, metacognitive and strategic knowledge are acquired primarily through appropriating the intellective patterns manifest in social interaction—a theoretical orientation that connects their research to Vygotsky. Vygotsky (1978) proposed that learning occurs initially through social interaction and that, with time, the cognitive patterns manifest in the social milieu become internalized, going "underground" (p. 33). In the same theoretical vein, Brown and Campione saw individual differences in intelligence as abiding not only in the differential possession of strategic and metacognitive knowledge, but also in the more causally important differences in learners' abilities to acquire metacognitive strategies from social experience, and how readily learners transfer strategies to new contexts once they are acquired (Belmont, 1989). This perspective implies an approach to assessment that departs radically from traditional psychometric ability testing. A learner's cognitive ability is suitably assessed *dynamically* by measuring the social assistance needed to achieve a given performance level (cf. Feuerstein, 1979, 1980). Campione and Brown found that the degree of assistance needed to bring learners to some criterion of cognitive performance is consistently greater among low-IQ than high-IQ subjects. Intelligence seems therefore to consist significantly in the ability to supplement incomplete information about tasks with strategies needed to complete them (Campione & Brown, 1984). The idea that high-ability learners are, as a rule, more able to profit from nonexplicit instruction is consistent with the long record of research on aptitude-treatment interactions (Cronbach & Snow, 1977).

Another difference between high- and low-ability learners concerns the propensity to transfer knowledge to new situations. In one illustrative study, Brown, Campione, and Barclay (1979) trained 9-year-old and 11-year-old children on strategies to remember a set of pictures. Both the younger and older students' mental age was about 3 years less than their chronological age. Two memory and monitoring strategies were taught. One was a rehearsal strategy, which entailed dividing a large set of pictures into subsets, and asking participants to rehearse the subsets until they were sure they could recall all items. The second was an anticipation strategy, in which subjects tried to recall the nature of a picture in a particular location before actually viewing it. Both the rehearsal and anticipation strategies boosted recall of pictures. Although the use of strategies was short-lived among the younger children, the older subjects continued to employ them. Consequently, the elevated performance of the older subjects was maintained through subsequent posttests, the last posttest occurring a full year after the training ended. The strategies also transferred to the school-like task of recalling the gist of prose passages. Children trained in rehearsal and anticipation strategies again outperformed controls on amount recalled, the ability to remember important ideas, and the use of strategies to support learning.

Through their research, Brown and Campione demonstrated the learnability of intelligence—not by raising IQ scores as such, but by showing that metacognitive abilities that distinguish high-IQ from low-IQ subjects can be learned by those of lower abilities. Studies by other investigators in the same research stream have also confirmed that superordinate metacognitive functions can be learned and transferred to contexts quite different from that of the initial learning (Belmont et al., 1982). Brown and Campione's work has contributed both to the identification of the cognitive constituents of intelligent thought and to the demonstration that intelligence (in the form of those constituents) is learnable. It should be noted, however, that even when metacognitive strategies are taught and learned they do not necessarily reduce differences in the efficiency of learning or in the propensity to transfer new strategies to other contexts. The cognitive rigidity of lower-ability learners implies that any instruction designed to improve the cognitive processes composing intelligence may need to be quite explicit in identifying the most important kinds of strategic and metacognitive knowledge. That the ease of acquisition and use of such knowledge so clearly differentiates high- and low-ability children reinforces the view that "such skills are . . . major components of intelligent behavior" (Campione et al., 1982, p. 430).

Feuerstein's Instrumental Enrichment

Israeli psychologist Reuven Feuerstein developed one of the most theoretically and programmatically elaborate systems for enhancing general cognitive functionality. Born in Bucharest, Romania, Feuerstein received his early psychological training under the guidance of Andre Rey, a colleague of Piaget in Geneva. In Feuerstein's theory, the influence of Genevan psychology is evident: Many of the tasks Feuerstein used in assessing and training learners have strong logical-mathematical demands that are reminiscent of Piagetian theory. Many of these same tasks also either resemble or actually are instruments used in IQ tests.

Feuerstein's theory and method can be traced to post-WWII Europe. Just after the war, many children of Holocaust victims were cared for in refugee facilities in southern France. Whether from psychological trauma, a lack of rich experience, or both, many of these children were judged to be retarded and without any real prospect for recovery. When Feuerstein was invited to assess these children, he found that they were more cognitively capable than they were credited. It is in *how* the children were judged to be capable that marks Feuerstein's theory: Their capability was demonstrated not so much by what they were able to do on their own, but in what they could *learn* to do given appropriate guidance during the course of assessment. The difference is crucial because it divides Feuerstein's framework from traditional theories—Feuerstein was interested not in performance per se, but in the *modifiability* of performance. What followed from this principle is that Feuerstein minimized traditional psychometric assessment in his own work and emphasized *dynamic* assessment, in which cognitive modifiability is evaluated during the course of testing. In fact, Feuerstein abjured the implicit assumptions of traditional assessment, including the belief that psychological testing reveals capacities that resist change.

Another cornerstone of Feuerstein's theory concerns the mechanism by which cognitive development occurs. According to Feuerstein, cognitive development is a function of the quality of social mediation in the child's learning experience. The primacy of social mediation and its internalization aligns considerably with Vygotskyan theory—although Feuerstein claimed to have developed his conceptualization independently of Vygotsky (Feuerstein, Rand, & Hoffman, 1979; Feuerstein, Rand, Hoffman, & Miller, 1980). One especially potent form of social mediation is what Feuerstein called *mediated learning*. *Mediation* refers to the structuring of the environment or experience by another person, such as a teacher or parent. Mediation might take the form of naming objects, asking questions, posing problems, selecting relevant stimuli, or ordering events temporally— essentially offering any cue that lends structure to the external environment. Mediation is said to vary in *distance*; sometimes it is quite close, as when a young child's hand is physically manipulated by an adult to write the letters of his or her name, or distant, as when a child is reminded to go slowly or to be careful. Gradations of mediational distance are reminiscent of hierarchical hint structures used to promote learning in Campione's and Brown's theory, which is also Vygotskian in character. In Feuerstein's terms, a skillful mediator understands just how much mediation is needed in a given situation, evoking Vygotsky's zone of proximal development.

Given the importance Feuerstein placed on mediated learning, it is not surprising that he rejected the idea that intelligence is an inevitable expression of biological programming. Rather, Feuerstein saw deficient intellectual performance as resulting from an inadequate quantity or quality of socially mediated learning experiences. In extreme form, this kind of deprivation could account for the poor performance of the Holocaust children. Feuerstein acknowledged that some learners are less modifiable than others, and are therefore less likely to learn from direct experience without mediation. However, Feuerstein's characteristic optimism was evident again in his belief that even low modifiability is modifiable, and that given appropriate mediated experiences a learner's cognition can be restructured such that in the future he or she would be better able to profit from both mediated and direct experience.

Feuerstein identified a set of cognitive functions that can account for deficiencies in performance on cognitive tasks. These functions include blurred and sweeping perception, failure to perceive the nature of a problem, difficulty in testing hypotheses, and impulsive and unsystematic exploratory behavior. Performance on these functions is assessed using a battery of tests known as the Learning Propensity Assessment Device, or LPAD. As mentioned earlier, instruments constituting the LPAD have a strong logicomathematical character, and some are quite similar or even identical to instruments associated with IQ testing (e.g., Raven's Progressive Matrices). The object of LPAD assessment is to identify a learner's deficient cognitive functions, including whether these are grouped according to the stage of processing or modality (e.g., visual, auditory, figural). Because the LPAD is intended to be administered dynamically, it is important to determine to what degree that learner's performance improves during the course of assessment. After characterizing the nature and limits of a learner's cognitive modifiability, the next step is to actually modify the learner's cognitive structures through the intervention program known as Instrumental Enrichment.

Instrumental Enrichment is guided by a series of exercises that correspond largely, but not completely, to the instruments composing the LPAD. For example, just as Raven's Matrices are used in the LPAD, Raven-like problems are used in Instrumental Enrichment. The Instrumental Enrichment curriculum consists of relatively content-independent paper-and-pencil exercises. These exercises are grouped into 15 units, or instruments, and each exercise addresses one or more deficient cognitive functions. For example, in the exercise known as "Organization of Dots," the learner is presented with a set of dot patterns. The objective is to find identified shapes, such as squares or triangles (possibly rotated or overlapping), in the dot pattern. The teacher, or mediator, gives the learner just enough assistance, often in the form of questions, to permit success. Mediation, then, has a central role in Instrumental Enrichment, just as it does in the LPAD.

It is important to understand that the exercises themselves are not sufficient for remediation; rather, it is the mediated learning experience used in combination with the exercises that moves the learner forward. Learners can work collaboratively or alone, but always under the eye of a mediator. Instrumental Enrichment is often intense and demanding, requiring participants to concentrate on tasks that are sometimes abstract and complex, and often for longer periods of time than what they are used to. Besides addressing specific cognitive deficiencies, remediation is designed to encourage learners to attend to their own thinking—and to become *self*-mediating. Thus, one product of a successful mediated learning experience is a greater capacity to learn and a greater awareness of when and how one is learning. Greater learning capacity arises as the learner internalizes the dialog structure and inquiry processes initiated by the mediator. As capacity grows, the learner follows a new intellectual trajectory in which structural changes in cognition lead to differences among learners that grow over time. Feuerstein called this the *hypothesis of divergent effects* (Feuerstein et al.,1980).

Although data on the effectiveness of Instrumental Enrichment are not quite as convincing as those of other cognitive intervention programs, Feuerstein's theory and method have received some empirical support (Blagg, 1991). In one study, Feuerstein and his colleagues (Feuerstein et al., 1980) separated 114 retarded Israeli students, aged 12 to 15 years, into a treatment group that received instruction in Instrumental Enrichment, and a control group that received extra help in school subjects. Participants were matched initially for performance on Thurstone's test of Primary Mental Abilities (PMA mean IQ = 80 for both groups). After 2 years of instruction in Instrumental Enrichment, posttests were administered. Mean total PMA scores (not IQ) were 172.7 for the Instrumental Enrichment group and 163.9 for the control group ($p < 0.01$). On cognitive ability tests administered as posttests only, experimentals again outperformed controls. Superior gains for the treatment group were also evident on measures of self-sufficiency, adaptiveness to work demands, and future planning (Nickerson, Perkins, & Smith, 1985; Rand, Mintzker, Miller, Hoffman, & Friedlender, 1981).

The IQ advantage of Instrumental Enrichment subjects was sustained after the treatment ended. About 18 months later, when students were inducted into the military, they were given the Israeli military intelligence test, DAPAR, which contains both fluid and crystallized components. Mean scores on the DAPAR were 52.58 and 45.11 for treatment and control groups, respectively, over a possible range of 10 to 90 (Rand et al., 1981). The differences between means were statistically significant (p < .01), as well as practically important. Treatment and control subjects were median split according to the PMA pretest. In the high-PMA group, 88% of experimentals and 53% of controls scored above the DAPAR mean for the military as a whole, thus making them eligible for selection as officers; in the low-PMA group, 46% of experimentals and 13% of controls met the DAPAR cutoff for officer eligibility. Interestingly, the gap between the treatment group and control groups grew linearly with the time between the initial intervention and induction into the military, a trend consistent with Feuerstein's hypothesis of divergent effects (Feuerstein et al., 1980). The rate of divergence between the experimental and control groups, translated to an IQ scale, amounted to just over 3 points per year.

Evaluations of Instrumental Enrichment conducted by other investigators have been somewhat mixed. For example, Blagg's (1991) evaluation demonstrated positive effects for Instrumental Enrichment on one cognitive ability test (Block Design—Power) and on certain critical thinking skills, but not on aggregate IQ or academic achievement. In this study, the power to detect treatment effects may have been limited by the abbreviated nature of the intervention and by the smallish size of the control group (13 to 19, depending on the measure). In a pilot study, Haywood and Arbitman-Smith (1981) found small but statistically significant differences in nonverbal IQ gains by treatment subjects (on the order of 5 to 9 points) compared to control subjects (about 2 to 3 points). When the pilot study was followed by a larger intervention, the results were less clear: At some experimental sites, the effects of Instrumental Enrichment were minimal or negligible, but at other sites the cognitive growth of experimentals was superior to that of controls. In a study conducted in South Africa, Mehl (1991) found that Feuerstein's Instrumental Enrichment could be used to guide the design of a curriculum for introductory physics at the university level. Prior to the intervention, Black students as a whole performed dismally in the physics course and a majority failed. Mehl showed the comprehension of physics (mechanics) was dramatically higher for Black students who used the IE-based curriculum guides than for students in a control group.

Despite some inconsistent findings, Instrumental Enrichment has tended to produce significant, if not always large, effects, including the enhancement of nonverbal IQ (Feuerstein et al., 1986; Perkins, 1995; Savell, Twohig, & Rachford, 1986). However, Feuerstein's tasks are structurally quite similar to those used on some IQ tests, so when IQ effects are found it is hard to know how generalizable they are. Program effects have sometimes extended to more complex performances. For example, when asked to organize a field trip, students who received Instrumental Enrichment formed plans that were more systematically organized, precise, and thoughtful than did untrained peers (Delclos, Bransford, & Haywood, 1984). After surveying the cumulative evaluations of Feuerstein's program, Perkins (1995) concluded that "Instrumental Enrichment in full and careful implementations can have a significant and worthwhile impact on the cognitive functioning of slow learners. Intelligence can be taught by Instrumental Enrichment" (p. 191).

Kvashchev's Experiments

Stankov (1986) reported on research by Kvashchev involving the training of cognitive abilities through creative problem solving. Stankov, who was a high school pupil of Kvashchev and later a collaborator, brought this body of research to light in the international community by presenting in English work that was originally published in Serbocroatian. Kvashchev's work was conducted among academically able high school students in the former Yugoslavia. A series of at least eight interventions resulted in the durable enhancement of either fluid or crystallized intelligence, or both (Kvashchev, 1980). Kvashchev's most ambitious project involved training almost 300 students over a 3-year period, and assessing changes in their cognitive ability with a battery of 37 cognitive tests. As Stankov pointed out, interventions of such duration and intensity are rare among studies designed to test the hypothesis of learnable intelligence.

Kvashchev's intervention entailed practice in creative problem solving rather than work on tasks that closely resembled tests of cognitive ability. In solving Kvashchev's problems, students had to think of a practical solution to a hypothetical problem, or to organize information to see a problem from a variety of perspectives. Stankov (1986) provided a helpful example: "List all possible scientific means that can be used to solve the problem of feeding a world population which will double in the next 30 years" (p. 216). After the initial production of potential solutions, Kvashchev encouraged students to generate still more ideas. Kvashchev himself taught some of the lessons in creative problem solving, but also trained regular high school teachers to pose similar problems in teaching in their subject areas. On average, students in the experimental group received about 3 or 4 hours of practice on creative problem-solving exercises per week.

A battery of cognitive tests was administered prior to the intervention and on its completion almost 3 years later. Kvashchev also administered two follow-up assessments at the beginning and end of the fourth (final) year of high school. In the initial pretesting, control subjects scored slightly higher across tests than did students in the experimental group. Using initial scores as covariates, Kvashchev compared means on the initial posttest, first follow-up, and second follow-up assessments. In each of these test administrations, students in the experimental group outperformed controls. The overall magnitude of the effects, based on standard deviations of scores on pretests, was a relative gain of 5.7 IQ points on the initial posttest and 7.8 IQ points on the second follow-up test administered 1 year later. The intervention effects were generally more pronounced on tests of fluid ability, such as Cattell's Matrices.

The widening of cognitive differences between experimentals and controls *after* the intervention is especially provocative. Although Stankov was more confident in the validity of the immediate posttest data than in the follow-up data, a growth in subsequent effects is consistent with findings by Feuerstein and his hypothesis of divergent effects (Feuerstein et al., 1980). Another interesting aspect of the Kvashchev data is that in the final testing, standard deviations of scores in the experimental group were smaller than those of controls, hinting that training reduced variability among students. The data are suggestive: It is possible, at least, that a large-scale enhancement of cognitive abilities would not lead to greater divergence of cognitive attainments.

Kvashchev's research is provocative on other counts as well. As Stankov (1986) pointed out, the follow-up data show that cognitive effects can be long-lasting and possibly even magnified over time. The research also demonstrates that increases in general cognitive ability can be achieved in students who are above average in IQ and who are older than is typical in cognitive intervention studies. Kvashchev's use of creative problem solving in high-ability students can be contrasted with Feuerstein's concentration on more basic abilities in populations that have learning problems. The use of different strategies for populations that differ in cognitive characteristics suggests that the teaching and learning of intelligence will ideally take different forms for different learners. That is, an aptitude-treatment interaction (ATI) is implicated (Cronbach & Snow, 1977). Finally, because Kvashchev's training program was quite unlike the cognitive ability tests used to assess its effects, we know that "general, rather than specific, transfer is . . . implicated, [because] training was not devised to improve IQ test performance as such" (Stankov, 1986, p. 228). This finding answers one critique of cognitive intervention research, which is that it amounts, essentially, to "teaching to the test" and thus "shows remarkably limited transfer beyond the specific class of tasks on which the particular skill were trained" (Jensen, 1992b, p. 293). Finally, Kvashchev's use of both domain-based and domain-independent teaching of thinking suggests that the two need not be viewed as rivals, but instead can be compatible and complementary.

SUMMARY AND CONCLUSIONS

Taken together, the projects described in this chapter (and others not examined here, e.g., Bereiter, 1969; Bereiter & Engelmann, 1966; Blank & Solomon, 1968; Budoff, 1974; Klaus & Gray, 1968; Staats & Burns, 1981; Sternberg, 1986) demonstrate that IQ and the cognitive proficiencies associated with intelligence can be enhanced through direct intervention. Existence proofs for the modifiability of intelligence can be found at every stage of childhood and youth (Nisbett, 1995). However, such effects are not limited to children and adolescents, but have also been demonstrated among the elderly (Willis, Blieszner, & Baltes, 1981). Not included in the review are studies of "coaching effects" for SATs and similar tests, although these too might be considered because of the close association between such tests and IQ batteries. Briefly, the effects of coaching on verbal SAT scores is consistent with a gain of about 3 IQ points following 50 hours of instruction, an effect that is "modest but scarcely trivial" (Nisbett, 1995, p. 46). Together, the research literature supports the following two conclusions: Intelligence can be characterized as a repertoire of cognitive functions; and the teaching of those functions can raise intellectual proficiency, sometimes markedly.

None of the studies reviewed in this chapter are methodologically flawless, nor are their effects always large, clear, and robust. In general, interventions designed to enhance intelligence (or to prevent its decline) have been described as demonstrating weak effects that tend not to be sustained (Caruso, Taylor, & Detterman, 1982; Eysenck, 1998). Jensen (1987) argued that there is insufficient evidence that gains on cognitive tests transfer to superficially dissimilar, g-loaded tasks or to real-life achievements. Also, when IQ gains are achieved it is not always clear what aspects of the program are responsible (Bereiter, 1969). Yet, exceptions can be found for many of these criticisms. For example, evidence of transfer has been demonstrated in several projects (e.g., Brown et al., 1979; Delclos et al., 1984; Herrnstein et al., 1986). As for the typical, but not inevitable (e.g., Feuerstein et al., 1980; Stankov, 1986) fading of IQ gains following the cessation of intervention, this is hardly surprising. As Nisbett (1995) observed: "It should be obvious that, if the environmental factors are important at all, as indeed established by the very substantial effects of the intervention, then once the environment reverts to one that is non-enriched, the cognitive gains would be expected to fade. If the enrichment were to continue, perhaps the intellectual gains would too" (p. 45).

The point is sensible. No theory of human development assumes that an early cognitive intervention can sustain normative growth irrespective of the child's subsequent experience (Ramey & Ramey, 1992).[4] When early intervention programs are extended into the school-age years, initial gains are largely preserved. As important as the preschool years are, it is a fantasy—and a dangerous one—to believe that the environmental effects that guide and shape intellectual growth are only (or even mostly) operative during the preschool years. If anything is to be learned from Piaget, it is that important cognitive shifts mark the entire ladder of development through adolescence and, indeed, through the life span.

If cognitive gains can be obtained through direct intervention, how large are the effects? Detterman's (1982) conservative estimate of maximum IQ effects is on the order of 10 to 20 points. Although he spoke of this as an "upper limit," it is more properly regarded as an approximation (some have been higher) of positive effects that have been obtained to date, not on what is possible (Detterman, 1982, p. 43). Even so, IQ effects in the range of 10 to 20 points (or about one standard deviation) are not to be dismissed. At the low end of the cognitive ability spectrum, 90% of those identified as retarded are *mildly* retarded (IQ approximately 55 to 70) and lack a clear biological etiology for their disability. Raising the cognitive ability of children at risk for mild retardation, or preventing its decline, is likely to have substantial effects on their adaptive competence. This is not to ignore the difficulty of raising cognitive ability, or of preventing its normative decline among those at risk (Spitz, 1986); the point is that an effect of one standard deviation is consequential.

Consequential effects might also be found in that large slice of the normal curve just above the mean (IQ between 100 and 115). Enhancing cognitive effectiveness the equivalent of one standard deviation might equip a much larger segment of the population with the cognitive foundation needed to pursue cognitively complex careers, which happen to be the most prestigious and best rewarded. Even gains smaller than one standard deviation could be important because shifts in the mean of a normal distribution are, in terms of representation, magnified at the tails. Assuming a constant standard deviation, a rightward shift of the population IQ curve, even if modest, would result in a large decrease in representation at the low end of the curve and a many-fold increase at the high end. Such an incremental transformation could go a long way toward addressing social problems associated with differing cognitive preparedness, and might prepare a larger and more diverse segment of the population to participate fully in a society whose universal passkey is a very able mind.

NOTES

1. Page and Grandon (1981) also noted that treatment and control groups differed in mean height at 24 months (even though no such differences were found at birth). However, as they pointed out, children in the *control* group were taller. Although this fact does not invalidate their suggestion about group nonequivalence, it does seem less alarming than if height differences were found favoring children in the treatment group, which would suggest more favorable nutrition and better health care.

2. The critique of the Milwaukee Project extends to other aspects of design and procedure, such as whether the measurement of IQ was done objectively. Page and Grandon (1981) seemed to assume that the Milwaukee Project staff intentionally dissembled and deceived readers. They noted, for instance, that the on the Metropolitan Achievement Tests, "The results appear to have been far less satisfactory [than IQ test results], so much so that the project directors do not give much interpretable data" (p. 253).

3. Like Herrnstein, the hereditarian William Shockley also conducted interventions designed to enhance general thinking competencies. Shockley (1972) taught a freshman seminar on "mental tools for scientific thinking" at Stanford, and found a general effect of 0.6 standard deviations for participants over controls on course grades earned in the four subsequent quarters. That both Herrnstein and Shockley would hold such strong hereditarian views in light of their own data is, to say the least, "puzzling" (Sternberg, 1995, p. 259).

4. Feuerstein's hypothesis of divergent effects may seem to be an exception to this claim, but Feuerstein would reject the proposal that the quality of experience subsequent to intervention is immaterial (Feuerstein et al., 1980).

Part IV

Learnable Intelligence and Society

10
Cultivating Intelligence

In lamenting the misguided antipathy between proponents of traditional education and advocates of progressive education, Dewey (1938) held out the possibility that, in certain cases, neither approach was educative. In making this claim, Dewey was asserting that the word *education* carries independent standards that experiences in schools may or may not meet. To Dewey, the important question was not whether progressive or traditional education was to be preferred, "but a question of what anything whatever must be to be worthy of the name education" (p. 91).

As we approach the idea of education as a way to cultivate intelligence, it becomes necessary to decouple the terms *education* and *schooling*. In common parlance they are used synonymously, as if schooling "constitutes *the* educational system" (Brandwein, 1981, p. 9), but philosophers of education from Plato to Dewey have recognized the difference. Brandwein (1981) divided the two terms, explaining that:

> Schooling attempts to transmit the concepts, values, and skills prized by a community acting under constraints of public custom, rule, and law (local, state, and federal). Education, on the other hand, affects all of life and living and comprises all influences, in school and out, that affect and effect changes in the individual—whether of habituation, of character, or of intellect. These changes in behavior occur throughout life. (p. 9)

The meaning of the Latin root *educere* is "to draw out." Education can be construed as any process that extends a human being in directions that build capacity and that lead to yet further growth, wherever and however that occurs. Educative experiences build competencies that are, in Snow's (1991) terminology, *propaedeutic*, or "needed as preparation for . . . [some future] success" (p. 257). A broad definition of education does not specify curriculum or venue.

Dewey's question as to what constitutes education is provocative on two counts. First, it implies that the institution of schooling is not equivalent to education. The school, as the primary site of institutional education, can in fact be miseducative, failing its mission as an educative agent, and perhaps even reinforcing inequities in the larger society (Shujaa, 1993). Cognitive differences among people are also traceable to experiences that precede and parallel schooling; through those experiences, cognitive abilities are stimulated or stunted all along the life span. The second implication of Dewey's question is that experiences can be evaluated as to their educative value. Dewey offered some guidance on this point.

In particular, he suggested that the most important quality of experience is its *continuity*, which is the ability of experience "to live fruitfully and creatively in subsequent experiences" (1938, p. 28). If intelligence consists of cognitive and noncognitive functions that lead to effectiveness across a wide situational spectrum, then experiences that cultivate intelligence satisfy the principle of continuity.

How can intelligence be cultivated? The chapters on experiential factors associated with IQ and on specific interventions that led to IQ gains are replete, conceptually and strategically, with ideas on how future interventions might be organized. Existing theories of intelligence, perhaps including the model that I have advanced, can help structure efforts to enhance intelligence more programmatically and deliberately. In this chapter, I have distilled some of the research literature on intelligence-promoting experiences to propose ten strategies that can organize efforts to enhance intelligence.

TEN STRATEGIES FOR CULTIVATING INTELLIGENCE

The School

1. Establish an Intelligence-Enhancing Curriculum for Every School. If the goal of raising intelligence were recognized by society as achievable and important, schools would have a vital role to play. When human intelligence is reinterpreted to be teachable and learnable, formal education can take on new meaning. In particular, it becomes conceivable that the direct enhancement of intelligence could be adopted as an explicit or even primary goal of schools. If the deliberate cultivation of intelligence were embraced as a central goal of formal education, the very meaning of education would by that fact be transformed. Intelligence would no longer be seen as only an input or raw material for education, but also, and more importantly, as a product.

Historically, educational systems have not adopted the teaching and learning of intelligence as an explicit goal, nor have educational systems been conceptually equipped with the necessary models of cognitive functions underlying intelligence. Instead, those functions have been learned incidentally and incorporated into the intelligence repertoire as *tacit* knowledge. A. D. deGroot (1948) observed that intelligence consists largely of "methods of thinking, . . . of searching and finding new solutions to problems" (p. 315). The intelligent person "adopts them, largely unconsciously, from others" (p. 316). At the level of the individual learner, the acquisition of the intelligence repertoire has amounted to a kind of code breaking, a quiet extraction of cognitive functions that are encrypted in the surrounding culture. But there is no reason why knowledge acquired incidentally through passive enculturation must remain tacit. Intelligence should be taught directly.

Cognitive theory now supplies an account of the cognitive functions composing intelligence. An appreciation of the functions most characteristic of intelligence makes them candidates for the organizing elements of the curriculum, or what Perkins (1992) called the *metacurriculum*. Some curricula have been explicitly organized around the goal of developing intelligence or intelligences. Gardner's (1983) theory of multiple intelligences, for example, has inspired the mission and curriculum of the Key School in Indianapolis (Gardner, 1993b; Gardner & Hatch, 1989), and has been used by thousands of teachers in diversifying symbol modalities and modes by which learners express proficiency. Many other curricula that aim to develop cognitive strategies, thinking skills, critical thinking, and the like probably also serve to develop the repertoire of intellectual functions that are general and powerful enough to be called *intelligence* (Nickerson, Perkins, & Smith, 1985; Paul, 1993; Perkins, Goodrich, Tishman, & Owen, 1994; Pressley & Harris, 1990; Whimbey & Lochhead, 1991).

The typical school curriculum already develops intelligence to some degree. Mathematics is a good example. Clearly, much or most of high school and college mathematics exceeds the numeracy needed by citizens in their daily lives or on the job. The study of advanced algebra, trigonometry, and calculus might now perform the function once ascribed to Latin.[1] Although not justified in these terms, the mathematics studied by academically oriented high school students probably serves to "exercise" the mind's capacity to think abstractly, to apprehend complexity, and to solve problems through the manipulation of symbols—just the sorts of cognitions that conform to information-processing characterizations of intelligence and to the work of the symbolic analyst. As Cattell (1987) observed, it is "no accident" that schools "concentrate on intelligence-demanding subjects" (p. 147).

The cultivation of intelligence can become much more focused by targeting the associated intellective functions either independent of specific content or in conjunction with subject matter. Although much is made over whether thinking-based curricula ought to be content independent or embedded in school subjects, the important thing is that it be done. If the regular curriculum incorporated the teaching of intelligent cognitive functions directly, those functions could be built into the design of curricula as cross-cutting cognitive objectives. In assessment, the measurement of cognitive outcomes could take advantage of a long tradition of designing test specifications to include both content and process dimensions. If subscores were reported along content and process dimensions, test results could directly contribute to the goal of teaching intelligence. All these changes would involve shifting curriculum and assessment to support not only academic achievement in subject areas, but also the development of cognitive abilities (Kvashchev, 1980).

Theories of cognitive development and the history of cognitive interventions show that the quality of early childhood experience is crucial. Many investigators have stressed the importance of developing cognitive abilities in preschools (Barnett, 1995, cited in Jencks & Phillips, 1998a; Ceci & Williams, 1998; Kornhaber, 1998). The proposal to emphasize cognition in preschool is controversial, but given the social consequences of differing experiences before a child first sets foot in a classroom, the potential benefits of a cognitively oriented program are compelling, especially for children who are at risk for failure in school. Successful preschool programs have, in general, created an environment of high complexity, to which children were expected to respond (Detterman, 1982). The quality of interactions between children and preschool staff is crucial: Children's language comprehension abilities have been found, for example, to be related to caregivers' mean sentence length and use of complex sentence structures (Tizard, Cooperman, Joseph, & Tizard, 1972).

Teaching for intelligence means engaging in an entirely new enterprise; it calls for a redefinition of what constitutes an educated person and what constitutes an educative experience. Should this goal be adopted, the meanings of both *education* and *intelligence* must both expand. That is because the universe of cognitive competencies composing intelligence is not yet fully known, nor are the kinds and qualities of educative experiences that engender them completely understood. Thus the questions: "What is intelligence?" and "What is education?" must remain open.

2. *Recognize the Convergence of Racial/Ethnic Cognitive Distributions as Achievable and Desirable.* For decades, a span of one standard deviation has separated the IQ distributions of Black and White Americans, and has persisted with such tenacity that it had seemed to be a permanent fixture. However, recent data on cognitive differences between Black and White students as manifest in IQ scores and academic achievement have shown that the cognitive gap is not permanent—and that it has in fact shrunk since 1970. This documentable narrowing of the gap makes an environmental explanation of Black-White cognitive differences more plausible now than ever (Jencks & Phillips, 1998a; Kaus, 1995).

The inferences are hopeful: The fact that the gap *has* narrowed means that it *can* narrow, and because the gap *can* narrow it is conceivable that it can close completely. On this point, even the hereditarians Herrnstein and Murray (1994, p. 293) made a startling concession, granting that "there is no reason why [the gap] shouldn't" continue to converge, with parity reached "sometime in the middle of the twenty-first century" (p. 293). However, their optimism was short-lived. Before they completed that sentence, they cast aside the monumental implications of what they had just written with the half-hearted hedge that "linear implications over such long periods are not worth much"!

Those particular linear implications are worth quite a lot—although Herrnstein and Murray (1994) were actually making a technical point, referring to the limited dependability of trend extrapolations. Nonetheless, a shrinking cognitive gap bodes well for the cause of equity. Reducing differences in cognitive ability and achievement, for example, is likely to influence racial disparities in educational attainment. High-scoring Black students are actually *more* likely to complete college than are White students with comparable test scores (Jencks & Phillips,

1998a). Jencks and Phillips (1998b) asserted that between-race differences in cognitive abilities can explain the entire Black-White gap in college graduation, and most of the discrepancy in earnings. The implication here is that Black and White populations are not so different on noncognitive influences on achievement, such as aspirations for success. The fact that the gap between Black and White students is narrowing on measures of cognitive achievement and ability, and that the abilities tapped by tests appear to be instructionally tractable, "could be very good news" (Jencks & Phillips, 1998b, p. 71).

3. Cultivate Fluid Intelligence Through Problem Solving. Problem solving and problem finding can serve as a general model for intelligent thought and action. Models of problem solving in novel situations, in particular, strongly resemble models of fluid intelligence. When the family resemblance between problem solving and fluid intelligence is recognized, this knowledge can be used to design intelligence-enhancing experiences. Tradition, however, may present a hurdle. In schools, crystallized intelligence tends to be emphasized at the expense of fluid intelligence (Lohman, 1993). Snow (1982a) showed that highly structured direct teaching can produce large gains in crystallized intelligence, but in some cases these gains are accompanied by declines in fluid intelligence with respect to control groups. Correcting the crystallized/fluid imbalance can be tricky because it depends on posing problems that are sufficiently novel such that students cannot rely on already learned procedures, yet not so novel that the students flounder. Balancing novelty and familiarity requires a delicate calibration of environmental demands to a student's zone of proximal development (Vygotsky, 1986/1934) along the novelty-familiarity continuum (Sternberg, 1985a). What complicates the matter is that this calibration point not only varies from student to student, but is itself a moving target because it can change rapidly with experience (Lohman, 1993). The ability to identify and hit that target consistently is a skill belonging to the very expert teacher.

If problem solving is to be used as a general model against which educative activities are compared, it is important that the nature and scope of problems typical to academic settings be reconsidered. Fig. 10.1 displays two dimensions of the space in which problem solving takes place. On the horizontal axis is the timeline over which problems are posed and solved. This timeline ranges from a single second to a life span. The vertical axis describes the complexity and teleological reach of the problem, and this dimension stretches from simple perception to the construction of values and meaning. Between the two axes is the problem space in which intelligence is exercised, and this space is divided by an arc that separates the "academic culture problem space" from the "life problem space." This division signifies that intelligence tests and school curricula have been mostly concerned with the lower-left corner of the problem space, whereas intelligent thought and action that make for successful lives stretch up and to the right. The diagram implies a need to revise education systems not only to emphasize

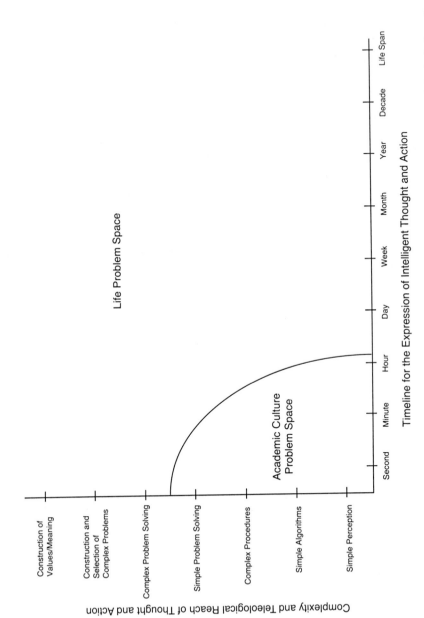

FIG. 10.1. Contrast of academic and life problem spaces along dimensions of timeline and complexity/teleological reach.

problem solving as the essence of intelligence, but also to more fairly represent the range of problems on which intelligence operates.

Besides recognizing that the full problem space of intelligence is far larger than the reach of most academic tests and tasks, it may be important to consider "noncognitive" aspects of broad-sense intelligence. Broadening the criteria for recognizing intelligent thought and action might mean expanding the range of psychological functions constituting intelligence to include conational (i.e., motivational and volitional) and emotional aspects (Hilgard, 1980; Snow, 1980b; Snow, Corno, & Jackson, 1996). This is because movement within a problem space is impelled and sustained by all manner of "hot" needs and rewards, not just coolly stated rational objectives.

4. Cultivate Crystallized Intelligence Through Deep Literacy and the Pursuit of Schema Quality. The strong connection between crystallized intelligence and proficiency with language, especially text comprehension, reinforces the primacy of literacy as an organizing goal of formal education. Although the promotion of crystallized intelligence can be accomplished through many forms of experience, the medium of text is especially potent. The amount of reading engaged in by students is associated with school achievement across race, gender, and SES (Heyns, 1978). Gains in crystallized intelligence over a lifetime appear to be strongly associated with exposure to print; that is, to reading habits (Stanovich, West, & Harrison, 1995). Crystallized intelligence can be cultivated more widely as a greater proportion of the population learns not just the skill of reading, but also the love of it. Developing that love poses a challenge. People who are able to read vary considerably in the extent to which they actually do read. The problem is not so much illiteracy, but *aliteracy*—the ability to read but an unwillingness to do so. There is evidence of a steady decline in reading engagement from the mid-1970s to the present, and a decline in newspaper reading beginning in the early 1900s (Glenn, 1994).

A study of the experiential histories of low-achieving college students illuminated the origins of text avoidance. Duchein and Mealey (1993) found that, as children, many students had been read to by their parents, and that in many cases their primary school teachers had read aloud to them. These experiences were remembered with considerable pleasure. Unfortunately, the frequency of being read to tapered off dramatically in the later grades and in high school. Competing activities and diversions, including television, led many students to reject any book reading that was not required as coursework. Many participating college students had not read for pleasure in years, and some felt aversion or dread about the prospect of reading a novel. The pleasure of text, however, can be recovered. When assigned to read the novel *The Prince of Tides* (Conroy, 1986), many students were surprised to discover that they actually enjoyed it. Some even began to read other books for pleasure.

Although text can serve as a strong medium for growing crystallized intelligence, the mechanism by which intelligence is crystallized is through the development of schemas. Learning, understanding, and critical thinking can all be gathered under the umbrella of improving schema quality. Likewise, the primary function of metacognitive thought can be seen as the improvement of schema quality. In my model, I have cast the pursuit of schema quality as depending on standards against which existing schemas can be judged. This comparative function is described in somewhat different terms in Perkins' (Perkins, Jay, & Tishman, 1993) theory of thinking dispositions, Paul's (1993) identification of intellectual virtues, and Baron's (1985) proposal that the central activity of rational intelligence is cognitive search. To the degree that such standards as clarity, efficiency, and integrity can be internalized and deployed as self-test procedures that are habitual, crystallized intelligence will grow.

Teachers can do a lot to promote the kind of intellectual search that promotes schema quality. Doing so depends partly on establishing a suitable classroom environment. Building a tolerance for uncertainty and ambiguity is important contextually, but this is likely to make the classroom environments less structured and less predictable, a potential worry if the social control of students is an issue (Nickerson, 1986a). In this vein, the curricular overemphasis on crystallized knowledge, often without understanding, may largely function to establish and maintain a "safe" social order because, for the teacher at least, the conceptual ground to be covered is familiar and predictable. Tidy conceptual structures can reinforce neat and predicable social structures. Students may wish to cooperate with this arrangement because by it they suffer less discomfort of effort, complying with an unspoken contract that Gardner (1991, p. 141) called "correct-answer compromises." When such a compact is reached, real understanding is unlikely to be attained (Gardner, 1991; Schank, 1986), and the development of fluid abilities is completely thwarted.

5. Abandon the False and Destructive Antithesis of Higher-Order and Lower-Order Cognitive Skills. The perpetual war between proponents of basic skills and champions of higher-order thinking can lead an observer to believe that educational reform can never be more than the oscillation of a pendulum. The problem lies in the misunderstanding that lower-order and higher-order processes are antagonistic. In reality, they are complementary. Higher-order processes depend on the skillful exercise (and sometimes, automatization) of lower-order abilities, but the teaching of lower-order abilities is, as an end in itself, an impoverished sort of educational objective. Moreover, it is false to think that lower-order abilities must be developed before higher processes. Their development can and should proceed in parallel.

There is some evidence that skill automatization predicts academic success (Whang, 1991, cited in Jensen, 1992b). Automated skills have value because they free up working memory for the operation of higher-order strategic planning and monitoring, and for creative work. Because the acquisition of automaticity is time intensive, it should target only those processes and knowledge structures that have wide importance. Decoding text is probably the best example of this kind of skill, because if decoding is laborious the cognitive system will have very little capacity left over for comprehension. At their best, reading and other forms of complex cognition combine automated knowledge with more open-ended search in which automated abilities liberate sufficient working memory for proficient, even expert, performance. When viewed in this light, higher-order cognitive activities are not antagonists of "basic skills"—as if there were a forced choice between them—rather, the most creative and proficient thinking always involves a concert of both higher-order and lower-order abilities.

Sternberg's (1985a) experiential subtheory of intelligence is relevant here. The subtheory holds that intelligence is most clearly demonstrated at the endpoints of a continuum of novelty and familiarity. On the familiarity end, intelligence is manifest in the process of skill automatization. At the novelty end, fluid intelligence is exercised. One might speculate that schools give too little attention to the two ends of the experiential continuum. The flow of experience in schools seems rather to bisect the continuum, requiring neither much adaptive problem solving nor many activities that lead to automaticity or "mastery." If this is an accurate appraisal, and if raising intelligence is adopted as a goal, then more attention should be channeled toward the poles of the experiential continuum.

The Home

6. Recognize the Home as at Least Equal to Schools in Educative Importance. Because intelligence is developed through a broad spectrum of life experience, schools cannot possibly compensate for variation in the experiences that precede, parallel, and follow the school experience. Differences in the intellectual quality of home life are large and relate strongly, although not exclusively, to the nature of parent-child interactions. According to some observers, changing the way parents relate to their children is the "single most important thing we can do to improve children's cognitive skills" (Jencks & Phillips, 1998a, p. 53).

Although reflective thinking is not taught systematically in the home, families differ in the quality of their dinner-table conversations, and in the expectations placed on children for clear thinking (Perkins, 1995). Intelligent habits of mind—ways of thinking about the world, including the kind of questions worth asking and problems worth solving—have a quiet but potent presence in social contexts, including home life. In the long run, the intellectual ambiance of the home carries enormous power and can impede or encourage creative accomplishment. Outstanding contributors to science and culture have typically been raised in homes that were intellectually stimulating and imbued with values encouraging independence, personal expression, and a strong work ethic (Mumford & Gustafson, 1988).

One way to foster intelligence in families is to equip parents with strategies that can advance children's cognitive development. Indeed, parenting "skills" of this sort are a recognized aspect of many cognitive interventions (Ramey & Ramey,

1992). Children's questions, for example, can be addressed at different levels. Parents can ignore or reject a question, furnish an answer outright, or help the child form and test hypothetical answers to the question (Sternberg, 1994a). Parents can learn to adopt "distancing" strategies in their social interactions with children, such that questions and prompts can help children transcend the limitations of the here and now, and extend their cognitive reach to ideas, associations, and relations that are more complex and abstract (Sigel, Stinson, & Kim, 1993). Distancing strategies, initially experienced in the social space of family interactions, can eventually be internalized so that the child can independently discern cause and effect, generate plans, and anticipate consequences. One might think of experiences of this sort as constituting a college-preparatory childhood.

Ramey and Ramey (1992) identified six qualities of experience that should characterize the daily lives of young children: Encouragement to explore; mentoring by adults in basic cognitive skills, such as comparing and labeling; celebration of developmental advances; practice and extension of new skills; protection from discouraging negative experiences, such as unnecessary disapproval; and a rich linguistic environment. These qualities of experience were distilled from dozens of research studies and interventions spanning decades. If applied in the home and elsewhere, they can help ensure that children, even those at risk for failure, will be prepared for success, academic and otherwise.

7. Restrict Cognitively Poor Default Activities. Anti-educational aspects of home life also must be considered. Here I refer to those activities that have a tendency to absorb large amounts of time with little cognitive payoff. Television is an obvious example. It is well known that American children, on average, spend huge amounts of time watching television. In 1988, about one quarter of all fourth-grade children watched television for 6 or more hours each day—and half of all of Black fourth graders watched this much television (Martinez & Lahart, 1990). Television is not categorically bad—viewing may have cognitive benefits up to about 10 hours per week (Williams, Haertel, Haertel, & Walberg, 1982). Beyond a certain point, however, television has a negative effect on school achievement—especially among high-IQ children—possibly because it squeezes out more intellectually rich and demanding activities, such as reading and interaction with adults (Huston & Wright, 1998). Extensive viewing has small but reliable negative effects on reading proficiency, and these effects tend to be more serious in older children (Huston & Wright, 1998). There is some evidence, in fact, that average vocabulary levels (adjusted for education level) declined steadily during the 20th century; during the same period, reading engagement also declined whereas television viewing increased (Glenn, 1994).[2] These data corroborate anecdotal reports. In a study of television's effects, one subject admitted, "After awhile, I lost interest in reading. I got hooked on television and couldn't get off of it" (Duchein & Mealey, 1993, p. 22).

There is also evidence that reducing time spent on viewing television can have a positive effect on children's IQ and cognitive style (reflectivity/impulsivity). Gadberry (1980) matched 6-year-olds on age, gender, IQ, and TV viewing habits, and randomly assigned them to restricted or unrestricted viewing conditions. In the restricted condition, parents limited their children's TV viewing time to half of what it was at baseline levels. The intervention lasted 6 weeks, during which TV viewing averaged 350 minutes per week in the restricted group, and 706 minutes per week in the unrestricted group. During this period, children in the restricted group voluntarily increased the time they spent reading books, a shift that supports the hypothesis that TV displaces other cognitively beneficial activities. Pre- and posttests on the Wechsler Preschool and Primary Scale of Intelligence (WPPSI) revealed a larger performance IQ gain for children in the restricted condition as compared to controls, especially among males. Posttest comparisons on the Matching Familiar Figures Test showed that the two groups also differed in cognitive style, with the TV-restricted group displaying greater reflectivity, and the TV-unrestricted group showing greater impulsivity.

It is possible that television viewing encourages a mental state of passive, uncritical information processing. Research by Salomon (1983) showed that children perceive television to be less demanding than text. Even when information-rich TV programs are presented, children tend to expend little effort to process these programs critically. This may be partly the nature of the medium: Television limits the opportunity to control the allocation of time and effort to reflection by virtue of its programmed pacing of information (Gadberry, 1980); reading, by contrast, engages self-regulation in how time and effort are allocated. Slowing down, skipping ahead, and re-reading are all possible.

The discussion of television raises the larger issue of the impact of mass media and electronic entertainment on cognition. From one point of view, there is a curious contradiction between rising IQ levels and a shift of underlying values toward ever-greater commitment to the intellectually shallow entertainment culture. The culture of the mass media may simply be an expression of abiding cultural commitments. America has always been unfriendly to intellectualism as a form of elitism (and therefore an expression of European values). Nonetheless, some commentators see a decline (Gabler, 1998). Erstwhile "serious" news media are increasingly acceding to the entertainment culture, as depth of analysis gives way to the life dramas of celebrities in the hope of trapping the attention, if only for a moment, of an ever-more-distractible audience. Nowadays, there is little patience with "serious literature, serious political debate, serious ideas, serious anything" (Gabler, 1998, p. 9). At risk is what Kermode (1996, p. 32) called "the highest pleasure, the pleasure of complexity," which is an acquired taste.

The ascendance of an image-rich mass entertainment culture might correspond to a decline in high-level verbal processing ability. Exposure to television can produce gains in word knowledge, but only to a point. Television vocabulary seems to top out at about the fourth-grade level; for a child to make gains beyond that seems to depend on significant exposure to more complex forms of language, especially as found in text. This is true partly because the kind of language used in the mass media is poor not only in vocabulary, but also in syntax. Mass media syntax is typically simple, consisting mostly of incomplete sentences that depend heavily on the presence of an image for comprehension of meaning. That is, TV and allied media do not present the kind of context-independent and explicit kinds of language that readers of text must rely on to construct, mentally, a model of what is being described. Unfortunately, and probably partly because of a shift to iconic mass media, there is less incidence of book reading than there has been in the past. Greenfield (1998) blamed the decline in high-level verbal ability, as manifest in SAT scores, on this shift toward nonprint media. Thus, iconic media may have mixed effects on verbal ability—raising the floor, but lowering the ceiling.

8. Ensure That, for All Children, Nutrition Is Optimized and Exposure to Toxins is Minimized. The cumulative research on nutrition and cognition has established a linkage between the two. In fact, global improvements in nutrition during the 20th century may have contributed to the worldwide increase in IQ known as the *Flynn effect.* That nutrition has played some role in the Flynn effect is supported also by the finding that smaller-scale nutritional improvements tend to enhance spatial or fluid abilities more than verbal abilities, a pattern that corresponds to the global pattern of rising cognitive abilities (Flynn, 1996).

In several experimental studies, vitamin and mineral supplementation resulted in cognitive gains. In developing countries, protein supplementation in childhood produced cognitive benefits lasting into adolescence and early adulthood. In New York City schools, attempts to improve the nutritional quality of foods led to discernible increases in school achievement. Although the agenda of cognitive enhancement must engage symbol processing activity, a healthy neurological base is a prerequisite. These findings warrant that every child should be assured of a daily nutrient intake defined not by what is minimal, but by what is optimal. The level of a particular nutrient that would prevent a deficiency disease, such as rickets or night blindness, may be different from the level that is ideal for health and cognitive growth. We should ensure that all children, especially those raised in poverty or inadequate social conditions, receive optimal levels of vitamins, minerals, protein, and other essential nutrients, and are spared exposure to toxins. Otherwise, a malnourished child might display apathy or irritability, and thus be unable to evoke sympathetic responsiveness from adults, leading to a cycle of interactional deprivation (Chávez & Martínez, 1975; Joffe, 1982).

The Workplace

9. Reconceptualize the Workplace as an Educational Institution. I have emphasized that nonschool learning environments are at least equal in importance to formal education in cognitive development (Ralph, Keller, & Crouse, 1994).

Educative environments include families, but also other settings, such as the workplace. General cognitive ability is relevant not only to what occupations are open to the individual—IQ has repeatedly been shown to predict workplace performance within jobs. The predictive validity of IQ on job performance is strongest when jobs are organized according to "complexity family" such that IQ best predicts proficiency in symbolic-analytic occupations. Given the connection between cognitive ability and workplace productivity at the level of the individual worker, it is necessary to reconceptualize the workplace as a facilitator of ongoing cognitive development; that is, as an educational institution in its own right (Secretary's Commission on Achieving Necessary Skills, 1991).

The connection between workplace activities and the growth or decline of cognitive abilities was established decades ago. Vernon (1948, p. 138) found, for example, that intelligence decreased for men in "lower-grade" occupations, but was maintained for those involved in "intellectual" occupations. More recently, Kohn and Schooler (1973; Schooler, 1998) found that workers whose jobs were intellectually challenging and entailed self-directed complex work developed greater intellectual flexibility, independent of workers' education level, than did less intellectually challenging jobs. Kohn and Schooler (1973) also found that the substantive complexity of jobs is related to positive feelings about work and toward self, even when controlling for other job characteristics and workers' education.

Work experience can lead to changes in cognitive abilities composing intelligence, including the capacity to deal with complex problems expressible in symbolic terms. It is just these abilities that have been recognized as central to worker effectiveness in the future. Hunt (1995), in analyzing trends in societal composition and the demands of the future workplace, concluded that what is needed most in the American workforce are problem-solving abilities and "learning to learn" skills, competencies that happen to map onto fluid and crystallized intelligence, respectively. United States government panels on the demands of the future labor market have arrived at similar conclusions, noting that learning and problem-solving skills are essential to the future workforce (Commission on the Skills of the American Workforce, 1990; Secretary's Commission on Achieving Necessary Skills, 1991).

Predictors of workplace success go beyond IQ. For example, certain personality dimensions of the "Big Five" theoretical model correlate with workplace performance (Landy, Shankster, & Kohler, 1994).[3] In particular, the superfactor known as *conscientiousness* predicts job performance quite widely, especially among workers whose jobs permit autonomy (Barrick & Mount, 1993). The conscientiousness dimension describes workers who are achievement oriented, responsible, and persistent. Conscientiousness and IQ are statistically independent; the combination of IQ and conscientiousness (and related measures of integrity) yields the best-known prediction of workplace performance (multiple $r = 0.65$) from two variables (Schmidt & Hunter, 1998).[4] Another predictive personality dimension, also one of the five superfactors, is *agreeableness* (Tett, Jackson, &

Rothstein, 1991). United States government reports have called for skills that can be collectively referred to as a "work ethic," which include the ability and commitment to meet deadlines and to do better work than is minimally necessary (Hunt, 1995). Under the broadest construal of intelligence, these characteristic behavior patterns might be included. Likewise, they too might be cultivated strategically in work settings.

There is another hugely important resource in determining workplace performance, and that is relevant knowledge. In terms of Cattell's fluid/crystallized intelligence dichotomy, domain knowledge is located on the crystallized side. Cognitive research has shown that the highest levels of performance in any domain rely on an extensive, well-organized knowledge base. Simon (1991) advanced parameters on the information-processing prerequisites of world class performance: 50,000 or more "chunks" of knowledge acquired over at least 10 years of full-time study. The importance of knowledge to the international economy was recognized by Stewart (1997), who called it the "primary ingredient of what we make, do, buy, and sell" (p. 12). Over the life span, as adults become invested in diverse roles requiring diverse funds of knowledge, broad-scale crystallized intelligence becomes less meaningful as a psychological construct (Ackerman, 1996). It is not that knowledge becomes less important over a lifetime; to the contrary, it is more important than ever to the development of expertise, but its contours become narrower and much deeper.

The Nation

10. Identify the Cultivation of Intelligence as a National Education Priority. Given more than a century of research on intelligence, it is somewhat surprising that only one nation has ever tried to raise the intelligence of its citizens. In the early 1980s, Venezuela adopted the cultivation of intelligence as a national goal, and that decision led to the short-lived, although successful, Project Intelligence. Given our understanding of how intelligence develops, and the importance of intelligence to individual and collective success, it is past time to develop what is arguably the most empowering technology of all—the technology of learnable intelligence. Recognition of this goal at a national level, followed by allocation of resources to achieve it, would help ensure a more strategic approach than that obtainable through many independent and uncoordinated efforts.

CONCLUSION

Although intelligence has long been regarded as inherited and immutable, the research evidence no longer supports that view. Experience plays a major and necessary role in the development of intelligence, and can account for much existing variation in IQ, including mean differences between racial/ethnic groups. Carroll (1997) spoke of these differences as, in part, "the resultant of opportunities afforded by schools, families, and everyday experiences" (p. 47). This realization opens the possibility that experience can be designed to encourage the growth of intelligence. Research has helped to make this possibility realizable through the analytical characterization of intelligence as definable competencies—a learnable repertoire (Perkins, 1995; Schank, 1986; Snow, 1996; Staats & Burns, 1981). Although there are dissenters and skeptics (e.g., Eysenck, 1998; Spitz, 1986), there is now an impressive accumulation of data showing that intelligence is definable and malleable. Cognitive psychology has contributed to this interpretive shift. Within the cognitive paradigm, it is now possible to define intelligence in terms compatible with information-processing models of the mind—namely, that intelligence consists in the variegated cognitive functions that facilitate effectiveness not only in formal education settings, but also in real-life problems and creative accomplishment. Traditional cognitive abilities—the kind studied by psychometricians—are implicated, but so are many other abilities, such as the complex and time-extended phenomena of problem solving and problem finding.

NOTES

1. The goal of education had long been viewed as the training of intellect in a generic sense, and only in the 20th century has this idea been questioned (Snow, 1982b). However, from antiquity to the beginning of the 20th century, intellectual development was thought to be accomplished through the exercise of mental faculties, much like physical strength is developed through the exercise of muscles. The rigor and complexity of Latin and other "disciplines" were thought to discipline the mind in a general way. It was assumed that this generic strength carried over, or transferred, to other intellectual pursuits, even those that were substantively remote. The transferability of Latin itself was cast into doubt when Thorndike (1924) published a paper showing that the study of Latin conferred no advantage to students' achievement in other subjects (however, cf. Judd's (1908) neglected rejoinder that far transfer is possible when the learner truly understands). This was the first step toward the demise of faculty theory and to a consensus of pessimism about transfer and the idea that education could develop general cognitive abilities.

2. Causal relations between education-adjusted vocabulary and reading habits cannot be proven by these data. However, deviations from linearity (i.e., residuals) between these variables and period of birth are correlated, adding support to a causal interpretation (Glenn, 1994).

3. The "Big Five" personality superfactors are extraversion, neuroticism, conscientiousness, agreeableness, and openness (Bouchard, 1994). These factors have been called by different names in different theories of personality.

4. The multiple correlation of IQ and conscientiousness to performance applies across a wide range of job types. The correlation is probably higher for the symbolic-analytic worker, because the predictive validity of IQ rises with job complexity and, similarly, the predictive validity of conscientiousness increases for jobs involving greater decision-making discretion.

11

Prospects for an Intelligent World

In navigating the complexity of day-to-day living, intelligence counts. The ability to separate important information from trivia, to order competing and conflicting priorities, and to select from innumerable options wisely but without undue deliberation—these everyday challenges demand intellectual readiness. Intelligence prepares the citizen of the modern world to accept complexity and to think and act rationally and purposefully within it. As the world complexifies, the ascendant value of intellect will increase (Ohlsson, 1998). Individual differences in intelligence will likely become more obvious and even more consequential (Bereiter, 1969), shunting people to differing opportunity paths. At a societal level, whether this leads to hope or to despair depends on whether intelligence can be cultivated.

Intelligence, long regarded as ontologically static and a direct expression of genotype, can now be seen more truly as a repertoire of learnable cognitive capabilities that develop over time and through experience. Genetics is surely implicated in individual differences in intelligence, but heritability in no way determines the level of intelligence in individuals or in populations. Intelligence is malleable. This is demonstrated in the 20th-century phenomenon of massive IQ escalation known as the *Flynn effect*. Although at some level genes must place limits on the phenotypic expression of intelligence, it is unlikely that any human being has ever reached his or her intellectual potential (Nickerson, Perkins, & Smith, 1985). It is time, therefore, to abandon the tired myth of immutable intelligence. By adopting a more elastic and realistic view of both intelligence and education, the deliberate cultivation of intelligence becomes a possibility.

TOWARD PRODUCTIVITY

In Reich's (1992) contemporary taxonomy of the labor force, the symbolic-analytic sector is closely identified with the intelligence repertoire. Those who work in this sector make their living by using their minds expertly to solve symbol-rich problems. The demand for symbolic-analytic ability is growing, as is the economic value attached to symbolic-analytic skills. This is demonstrated in the growing wage premium associated with advanced levels of education. In economic terms, higher education is a potent investment in human capital or "population quality" (Schultz, 1981). Companies are willing to pay for the services of intelligent minds because their economic competitiveness depends on their ability to recruit those who are best prepared to engage in symbolic-analytic work. Employees who hold the same title can differ markedly in productive output (a factor of 2:1 is not unusual), and these differences in productivity are moderately predicted by IQ (Schmidt & Hunter, 1998). Because strong economic implications follow, companies have a large stake in the recruitment and development of intellectual talent.

Intelligence, manifested as symbolic-analytic ability, creates opportunity at the level of the individual. Although career choice is essentially unconstrained for those with IQs of 120 or more, options "drop dramatically" as one moves lower in the IQ distribution (Gottfredson, 1997, p. 90). To become expert or even to reach creative eminence in most fields does not require a stratospheric IQ, but instead a moderately high threshold of about 120 (Ochse, 1990). As IQ distributions shift rightward in comparison to the norms of previous generations, it is possible that an increasing percentage of future populations will be prepared to succeed in work that requires complex symbolic thought. The Flynn effect hints that a growing population segment has acquired the prerequisite competencies for symbolic-analytic success. Indeed, in the United States and around the world, a rising percentage of the population has entered into the labor sector that Reich called *symbolic analysis.*

As cognitive fitness rises in economic importance, so do the institutions responsible for its development. Economics and education now rise and fall together. Marshall and Tucker (1992), among others (e.g., Thurow, 1985), recognized that the economic prospects of nations depend vitally on the quality of their schools. "The future now belongs to societies that organize themselves for learning," they asserted, "where all institutions are organized to learn and to act on what they learn" (1992, pp. xiii). As important as schools are, other institutions—notably the family and the workplace—also carry tremendous responsibility and potential to grow the intelligence of future generations.

TOWARD EQUITY

Although non-IQ factors account for much of the income variance in the United States (Ceci & Williams, 1997), cognitive abilities play a prominent role, independent of SES and educational attainment, in explaining income differences. Societal fractionation along the axis of cognitive abilities begins at birth (and even earlier through differences in prenatal experience) and traces though the entire life span. The deliberate cultivation of the mind's most important abilities, the intelligence repertoire, could transform the structure of society. In particular, because entry into the labor sector of symbolic analysis carries economic rewards, the cultivation of intelligence among all people could contribute to a more equitable society—not by erasing socioeconomic differences, but instead by curtailing the association of wealth and opportunity with race and ethnicity.

It is likely that the social gains that followed the Civil Rights movement had substantial effects on how millions of minority children were raised. The entry of underrepresented minority students, African Americans in particular, into universities and then into professional occupations may have caused them to become different kinds of parents than those of the previous generation. Evidence for the efficacy of laws, court decisions, and social policies supporting greater equity of opportunity is found in the academic gains made by Black students since 1970, and in the shrinking Black-White cognitive gap in academic achievement and IQ. The possibility of cognitive convergence—the merging of IQ and achievement curves that have for centuries segregated Black and White populations along the psychometric axis—has become thinkable.

TOWARD CREATIVITY

Creative masterpieces are manifest in a deeper understanding of the natural world, by insights into the human realm, and by rebirthings of artistic expression. Creative productivity has differed markedly across cultures, and fluctuates widely within cultures across time (McClelland, Atkinson, Clark, & Lowell, 1953). Is intelligence relevant? Creativity and intelligence are surely not the same thing. High intelligence never guarantees creativity; however, major advances in science and creative expression seem to require a threshold of at least moderately high intelligence (Guilford, 1967; Ochse, 1990; Simonton, 1984). Exceptionally creative people seldom obtain low scores on tests of mental ability (Hunt, 1995). In more demanding fields that require facility with abstract concepts, a moderately high degree of intelligence is arguably a "minimal precondition" for the generation of significant creative products (Mumford & Gustafson, 1988, p. 32). The cultivation of intelligence could increase the likelihood of a modern Renaissance, although perhaps of a kind and to a degree not yet known (Solso, 1995).

Expertise, world-class performance, and genius are all richly complex phenomena that we have only begun to understand. Research on world-class performance makes that phenomenon a little less mysterious than in the past. For example, there is more evidence supporting the view that high ability is developed through sustained, intense experience than through initial differences in talent (Bloom, 1985; Ericsson, Krampe, & Heizmann, 1993). World-class performance requires extreme dedication, access to the best teachers, robust confidence, and identification with the talent field (Bloom, 1985; Ochse, 1990). In the evolution of the world-class performer, habitual engagement in deliberate practice is instrumental in such diverse fields as chess, music, and sports (Ericsson, 1996). The ability to tolerate high-effort activities that are not always intrinsically enjoyable is a self-regulatory function that might be taught and learned systematically. This raises a uniquely provocative question: "Can we create gifted people?" (Ericsson, Krampe, & Heizmann, 1993). An affirmative answer seems more defensible now than ever before. Benjamin Bloom (1985), after chronicling the lives of world-class performers in such diverse fields as neurology, mathematics, tennis, art, and concert piano, concluded that "there is enormous human potential in each society [and] only a small amount of this human potential is ever fully developed. We believe that each society could vastly increase the amount and kinds of talent it develops" (p. 549).

TOWARD WISDOM

In the modern world, the core intellectual functions constituting intelligence have special importance as prerequisites to individual and societal effectiveness. More significant, intelligence can be directed toward the world problematique, the tangle of dilemmas that threatens to disrupt and even to destroy the world's biological and social spheres. In confronting the menace, the full engagement of the human mind is not just part of the puzzle's denouement, but instead is the key—the "issue of issues" (Botkin, Elmandjra, & Malitza, 1979, p. 9). Features that define intelligence—the capacity to think flexibly, to welcome complexity, and to bring knowledge to bear on important problems—are precisely the kinds of cognition that are needed to untangle the world problematique (Botkin et al., 1979).

A more intelligent population is better prepared to secure a good future for generations to come. The ability to think well is a fundament of democratic order and insurance against challenges to democracy (Nickerson, 1994). A more intelligent electorate is also better prepared to "judge men and measures wisely," and is less susceptible to manipulation (Dewey, 1916, p. 120). To be sure, enduring social problems defy simple solutions, but without a foundation of intelligence there is little hope of making reasonable progress against them. Gaining ground against poverty, disease, pollution, and war is unlikely without qualities of intelligence: imagination, insight, flexible thinking, perseverance, and commitment—and, above all, wisdom. Although wisdom, like creativity, is never the same as intelligence, neither are they unrelated. With wisdom, would-be solvers of the world's problems will be able to weigh competing interests judiciously and to envision solutions that range from gentle adjustments to radical reconfigurations of the existing order (Sternberg, 1998b).

CONCLUSION

In this book, I have attempted to invert commonsense ideas about intelligence. Although we often think of intelligence as static, the claim here is that it is malleable. Intelligence is often presumed to be genetically transmitted, but there are plentiful data showing that differences in experience are "just as important as genes" (Plomin & DeFries, 1998, p. 66). Intelligence is commonly regarded as a raw material to education, but there is now abundant evidence that intelligence is also a product of education, and can be so to a greater degree in the future.

The authors of *The Bell Curve*, a book strongly associated with the hereditarian position, inverted their own thesis when they acknowledged: "Limitless possibilities for improving intelligence environmentally wait to be uncovered by science: improved educational methods, diets, treatments for disease, prenatal care, educational media, and even medicines to make one smarter. In principle, intelligence can be raised environmentally to unknown limits" (Herrnstein & Murray, 1994, p. 390).

These conceptual inversions are all consequential, holding "massive implications for our child-rearing practices, for our educational system, and for the whole complex of fields that bear on the development and management of human potential" (Horn, 1967, p. 31). As one race, let us be unafraid to enter the problem space of our own future, to decide what ends we truly desire, and then to construct, intelligently, the means to achieve them.

REFERENCES

Ackerman, P. L. (1996). Knowledge structures: Successive glimpses of an elusive theory of adult intelligence. In D. K. Detterman (Ed.), *Current topics in human intelligence, vol. 5: The environment* (pp. 105-111). Norwood, NJ: Ablex.

Alexander, C. N., Druker, S. M., & Langer, E. J. (1990). Introduction: Major issues in the exploration of adult growth. In C. N. Alexander & E. J. Langer (Eds.), *Higher stages of human development: Perspectives on adult growth* (pp. 3-32). New York: Oxford University Press.

Alexander, C. N., & Langer, E. J. (Eds.). (1990). *Higher stages of human development: Perspectives on adult growth*. New York: Oxford University Press.

Anastasi, A. (1986). Intelligence as a quality of behavior. In R. J. Sternberg & D. K. Detterman (Eds.), *What is intelligence?: Contemporary viewpoints on its nature and definition* (pp. 19-21). Norwood, NJ: Ablex.

Anderson, J. R. (1983). *The architecture of cognition*. Mahwah, NJ: Lawrence Erlbaum Associates.

Anderson, J. R. (1985). *Cognitive psychology: And its implications* (2nd ed.). New York: Freeman.

Anderson, J. R. (1996). ACT: A simple theory of complex cognition. *American Psychologist, 51*, 355-365.

Angoff, W. H. (1988). The nature-nurture debate, aptitudes, and group differences. *American Psychologist, 43*, 713-720.

Arlin, P. K. (1989a). Problem solving and problem finding in young artists and young scientists. In M. L. Commons, J. D. Sinnott, F. A. Richards, & C. Armon (Eds.), *Adult development, 1, Comparisons and applications of adolescent and adult development models* (pp. 197-216). New York: Praeger.

Arlin, P. K. (1989b). The problem of the problem. In J. D. Sinnott (Ed.), *Everyday problem solving: Theory and applications* (pp. 229-237). New York: Praeger.

Arvey, R. D. (1986). General ability in employment: A discussion. *Journal of Vocational Behavior, 29*, 415-420.

Atkinson, R. C., & Shiffrin, R. M. (1971). The control of short-term memory. *Scientific American, 224*(2), 82-90.

Baddeley, A. (1986). *Working memory*. Oxford: Clarendon.

Baddeley, A. (1992). Working memory. *Science, 155*, 556-559.

Balke-Aurell, G. (1982). *Changes in ability structure as related to educational and occupational experience*. Göteborg, Sweden: Acta Universitatis Gothoburgensis.

Baltes, P. B. (1986). Notes on the concept of intelligence. In R. J. Sternberg & D. K. Detterman (Eds.), *What is intelligence?: Contemporary viewpoints on its nature and definition* (pp. 23-27). Norwood, NJ: Ablex.

Baltes, P. B., & Schaie, K. W. (1976). On the plasticity of intelligence in adulthood and old age: Where Horn and Donaldson fail. *American Psychologist, 31*, 720-725.

Bandura, A. (1986). *Social foundations of thought and action: A social cognitive theory*. Englewood Cliffs, NJ: Prentice-Hall.

Baron, J. (1985). *Rationality and intelligence*. New York: Cambridge University Press.

Baron, J. (1987). An hypothesis about the training of intelligence. In D. N. Perkins, J. Lochhead, & J. Bishop (Eds.), *Thinking: The second international conference* (pp. 60-67). Hillsdale, NJ: Lawrence Erlbaum Associates.

Barrick, M. R., & Mount, M. K. (1993). Autonomy as a moderator of the relationships between the big five personality dimensions and job performance. *Journal of Applied Psychology, 78*, 111-118.

Bartlett, F. C. (1932). *Remembering: A study in experimental and social psychology*. Cambridge, England: Cambridge University Press.

Belmont, J. M. (1989). Cognitive strategies and strategic learning: The socio-instructional approach. *American Psychologist, 44*, 142-148.

Belmont, J. M., Butterfield, E. C., & Ferretti, R. P. (1982). To secure transfer of training instruct self-management skills. In D. K. Detterman & R. J. Sternberg (Eds.), *How and how much can intelligence be increased* (pp. 147-154). Norwood, NJ: Ablex.

Benton, D., & Roberts, G. (1988). Effect of vitamin and mineral supplementation on intelligence of a sample of schoolchildren. *The Lancet, 1*, 140-143.

Bereiter, C. (1969). The future of individual differences. *Harvard Educational Review, 39*, 310-318.

Bereiter, C., & Engelmann, S. (1966). *Teaching disadvantaged children in the preschool.* Englewood Cliffs, NJ: Prentice-Hall.

Bereiter, C., & Scardamalia, M. (1979). Pascual-Leone's *M* construct as a link between cognitive-developmental and psychometric concepts of intelligence. *Intelligence, 3*, 41-63.

Bernstein, B. (1961). Social class and linguistic development: A theory of social learning. In A. H. Halsey, J. Floud, & C. A. Anderson (Eds.), *Education, economy, and society: A reader in the sociology of education* (pp. 288-314). New York: The Free Press.

Berry, J. W. (1974). Radical cultural relativism and the concept of intelligence. In J. W. Berry & P. R. Dasen (Eds.), *Culture and cognition: Readings in cross-cultural psychology* (pp. 225-229). London: Methuen.

Bidell, T. R., & Fischer, K. W. (1997). Between nature and nurture: The role of human agency in the epigenesis of intelligence. In R. J. Sternberg & E. L. Grigorenko (Eds.), *Intelligence, heredity, and environment* (pp. 193-242). New York: Cambridge University Press.

Binet, A. (1894). *Introduction à la psychologie expérimentale.* Paris: F. Alcan.

Binet, A. (1909). *Les idées modernes sur les enfants.* Paris: Ernest Flamarion.

Birch, E. E., Hoffman, D. R., Uauy, R., Birch, D. G., & Prestidge, C. (1998). Visual acuity and the essentiality of docosahexaenoic acid and arachidonic acid in the diet of term infants. *Pediatric Research, 44*(2), 201-209.

Blagg, N. (1991). *Can we teach intelligence? A comprehensive evaluation of Feuerstein's Instrumental Enrichment program.* Hillsdale, NJ: Lawrence Erlbaum Associates.

Blank, M., & Solomon, F. (1968). A tutorial language program to develop abstract thinking in socially disadvantages preschool children. *Child Development, 39*, 379-389.

Bloom, B. S. (1985). Generalizations about talent development. In B. S. Bloom (Ed.), *Developing talent in young people* (pp. 507-549). New York: Ballantine.

Bock, R. D., & Moore, E. G. J. (1986). *Advantage and disadvantage: A profile of American youth.* Hillsdale, NJ: Lawrence Erlbaum Associates.

Boring, E. G. (1923, June 6). Intelligence as the tests test it. *The New Republic*, pp. 35-37.

Botkin, J. W., Elmandjra, M., & Malitza, M. (1979). *No limits to learning: Bridging the human gap* (a report to the Club of Rome). New York: Pergamon.

Bouchard, T. J. (1994). Genes, environment, and personality. *Science, 264*, 1700-1701.

Bouchard, T. J., & McGue, M. (1981). Familial studies of intelligence: A review. *Science, 212*, 1055-1059.

Bower, G. H. (1972). Mental imagery and associative learning. In L. Gregg (Ed.), *Cognition in learning and memory* (pp. 51-88). New York: Wiley.

Bower, G. H. (1995). Empowering people through friendly technology: Psychology in the twenty-first century. In R. L. Solso & D. W. Massaro (Eds.), *The science of the mind: 2001 and beyond* (pp. 18-34). New York: Oxford University Press.

Bowles, S., & Nelson, V. I. (1974). The "inheritance of IQ" and the intergenerational reproduction of economic inequality. *Review of Economics and Statistics, 56*, 39-51.

Bradley, R. H., Caldwell, B. M., Rock, S. L., Ramey, C. T., Barnard, K. E., Gray, C., Hammond, M. A., Mitchell, S., Gottfried, A. W., Siegel, L., & Johnson, D. L. (1989). Home environment and cognitive development in the first 3 years of life: A collaborative study involving six sites and three ethnic groups in North America. *Developmental Psychology, 25* 217-235.

Brandwein, P. F. (1981). *Memorandum: On renewing schooling and education.* New York: Harcourt Brace Jovanovich.

Breitmayer, B. J., & Ramey, C. T. (1986). Biological nonoptimality and quality of postnatal environment as codeterminants of intellectual development. *Child Development, 57*, 1151-1165.

Brody, N. (1992). *Intelligence*. San Diego: Academic Press.

Brooks-Gunn, J., Klebanov, P. K., Liaw, F., & Spiker, D. (1993). Enhancing the development of low-birthweight, premature infants: Changes in cognition and behavior over the first three years. *Child Development, 64*, 736-753.

Brown v. Board of Educ., 347 U.S. 483 (1954).

Brown, A. L. (1978). Knowing when, where, and how to remember: A problem of metacognition. In R. Glaser (Ed.), *Advances in instructional psychology: Vol. 1* (pp. 77-165). Hillsdale, NJ: Lawrence Erlbaum Associates.

Brown, A. L., & Campione, J. C. (1982). Modifying intelligence or modifying cognitive skills: More than a semantic quibble? In D. K. Detterman & R. J. Sternberg (Eds.), *How and how much can intelligence be increased* (pp. 215-230). Norwood, NJ: Ablex.

Brown, A. L., & Campione, J. C. (1986). Academic intelligence and learning potential. In R. J. Sternberg & D. K. Detterman (Eds.), *What is intelligence?: Contemporary viewpoints on its nature and definition* (pp. 39-43). Norwood, NJ: Ablex.

Brown, A. L., Campione, J. C., & Barclay, C. R. (1979). Training self-checking routines for estimating test readiness: Generalization from list learning to prose recall. *Child Development, 50*, 501-512.

Bruer, J. T. (1997). Education and the brain: A bridge too far. *Educational Researcher, 26*(8), 4-16.

Bruner, J. S. (1990). *Acts of meaning*. Cambridge, MA: Harvard University Press.

Budoff, M. (1974). *Learning potential and educability among the educable mentally retarded* (Final Report No. 312312). Cambridge, MA: Research Institute for Educational Problems, Cambridge Mental Health Association.

Burt, C. (1940). *The factors of the mind: An introduction to factor-analysis in psychology*. London: University London Press. [New York: Macmillan, 1941].

Butterfield, E. C., Slocum, T. A., & Nelson, G. D. (1993). Cognitive and behavioral analyses of teaching and transfer: Are they different? In D. K. Detterman & R. J. Sternberg (Eds.), *Transfer on trial: Intelligence, cognition, and instruction* (pp. 192-257). Norwood, NJ: Ablex.

Cahan, S., & Cohen, N. (1989). Age versus schooling effects on intelligence development. *Child Development, 60*, 1239-1249.

Callahan, C. M., Tomlinson, C. A., Moon, T. R., Tomchin, E. M., & Plucker, J. (1995). *Project START: Using a multiple intelligences model in identifying and promoting talent in high-risk students* [Research Monograph 95136]. Storrs: University of Connecticut, The National Research Center on the Gifted and Talented.

Campione, J. C., & Brown, A. L. (1984). Learning ability and transfer propensity as sources of individual differences in intelligence. In P. H. Brooks, R. Sperber, & C. McCauley (Eds.), *Learning and cognition in the mentally retarded* (pp. 265-293). Hillsdale, NJ: Lawrence Erlbaum Associates.

Campione, J. C., & Brown, A. L. (1990). Guided learning and transfer: Implications for approaches to assessment. In N. Frederiksen, R. Glaser, A. Lesgold, & M. G. Shafto (Eds.), *Diagnostic monitoring of skill and knowledge acquisition* (pp. 141-172). Hillsdale, NJ: Lawrence Erlbaum Associates.

Campione, J. C., Brown, A. L., & Ferrara, R. A. (1982). Mental retardation and intelligence. In R. J. Sternberg (Ed.), *Handbook of human intelligence* (pp. 392-490). New York: Cambridge University Press.

Capron, C., & Duyme, M. (1989). Assessment of effects of socio-economic status on IQ in a full cross-fostering study. *Nature, 340*, 552-554.

Carnevale, A. P., & Rose, S. J. (1998). *Education for what?: The new office economy* (Executive Summary). Princeton, NJ: Educational Testing Service.

Carpenter, P. A., Just, M. A., & Shell, P. (1990). What one intelligence test measures: A theoretical account of the processing in the Raven Progressive Matrices Test. *Psychological Review, 97*, 404-431.

Carroll, J. B. (1976). Psychometric tests as cognitive tasks: A new "structure of intellect." In L. B. Resnick (Ed.), *The nature of intelligence* (pp. 27-56). Hillsdale, NJ: Lawrence Erlbaum Associates.

Carroll, J. B. (1980). Remarks on Sternberg's "Factor Theories of Intelligence Are All Right Almost." *Educational Researcher, 9*(8), 14-18.

Carroll, J. B. (1993). *Human cognitive abilities: A survey of factor-analytic studies.* Cambridge University Press.

Carroll, J. B. (1996). A three-stratum theory of intelligence: Spearman's contribution. In I. Dennis & P. Tapsfield (Eds.), *Human abilities: Their nature and measurement* (pp. 1-17). Mahwah, NJ: Lawrence Erlbaum Associates.

Carroll, J. B. (1997). Psychometrics, intelligence, and public perception. *Intelligence, 24,* 25-52.

Caruso, D. R., Taylor, J. J., & Detterman, D. K. (1982). Intelligence research and intelligent policy. In D. K. Detterman & R. J. Sternberg (Eds.), *How and how much can intelligence be increased* (pp. 45-65). Norwood, NJ: Ablex.

Case, R. (1991). *The mind's staircase: Exploring the conceptual underpinnings of children's thought and knowledge.* Hillsdale, NJ: Lawrence Erlbaum Associates.

Cattell, R. B. (1941). Some theoretical issues in intelligence testing. *Psychological Bulletin, 38,* 592.

Cattell, R. B. (1963). Theory of fluid and crystallized intelligence: A critical experiment. *Journal of Educational Psychology, 54,* 1-22.

Cattell, R. B. (1971). *Abilities: Their structure, growth, and action.* Boston: Houghton Mifflin.

Cattell, R. B. (1987). *Intelligence: Its structure, growth, and action.* New York: North-Holland.

Ceci, S. J. (1991). How much does schooling influence general intelligence and its cognitive components? A reassessment of the evidence. *Developmental Psychology, 27,* 703-722.

Ceci, S. J. (1996). *On intelligence: A bioecological treatise on intellectual development* (Expanded edition). Cambridge, MA: Harvard University Press.

Ceci, S. J., & Williams, W. M. (1997). Schooling, intelligence, and income. *American Psychologist, 52,* 1051-1058.

Ceci, S. J., & Williams, W. M. (1998, November-December). Commentary on C. Jencks & M. Phillips, "American's next achievement test." *The American Prospect,* pp. 63-64.

Chávez, A., & Martínez, C. (1975). Nutrition and development of children from poor areas v. nutrition and behavioral development. *Nutrition Reports International, 11,* 477-489.

Chi, M. T. H. (1978). Knowledge structures and memory development. In R. S. Siegler (Ed.), *Children's thinking: What develops* (pp. 73-96). Hillsdale, NJ: Lawrence Erlbaum Associates.

Chorney, M. J., Chorney, K., Seese, N., Owen, M. J., Daniels, J., McGuffin, P., Thompson, L. A., Detterman, D. K., Benbow, C., Lubinski, D., Eley, T., & Plomin, R. (1998). A quantitative trait locus associated with cognitive ability in children. *Psychological Science, 9,* 159-166.

Cicirelli, V. G. (1969). *The impact of Head Start: An evaluation of the effects of Head Start on children's cognitive and affective development.* Bladensburg, MD: Westinghouse Learning Corporation and Ohio University.

Cole, M., Gay, J., Glick, J. A., & Sharp, D. W. (1971). *The cultural context of learning and thinking: An exploration in experimental anthropology.* New York: Basic Books.

Coleman, J. S., Campbell, E. Q., Hobson, C. J., McPartland, J., Mood, A. M., Weinfeld, F. D., & York, R. L. (1966). *Equality of educational opportunity.* Washington, DC: U.S. Office of Education.

Collins, A. M., & Loftus, E. F. (1975). A spreading activation theory of semantic processing. *Psychological Review, 82,* 407-428.

Commission on the Skills of the American Workforce. (1990). *America's choice: High skills or low wages!* Rochester, NY: National Center on Education and the Economy.

Conroy, P. (1986). *The prince of tides.* New York: Bantam.

Cooper, L. A. (1982). Strategies for visual comparison and representation: Individual differences. In R. J. Sternberg (Ed.), *Advances in the psychology of human intelligence* (Vol. 1, pp. 77-124). Hillsdale, NJ: Lawrence Erlbaum Associates.

Costa, A. (1991). Do you speak cogitare? In A. Costa (Ed.), *The school as a home for the mind* (pp. 109-119). Palatine, IL: IRI/Skylight.

Cotman, C. W., & Neeper, S. (1996). Activity-dependent plasticity and the aging brain. In E. L. Schneider & J. W. Rowe (Eds.), *Handbook of the biology of aging* (4th ed., pp. 283-299). San Diego, CA: Academic Press.

Crawford, J. R., Deary, I. J., Allan, K. M., & Gustafsson, J.-E. (1998). Evaluating competing models of the relationship between inspection time and psychometric intelligence. *Intelligence, 26,* 27-42.

Cronbach, L. J. (1957). The two disciplines of scientific psychology. *American Psychologist, 12,* 671-684.

Cronbach, L. J. (1975). Beyond the two disciplines of scientific psychology. *American Psychologist, 30,* 116-127.

Cronbach, L. J. (1977). *Educational psychology* (3rd ed.). New York: Harcourt Brace Jovanovich.

Cronbach, L. J. (1982). Prudent aspirations for social inquiry. In W. Kruskal (Ed.), *Social sciences in the twentieth century* (pp. 61-81). Chicago: University of Chicago Press.

Cronbach, L. J. (1984). *Essentials of psychological testing* (4th edition). New York: Harper & Row.

Cronbach, L. J., & Snow, R. E. (1977). *Aptitudes and instructional methods: A handbook for research on interactions.* New York: Irvington.

Datta, L. (1976). The impact of the Westinghouse/Ohio evaluation on the development of Project Head Start. In C. C. Abt (Ed.), *The evaluation of social programs* (pp. 129-190). Beverly Hills, CA: Sage.

Datta, L. (1979). Another spring and other hopes: Some findings from the national evaluations of Project Head Start. In E. Zigler & J. Valentine (Eds.), *Project Head Start: A legacy of the War on Poverty* (pp. 405-432). New York: The Free Press.

Dawe, H. C. (1942). A study of the effect of an educational program upon language development and related mental functions in young children. *Journal of Experimental Education, 11,* 200-209.

Deary, I. J., & Stough, C. (1997). Looking down on intelligence. *American Psychologist, 52,* 1148-1150.

deGroot, A. D. (1948). The effects of war upon the intelligence of youth. *Journal of Abnormal Social Psychology, 43,* 311-317.

deGroot, A. D. (1951). War and the intelligence of youth. *Journal of Abnormal Social Psychology, 46,* 596-597.

Dehaene, S., Spelke, E., Pinel, P., Stanescu, R., & Tsivkin, S. (1999). Sources of mathematical thinking: Behavioral and brain-imaging evidence. *Science, 284,* 970-974.

Delclos, V. R., Bransford, J. D., & Haywood, H. C. (1984). Instrumental enrichment: A program for teaching thinking. *Childhood Education, 60,* 256-259.

Denis, I., & Tapsfield, P. (Eds.). (1996). *Human abilities: Their nature and measurement.* Mahwah, NJ: Lawrence Erlbaum Associates.

DeParle, J. (1994, October 9). Daring research or "social science pornography"? *The New York Times Magazine,* pp. 48-53, 62, 70, 74, 78-79.

Detterman, D. K. (1982). Introduction: Questions I would like to have answered. In D. K. Detterman & R. J. Sternberg (Eds.), *How and how much can intelligence be increased* (pp. 41-44). Norwood, NJ: Ablex.

Detterman, D. K. (1993). The case for the prosecution: Transfer as an epiphenomenon. In D. K. Detterman & R. J. Sternberg (Eds.), *Transfer on trial: Intelligence, cognition, and instruction* (pp. 1-24). Norwood, NJ: Ablex.

Devlin, B., Daniels, M., & Roeder, K. (1997). The heritability of IQ. *Nature, 388,* 468-471.

De Vos, G., & Wagatsuma, H. (1966). Minority status and attitudes toward authority. In G. De Vos and H. Wagatsuma (Eds.), *Japan's invisible race: Caste in culture and personality* (pp. 258-272). Berkeley: University of California Press.

Dewey, J. (1916). *Democracy and education.* New York: The Free Press.

Dewey, J. (1938). *Experience and education.* New York: Macmillan.

Dietrich, K. N., Berger, O. G., & Succop, P. A. (1993). Lead exposure and the motor development status of urban six-year-old children in the Cincinnati Prospective Study. *Pediatrics, 91*, 301-307.

Dittmann-Kohli, F., & Baltes, P. B. (1990). Toward a neofunctionalist conception of adult intellectual development: Wisdom as a prototypical case of intellectual growth. In C. N. Alexander & E. J. Langer (Eds.), *Higher stages of human development: Perspectives on adult growth* (pp. 54-78). New York: Oxford University Press.

Duchein, M. A., & Mealey, D. L. (1993). Remembrance of books past . . . long past: Glimpses into aliteracy. *Reading Research and Instruction, 33*, 13-28.

Dumaret, A. (1985). IQ, scholastic achievement and behaviour problems of sibs raised in contrasting environments (J. Stewart, trans.). *Journal of Child Psychology and Psychiatry, 26*, 553-580.

Dunn, A. (1998, October 27). Merging of man and machine. *Los Angeles Times*, pp. A1, A28.

Einstein, A., & Infeld, L. (1938). *The evolution of physics: The growth of ideas from early concepts to relativity and quanta.* New York: Simon & Schuster.

Eisner, E. W. (1997). Cognitions and representation: A way to pursue the American dream? *Phi Delta Kappan, 78*, 349-353.

Embretson, S. E. (1995). The role of working memory capacity and general control processes in intelligence. *Intelligence, 20*, 169-189.

Ericsson, K. A. (1996). The acquisition of expert performance: An introduction to some of the issues. In K. A. Ericsson (Ed.), *The road to excellence: The acquisition of expert performance in the arts and sciences, sports, and games* (pp. 1-50). Mahwah, NJ: Lawrence Erlbaum Associates.

Ericsson, K. A., & Charness, N. (1994). Expert performance: Its structure and acquisition. *American Psychologist, 49*, 725-747.

Ericsson, K. A., Krampe, R. T., & Heizmann, S. (1993). Can we create gifted people? In G. R. Bock & K. Ackrill (Eds.), *The origins and development of high ability* (pp. 222-249). New York: Wiley.

Ericsson, K. A., Krampe, R. T., & Tesch-Römer, C. (1993). The role of deliberate practice in the acquisition of expert performance. *Psychological Review, 100*, 363-406.

Eriksson, P. S., Perfilieva, E., Björk-Eriksson, T., Alborn, A.-M., Nordborg, C., Peterson, D. A., & Gage, F. H. (1998). Neurogenesis in the adult human hippocampus. *Nature Medicine, 4*, 1313-1317.

Eyferth, K. (1961). Leistungen verschiedener Gruppen von Besatzungskindern im Hamburg-Wechsler Intelligenztest für Kinder (HAWIK). *Archiv für die gesamte Psychologie, 113*.

Eysenck, H. J. (Ed.). (1982). *A model for intelligence.* Berlin: Springer-Verlag.

Eysenck, H. J. (1991). Raising I.Q. through vitamin and mineral supplementation: An introduction. *Personality and Individual Differences, 14*, 329-333.

Eysenck, H. J. (1998). *Intelligence: A new look.* New Brunswick, NJ: Transaction.

Eysenck, H. J., & Schoenthaler, S. J. (1997). Raising IQ level by vitamin and mineral supplementation. In R. J. Sternberg & E. L. Grigorenko (Eds.), *Intelligence, heredity, and environment* (pp. 363-392). New York: Cambridge University Press.

Ferguson, G. A. (1954). On learning and human ability. *Canadian Journal of Psychology, 8*, 95-112.

Feuerstein, R., Hoffman, M. B., Rand, Y., Jensen, M., Tzuriel, D., & Hoffman, D. B. (1986). Learning to learn: Mediated learning experiences and instrumental enrichment. *Special Services in the Schools, 39*(1-2), 49-82.

Feuerstein, R., Rand, Y., & Hoffman, M. (1979). *The dynamic assessment of retarded performers.* Baltimore: University Park Press.

Feuerstein, R., Rand, Y., Hoffman, M., & Miller, R. (1980). *Instrumental enrichment: An intervention program for cognitive modifiability.* Baltimore: University Park Press.

Flavell, J. H. (1979). Metacognition and cognitive monitoring. *American Psychologist, 10*, 906-911.

Flynn, J. R. (1980). *Race, IQ and Jensen.* London: Routledge & Kegan Paul.

Flynn, J. R. (1987). Massive IQ gains in 14 nations: What IQ tests really measure. *Psychological Bulletin, 101*(2), 171-191.

Flynn, J. R. (1996). What environmental factors affect intelligence: The relevance of IQ gains over time. In D. K. Detterman (Ed.), *Current topics in human intelligence, vol. 5: The environment* (pp. 17-29). Norwood, NJ: Ablex.

Flynn, J. R. (1998) IQ gains over time: Toward finding the causes. In U. Neisser (Ed.), *The rising curve: Long-term gains in IQ and related measures* (pp. 25-66). Washington, DC: American Psychological Association.

Fodor, J. A. (1985). Precis of the modularity of mind. *The Behavioral and Brain Sciences, 8,* 1-42.

Folkard, S., & Monk, T. H. (1985). Circadian performance rhythms. In S. Folkard & T. H. Monk (Eds.), *Hours of work: Temporal factors in work-scheduling* (pp. 37-52). New York: Wiley.

Freeman, F. S. (1934). *Individual differences: The nature and causes of variations in intelligence and special abilities.* New York: Henry Holt.

Gabler, N. (1998). *Life the movie: How entertainment conquered reality.* New York: Knopf.

Gadberry, S. (1980). Effects of restricting first graders' TV-viewing on leisure time use, IQ change, and cognitive style. *Journal of Applied Developmental Psychology, 1,* 45-57.

Gall, C. M., Hess, U. S. & Lynch, G. (1998). Mapping brain networks engaged by, and changed by, learning. *Neurobiology of Learning and Memory, 70,* 14-36.

Galton, F. (1869). *Hereditary genius: An inquiry into its laws and consequences.* London: Macmillan.

Garber, H. L. (1988). *The Milwaukee Project: Preventing mental retardation in children at risk.* Washington, DC: American Association on Mental Retardation.

Garber, H., & Heber, R. (1982). Modification of predicted cognitive development in high-risk children through early intervention. In D. K. Detterman & R. J. Sternberg (Eds.), *How and how much can intelligence be increased* (pp. 121-137). Norwood, NJ: Ablex.

Garber, H. L., & Hodge, J. (1996). Misrepresentations and distortions in second-hand accounts of research. In D. K. Detterman (Ed.), *Current topics in human intelligence, vol. 5: The environment* (pp. 127-145). Norwood, NJ: Ablex.

Gardner, H. (1983). *Frames of mind: The theory of multiple intelligences.* New York: Basic Books.

Gardner, H. (1991). *The unschooled mind: How children think and how schools should teach.* New York: Basic Books.

Gardner, H. (1993a). *Creating minds.* New York: Basic Books.

Gardner, H. (1993b). *Multiple intelligences: The theory in practice.* New York: Basic Books.

Gardner, H. (1997). Are there additional intelligences? The case for naturalist, spiritual, and existential intelligences. *Gifted Education Press Quarterly, 11*(1), 2-5 & *11*(2), 2-8.

Gardner, H., & Hatch, T. (1989). Multiple intelligences go to school: Educational implications of the theory of multiple intelligences. *Educational Researcher, 18*(8), 4-10.

Gardner, H., Kornhaber, M. L., & Wake, W. K. (1996). *Intelligence: multiple perspectives.* Fort Worth: Harcourt Brace.

Getzels, J. W. (1979a). Problem finding: A theoretical note. *Cognitive Science, 3,* 167-172.

Getzels, J. W. (1979b). Problem-finding and research in educational administration. In G. L. Immegart & W. L. Boyd (Eds.), *Problem finding in educational administration: Trends in research and theory* (pp. 5-22). Lexington, MA: Lexington.

Getzels, J., & Csikszentmihalyi, M. (1976). *The creative vision: A longitudinal study of problem finding in art.* New York: Wiley.

Ghiselin, B. (Ed.). (1952). *The creative process.* New York: Mentor Books.

Gick, M. L., & Holyoak, K. J. (1980). Analogical problem solving. *Cognitive Psychology, 12,* 306-355.

Gladwin, T. (1970). *East is a big bird: Navigation and logic on Puluwat Atoll.* Cambridge, MA: Harvard University Press.

Glenn, N. D. (1994). Television watching, newspaper reading, and cohort differences in verbal ability. *Sociology of Education, 67,* 216-230.

Glick, J. (1975). Cognitive development in cross-cultural perspective. In D. Horowitz (Ed.), *Review of child development research* (Vol. 4., pp. 595-654). Chicago: University of Chicago Press.

Goldsmith, H. H. (1993). Nature-nurture issues in the behavioral genetics context: Overcoming barriers to communication. In R. Plomin & G. E. McClearn (Eds.), *Nature, nurture, & psychology* (pp. 155-160). Washington, DC: American Psychological Association.

Goleman, D. (1995). *Emotional intelligence*. New York: Bantam.

Gordon, H. (1970). The intelligence of English canal boat children. In I. Al-Issa & W. Dennis (Eds.), *Cross-cultural studies of behavior* (pp. 111-119). New York: Holt, Rinehart & Winston.

Gottfredson, L. S. (1997). Why g matters: The complexity of everyday life. *Intelligence, 24*, 97-132.

Gottfried, A. W. (1984). Home environment and early cognitive-intellectual development: The social environment. In A. W. Gottfried (Ed.), *Home environment and early cognitive development: Longitudinal research* (pp. 329-342). Orlando, FL: Academic Press.

Gould, S. J. (1981). *The mismeasure of man*. New York: Norton.

Granat, K., & Granat, S. (1978). Adjustment of intellectually below-average men not identified as mentally retarded. *Scandinavian Journal of Psychology, 19*, 41-51.

Green, R. L., Hofmann, L. J., Morse, R. J., Hayes, M. E., & Morgan, R. F. (1964). *The educational status of children in a district without public schools* (Cooperative Research Project No. 2321). East Lansing: Michigan State University College of Education.

Greenfield, P. M. (1978). Commentary and discussion. In H. W. Stevenson, T. Parker, A. Wilkinson, B. Bonnevaux, & M. Gonzalez (1978). Schooling, environment, and cognitive development: A cross-cultural study. *Monographs of the Society for Research in Child Development, 43* (Serial No. 175), 80-85.

Greenfield, P. M. (1998). The cultural evolution of IQ. In U. Neisser (Ed.), *The rising curve: Long-term gains in IQ and related measures* (pp. 81-123). Washington, DC: American Psychological Association.

Greenough, W. T., & Black, J. E. (1992). Induction of brain structure by experience: Substrates for cognitive development. In M. R. Gunnar & C. A. Nelson (Eds.), *Developmental behavioral neuroscience: The Minnesota symposia on child psychology* (pp. 155-200). Hillsdale, NJ: Lawrence Erlbaum Associates.

Grissmer, D. W., Flanagan, A., & Williamson, S. (1998). Why did the black-white score gap narrow in the 1970s and 1980s? In C. Jencks & M. Phillips (Eds.), *The black-white test score gap* (pp. 182-226). Washington, DC: Brookings Institution Press.

Grissmer, D. W., Williamson, S., Kirby, S. N., & Berends, M. (1998). Exploring the rapid rise in black achievement scores in the United States (1970-1990). In U. Neisser (Ed.), *The rising curve: Long-term gains in IQ and related measures* (pp. 251-285). Washington, DC: American Psychological Association.

Guilford, J. P. (1964). Zero correlations among tests of intellectual abilities. *Psychological Bulletin, 61*, 401-404.

Guilford, J. P. (1967). *The nature of human intelligence*. New York: McGraw-Hill.

Guilford, J. P. (1981). Higher-order structure-of-intellect abilities. *Multivariate Behavioral Research, 16*, 411-435.

Guilford, J. P. (1985). The structure of intellect model. In B. B. Wolman (Ed.), *Handbook of intelligence* (pp. 225-266). New York: Wiley.

Guilford, J. P. (1988). Some changes in the structure-of-intellect model. *Educational and Psychological Measurement, 48*, 1-4.

Guinagh, B. J. (1971). An experimental study of basic learning ability and intelligence in low-socioeconomic-status children. *Child Development 42*, 27-36.

Gustafsson, J.-E. (1999). Measuring and understanding G: Experimental and correlational approaches. In P. L. Ackerman, P. C. Kyllonen, & R. D. Roberts (Eds.), *Learning and individual differences: Process, trait, and content determinants* (pp. 275-289). Washington, DC: American Psychological Association.

Gustafsson, J.-E., & Undheim, J. O. (1996). Individual differences in cognitive functions. In D. C. Berliner & R. C. Calfee (Eds.), *Handbook of Educational Psychology* (pp. 186-310). New York: Macmillan.

Haier, R. J., Siegel, B. V., Nuechterlein, K. H., Hazlett, E., Wu, J. C., Paek, J., Browning, H. L., & Buchsbaum, M. S. (1988). Cortical glucose metabolic rate correlates of abstract reasoning and attention studied with positron emission tomography. *Intelligence, 12*, 199-217.

Halford, G. S. (1993). *Children's understanding: The development of mental models.* Hillsdale, NJ: Lawrence Erlbaum Associates.

Hammer, J. (2000, March 20). Hitler's children. *Newsweek*, pp. 34-36.

Harlow, H. F. (1953). Mice, monkeys, men, and motives. *Psychological Review, 60*, 23-32.

Härnqvist, K. (1959). Intelligensutveckling och skolresultat. *Ped. Forskn., 4*, 57-69.

Härnqvist, K. (1968). Relative changes in intelligence from 13 to 18. *Scandinavian Journal of Psychology, 9*, 50-64 (Part I) & 65-82 (Part II).

Harrell, R. F., Woodyard, E., & Gates, A. I. (1955). *The effect of mothers' diets on the intelligence of offspring.* New York: Teachers College, Columbia University.

Harris, J. R. (1995). Where is the child's environment? A group socialization theory of development. *Psychological Review, 102*, 458-489.

Harris, P., Clark, M., & Karp, R. J. (1993). Prevention and treatment of lead poisoning. In R. J. Karp (Ed.), *Malnourished children in the United States: Caught in the cycle of poverty* (pp. 91-100). New York: Springer.

Hart, B., & Risley, T. R. (1995). *Meaningful differences in the everyday experience of young American children.* Baltimore: Brookes.

Harvard University. (1983, October). *Project Intelligence Overview: The development of procedures to enhance thinking skills.* Final Report, submitted to the Minister for the Development of Human Intelligence, Republic of Venezuela.

Haskins, R. (1989). Beyond metaphor: The efficacy of early childhood education. *American Psychologist, 44*, 274-282.

Hayes, D. P., & Grether, J. (1983). The school year and vacations: When do students learn? *Cornell Journal of Social Relations, 17*(1), 56-71.

Hayes, K. J. (1962). Genes, drives, and intellect. *Psychological Reports, 10*, 299-342.

Haywood, H. C., & Arbitman-Smith, R. (1981). Modification of cognitive functions in slow-learning adolescents. In P. Mittler (Ed.), *Frontiers of knowledge in mental retardation. Vol. 1: Proceedings of the Fifth Congress of IASSMD I—Social, educational, and behavioral aspects* (pp. 129-140). Baltimore: University Park Press.

Hebb, D. O. (1949). *The organization of behavior: A neuropsychological theory.* New York: Wiley.

Heber, R., Garber, H., Harrington, S., Hoffman, C., & Falender, C. (1972). *Rehabilitation of families at risk for mental retardation* (Progress Report). Madison: University of Wisconsin, Rehabilitation Research and Training Center in Mental Retardation.

Herrnstein, R. J. (1987). Introduction, and the Venezuelan experiment. In D. N. Perkins, J. Lochhead, & J. Bishop (Eds.), *Thinking: The second international conference* (pp. 51-53). Hillsdale, NJ: Lawrence Erlbaum Associates.

Herrnstein, R. J., & Murray, C. (1994). *The bell curve: Intelligence and class structure in American life.* New York: The Free Press.

Herrnstein, R. J., Nickerson, R. S., de Sanchez, M., & Swets, J. A. (1986). Teaching thinking skills. *American Psychologist, 41*(11), 1283.

Heyns, B. (1978). *Summer learning and the effects of schooling.* New York: Academic Press.

Hick, W. E. (1952). On the rate of information gain. *Quarterly Journal of Experimental Psychology, 4*, 11-26.

Hilgard, E. R. (1980). The trilogy of mind: Cognition, affection, and conation. *Journal of the History of the Behavioral Sciences, 16*, 107-117.

Hirsh, E. D. (1987). *Cultural literacy.* Boston: Houghton Mifflin.

Ho, H.-Z. (1987). Interaction of early caregiving environment and infant developmental status in predicting subsequent cognitive performance. *British Journal of Developmental Psychology, 5*, 183-191.

Hoffman, D. D. (1998). *Visual intelligence: How we create what we see.* New York: Norton.

Hogaboam, T. W., & Pellegrino, J. W. (1978). Hunting for individual differences in cognitive processes: Verbal ability and semantic processing of words and pictures. *Memory and Cognition, 6,* 189-193.

Holland, J. H. (1995). *Hidden order: How adaptation builds complexity.* Reading, MA: Addison-Wesley.

Holloway, M. H. (1999). Seeking "smart" drugs. *Scientific American, 9*(4), 39-43.

Horgan, J. (1995). Get smart, take a test. *Scientific American, 273*(5), 12-14.

Horn, J. L. (1967, November). Intelligence—why it grows, why it declines. *Trans-Action,* pp. 23-31.

Horn, J. L. (1968). Organization of abilities and the development of intelligence. *Psychological Review, 75,* 242-259.

Horn, J. L. (1985). Remodeling old models of intelligence. In B.B. Wolman (Ed.), *Handbook of intelligence* (pp. 167-300). New York: Wiley.

Horn, J. L., & Knapp, J. R. (1973). On the subjective character of the empirical base of Guilford's structure of the intellect model. *Psychological Bulletin, 80,* 3-43.

Horwood, L. J., & Fergusson, D. M. (1998). Breastfeeding and later cognitive and academic outcomes. *Pediatrics, 101*(1), 1-7. (Available www: http://www.pediatrics.org/cgi/content/full/101/1/e9)

Hotz, R. L. (1999, February 23). Active mind, body linked to brain growth. *The Los Angeles Times,* pp. A1, A27.

Howard, R. W. (1999). Preliminary real-world evidence that average human intelligence really is rising. *Intelligence, 27,* 235-250.

Humphreys, L. G. (1989). Intelligence: Three kinds of instability and their consequences for policy. In R. L. Linn (Ed.), *Intelligence: Measurement, theory, and public policy* (pp. 193-216). Urbana: University of Illinois Press.

Hunt, E. B. (1995). *Will we be smart enough?: A cognitive analysis of the coming workforce.* New York: Russell Sage Foundation.

Hunt, E. (1986). The heffalump of intelligence. In R. J. Sternberg & D. K. Detterman (Eds.), *What is intelligence?: Contemporary viewpoints on its nature and definition* (pp. 101-107). Norwood, NJ: Ablex.

Hunt, E., Frost, N., & Lunneborg, C. (1973). Individual differences in cognition: A new approach to intelligence. In G. Bower (Ed.), *The psychology of learning and motivation: Vol. 7* (pp. 87-122). New York: Academic Press.

Hunt, J. McV. (1961). *Intelligence and experience.* New York: Ronald Press.

Hunter, J. E. (1986). Cognitive ability, cognitive aptitudes, job knowledge, and job performance. *Journal of Vocational Behavior, 29,* 340-362.

Hunter, J. E., & Hunter, R. F. (1984). Validity and utility of alternative predictors of job performance. *Psychological Bulletin, 96,* 72-98.

Husén, T. (1951). The influence of schooling upon IQ. *Theoria, 17,* 61-88.

Husén, T., & Tuijnman, A. (1991). The contribution of formal schooling to the increase in intellectual capital. *Educational Researcher, 20*(7), 17-25.

Huston, A. C., & Wright, J. C. (1998). Mass media and children's development. In I. E. Sigel & K. A. Renninger (Eds.), *Handbook of child psychology (5th ed.), Vol. 4: Child psychology in practice* (pp. 999-1058). New York: Wiley.

Inhelder, B., & Piaget, J. (1958). *The growth of logical thinking from childhood to adolescence.* New York: Basic Books.

Intelligence and its measurement: A symposium (1921). *Journal of Educational Psychology, 12,* 123-147, 195-216, 271-275.

Jacobs, P. I., & Vandeventer, M. (1972). Evaluating the teaching of intelligence. *Educational and Psychological Measurement, 32,* 235-248.

Jacobson, J. L., & Jacobson, S. W. (1996). Intellectual impairment in children exposed to polychlorinated biphenyls in utero. *The New England Journal of Medicine, 335*(11), 783-789.

James, W. (1896/1956). *The will to believe and other essays in popular philosophy.* New York: Dover.

Jay, E. S. (1996). The nature of problem finding in students' scientific inquiry (Doctoral dissertation, Harvard University, 1996). *Dissertations Abstracts International, 57,* 2953A.

Jay, E. S., & Perkins, D. N. (1997). Problem finding: The search for mechanism. In M. A. Runco (Ed.), *The creativity research handbook (Vol. 1,* pp. 257-293). Cresskill, NJ: Hampton Press.

Jencks, C. (1972). *Inequality: A reassessment of the effect of family and schooling in America.* New York: Basic Books.

Jencks, C., & Phillips, M. (1998a, September-October). America's next achievement test. *The American Prospect,* pp. 44-53.

Jencks, C., & Phillips, M. (1998b, November-December). Christopher Jencks and Meredith Phillips respond. *The American Prospect,* pp. 70-73.

Jencks, C., & Phillips, M. (1998c). The black-white score gap: An introduction. In C. Jencks & M. Phillips (Eds.), *The black-white test score gap* (pp. 1-51). Washington, DC: Brookings Institution Press.

Jennings, K. D., & Connors, R. E. (1989). Mothers' interactional style and children's competence at 3 years. *International Journal of Behavioral Development, 12,* 155-175.

Jensen, A. R. (1969). How much can we boost IQ and scholastic achievement? *Harvard Educational Review, 39,* 1-123.

Jensen, A. R. (1977). Cumulative deficit in IQ of blacks in the rural south. *Developmental Psychology, 13,* 184-191.

Jensen, A. R. (1982). Reaction time and psychometric g. In H. J. Eysenck (Ed.), *A model for intelligence* (pp. 93-132). New York: Springer-Verlag.

Jensen, A. (1987). The plasticity of "intelligence" at different levels of analysis. In D. N. Perkins, J. Lochhead, & J. Bishop (Eds.), *Thinking: The second international conference* (pp. 67-75). Hillsdale, NJ: Lawrence Erlbaum Associates.

Jensen, A. R. (1992a). Spearman's hypothesis: Methodology and evidence. *Multivariate Behavioral Research, 27,* 225-233.

Jensen, A. R. (1992b). Understanding g in terms of information processing. *Educational Psychology Review, 4,* 271-308.

Jensen, A. R. (1996). Giftedness and genius: Crucial differences. In C. P. Benbow & D. Lubinski (Eds.), *Intellectual talent: Psychometric and social issues* (pp. 393-411). Baltimore: Johns Hopkins University Press.

Jensen, A. R. (1998). *The g factor: The science of mental ability.* Westport, CT: Praeger.

Jensen, A. R., & Figueroa, R. A. (1975). Forward and backward digit span interaction with race and IQ: Predictions from Jensen's theory. *Journal of Educational Psychology, 67,* 882-893.

Joffe, J. M. (1982). Approaches to prevention of adverse developmental consequences of genetic and prenatal factors. In L. A. Bond & J. M. Joffe (Eds.), *Facilitating infant and early child development* (pp. 121-158). Hanover & London: University Press of New England.

Judd, C. H. (1908). The relation of special training to general intelligence. *Educational Review, 36,* 28-42.

Kamin, L. J. (1974). *The science and politics of I.Q.* Potomac, MD: Lawrence Erlbaum Associates.

Karmiloff-Smith, A. (1992). *Beyond modularity: A developmental perspective on cognitive science.* Cambridge, MA: The MIT Press.

Karp, R. J. (Ed.). (1993). *Malnourished children in the United States: Caught in the cycle of poverty.* New York: Springer.

Kaufman, M. (1999, June 7). Fight over formula additive heats up. *Los Angeles Times,* pp. S4-S5.

Kaus, M. (1995). The "it-matters-little" gambit. In S. Fraser (Ed.), *The bell curve wars* (pp. 130-138). New York: Basic Books.

Keating, D. P. (1996). Habits of mind: Developmental diversity in competence and coping. In D. K. Detterman (Ed.), *Current topics in human intelligence, vol. 5: The environment* (pp. 31-44). Norwood, NJ: Ablex.

Kermode, F. (1996, September 19). The pleasure of the text. *The New York Review,* pp. 31-33.

Klaus, R. A., & Gray, S. W. (1968). The early training project for disadvantaged children: A report after five years. *Monographs for the Society for Research in Child Development, 33*(4).

Kohn, M. L., & Schooler, C. (1973). Occupational experience and psychological functioning: An assessment of reciprocal effects. *American Sociological Review, 38,* 97-118.

Kornhaber, M. (1998, November-December). Commentary on C. Jencks & M. Phillips, "American's next achievement test." *The American Prospect*, pp. 63-64.

Kosslyn, S. M. (1980). *Image and mind*. Cambridge, MA: Harvard University Press.

Krugman, S., & Law, P. (1999). Breastfeeding and IQ. *Pediatrics, 103*, 193-194.

Kuhn, T. S. (1962). *The structure of scientific revolutions*. Chicago: University of Chicago Press.

Kvashchev, R. (1980). *Mogucnosti i granice razvoja inteligencije* [The feasibility and limits of intelligence training]. Belgrade: Nolit.

Kyllonen, P. C., & Christal, R. E. (1990). Reasoning ability is (little more than) working memory capacity?! *Intelligence, 14*, 389-433.

Kyllonen, P. C., Lohman, D. F., & Snow, R. E. (1984). Effects of aptitudes, strategy training, and task facets on spatial task performance. *Journal of Educational Psychology, 76*, 130-145.

Laird, J. E., Newell, A., & Rosenbloom, P. S. (1987). SOAR: An architecture for general intelligence. *Artificial Intelligence, 33*, 1-64.

Landy, F. J., Shankster, L. J., & Kohler, S. S. (1994). Personnel selection and placement. *Annual Review of Psychology, 45*, 261-296.

Langer, E. J. (1997). *The power of mindful learning*. Reading, MA: Addison-Wesley.

Larkin, J., McDermott, J., Simon, D. P., & Simon, H. A. (1980). Expert and novice performance in solving physics problems. *Science, 208*, 1335-1342.

Larson, G. E. (1990). Novelty as "representational complexity": A cognitive interpretation of Sternberg and Gastel (1989). *Intelligence, 14*, 235-238.

Larson, G. E., & Saccuzzo, D. P. (1989). Cognitive correlates of general intelligence: Toward a process theory of *g. Intelligence, 13*, 5-31.

Lesh, R., Post, T., & Behr, M. (1987). Representations and translations among representations in mathematics learning and problem solving. In C. Janvier (Ed.), *Problems in representation in the teaching and learning of mathematics* (pp. 33-40). Hillsdale, NJ: Lawrence Erlbaum Associates.

Lewontin, R. C. (1970). Race and intelligence. *Bulletin of the Atomic Scientists, 26*, 2-8.

Locurto, C. (1990). The malleability of IQ as judged from adoption studies. *Intelligence, 14*, 275-292.

Loehlin, J. C., Horn, J. M., & Willerman, L. (1997). Heredity, environment, and IQ in the Texas Adoption Project. In R. J. Sternberg & E. L. Grigorenko (Eds.), *Intelligence, heredity, and environment* (pp. 105-125). New York: Cambridge University Press.

Loehlin, J. C., Lindzey, G., & Spuhler, J. N. (1975). *Race differences in intelligence*. San Francisco: Freeman.

Loehlin, J. C., Vandenberg, S. G., & Osborne, R. T. (1973). Blood group genes and Negro-White ability differences. *Behavior Genetics, 3*, 263-270.

Lohman, D. F. (1989). Human intelligence: An introduction to advances in theory and research. *Review of Educational Research, 59*, 333-373.

Lohman, D. F. (1993). Teaching and testing to develop fluid abilities. *Educational Researcher, 22*(7), 12-23.

Lohman, D. F. (1994). Component scores as residual variation (or why the intercept correlates best). *Intelligence, 19*, 1-11.

Lohman, D. F. (1996). Spatial ability and *g*. In I. Dennis & P. Tapsfield (Eds.), *Human abilities: Their nature and measurement* (pp. 97-116). Mahwah, NJ: Lawrence Erlbaum Associates.

Lorge, I. (1945). Schooling makes a difference. *Teachers College Record, 46*, 483-492.

Lou, H. C., Hansen, D., Nordentoft, M., Pryds, O., Flemming, J., Nim, J., & Hemmingsen, R. (1994). Prenatal stressors of human iife affect fetal brain development. *Developmental Medicine and Child Neurology, 36*, 826-832.

Loury, G. C. (1998, November-December). Commentary on C. Jencks & M. Phillips, "American's next achievement test." *The American Prospect*, pp. 63-64.

Lynch, G. (1998). Memory and the brain: Unexpected chemistries and a new pharmacology. *Neurobiology of Learning and Memory, 70*, 82-100.

Lynn, R. (1990). The role of nutrition in secular increases in intelligence. *Personality and Individual Differences, 11*, 273-285.

Mackworth, N. H. (1965). Originality. *American Psychologist, 20*, 51-66.

Marsh, D. O., Clarkson, T. W., Myers, G. J., Davidson, P. W., Cox, C., Cernichiari, E., Tanner, M. A., Lednar, W., Shamlaye, C., Choisy, O., Hoarneau, C., & Berlin, M. (1995). The Seychelles study of fetal methlymercury exposure and child development: Introduction. *NeuroToxicology, 16*(4), 583-596.

Marshall, R., & Tucker, M. (1992). *Thinking for a living.* New York: Basic Books.

Marshall, S. P. (1995). *Schemas in problem solving.* New York: Cambridge University Press.

Martinez, M. E. (1999). Cognitive representations: Distinctions, implications, and elaborations. In I. E. Sigel (Ed.), *Development of mental representations: Theories and applications* (pp. 13-31). Mahwah, NJ: Lawrence Erlbaum Associates.

Martinez, M. E., & Lahart, C. (1990). *Profile: Student background characteristics from the 1986 and 1988 NAEP assessments* (Research Report No. RR-90-20). Princeton, NJ: Educational Testing Service.

Maslow, A. H. (1968). *Toward a psychology of being* (2nd ed.). New York: Van Nostrand Reinhold.

Mattson, S. N., Riley, E. P., Gramling, L., Delis, D. C., & Jones, K. L. (1997). Heavy prenatal alcohol exposure with or without physical features of fetal alcohol syndrome leads to IQ deficits. *The Journal of Pediatrics, 131*, 718-721.

Mayer, J. D., Caruso, D. R., & Salovey, P. (1999). Emotional intelligence meets traditional standards for an intelligence. *Intelligence, 27*, 267-298.

McClelland, D. C., Atkinson, J. W., Clark, R. A., & Lowell, E. L. (1953). *The achievement motive.* New York: Appleton-Century-Crofts.

Mehl, M. C. (1991). Mediated learning experience at university level—a case study. In R. Feuerstein, P. S. Klein, & A. J. Tannenbaum (Eds.), *Mediated learning experience (MLE): Theoretical, psychosocial, and learning implications* (pp. 157-178). London: Freund.

Meichenbaum, D. H. (1972). Cognitive modification of test anxious college students. *Journal of Consulting and Clinical Psychology, 39*, 370-380.

Meichenbaum, D. (1977). *Cognitive-behavior modification: An integrative approach.* New York: Plenum.

Melnick, M., Myrianthopolous, N. C., & Christian, J. C. (1978). The effects of chorion type on variation in IQ in the NCPP twin population. *American Journal of Human Genetics, 30*, 425-433.

Messick, S. (1987). *Assessment in the schools: Purposes and consequences* (Research Report RR-87-51). Princeton, NJ: Educational Testing Service.

Messick, S. (1992). Multiple intelligences or multilevel intelligence? Selective emphasis on distinctive properties of hierarchy: On Gardner's *Frames of Mind* and Sternberg's *Beyond IQ* in the context of theory and research on the structure of human abilities. *Psychological Inquiry, 3*, 365-384.

Messick, S. (1994). Cognitive styles and learning. In T. Husen & T. N. Postlethwaite (Eds.), *International encyclopedia of education* (2nd ed.) (pp. 868-872). New York: Pergamon.

Messick, S. (1996). *Bridging cognition and personality in education: The role of style in performance and development* (Research Report RR-96-22). Princeton, NJ: Educational Testing Service.

Miller, G. A. (1956). The magical number seven, plus or minus two. *Psychological Review, 63*, 81-97.

Miller, A. K. H., & Corsellis, J. A. N. (1977). Evidence for a secular increase in human brain weight during the past century. *Annals of Human Biology, 4*, 253-257.

Mumford, M. D., & Gustafson, S. B. (1988). Creativity syndrome: Integration, application, and innovation. *Psychological Bulletin, 103*, 27-43.

Nantais, K. M., & Schellenberg, E. G. (1999). The Mozart effect: An artifact of preference. *Psychological Science, 10*, 370-373.

Needleman, H. L., & Gatsonis, C. A. (1990). Low-level lead exposure and the IQ of children. *Journal of the American Medical Association, 263*, 673-678.

Neisser, U. (1976). General, academic, and artificial intelligence. In L. B. Resnick (Ed.), *The nature of intelligence* (pp. 135-144). Hillsdale, NJ: Lawrence Erlbaum Associates.

Neisser, U. (1997). Rising scores on intelligence tests. *American Scientist, 85,* 440-447.

Neisser, U. (1998). Introduction: Rising tests scores and what they mean. In U. Neisser (Ed.), *The rising curve: Long-term gains in IQ and related measures* (pp. 3-22). Washington, DC: American Psychological Association.

Neisser, U., Boodoo, G., Bouchard, T. J., Boykin, A. W., Brody, N., Ceci, S. J., Halpern, D. F., Loehlin, J. C., Perloff, R., Sternberg, R. J., & Urbina, S. (1996). Intelligence: Knowns and unknowns. *American Psychologist, 51*(2), 77-101.

Nelson, C. A. (1999). Neural plasticity and human development. *Current Directions in Psychological Science, 8,* 42-45.

Nettlebeck, T. (1987). Inspection time and intelligence. In P. A. Vernon (Ed.), *Speed of information processing and intelligence* (pp. 295-346). Norwood, NJ: Ablex.

Newell, A. (1980). Reasoning, problem solving, and decision processes: The problem space as the fundamental category. In R. S. Nickerson (Ed.), *Attention and performance VIII* (pp. 693-718). Hillsdale, NJ: Lawrence Erlbaum Associates.

Newell, A. (1990). *Unified theories of cognition.* Cambridge, MA: Harvard University Press.

Newell, A., & Simon, H. A. (1972). *Human problem solving.* Englewood Cliffs, NJ: Prentice-Hall.

Nickerson, R. S. (1986a). Project Intelligence: An account and some reflections. *Special Services in the Schools, 3*(1-2), 83-102.

Nickerson, R. S. (1986b). *Reflections on reasoning.* Hillsdale, NJ: Lawrence Erlbaum Associates.

Nickerson, R. S. (1994). The teaching of thinking and problem solving. In R. J. Sternberg (Ed.), *Thinking and problem solving* (pp. 409-449). San Diego: Academic Press.

Nickerson, R. S., Perkins, D. N., & Smith, E. E. (1985). *The teaching of thinking.* Hillsdale, NJ: Lawrence Erlbaum Associates.

Nisbett, R. (1995). Race, IQ, and scientism. In S. Fraser (Ed.), *The bell curve wars* (pp. 36-57). New York: Basic Books.

Nisbett, R. (1998). Race, genetics, and IQ. In C. Jencks & M. Phillips (Eds.), *The black-white test score gap* (pp. 86-102). Washington, DC: Brookings Institution Press.

Noble, D. F. (1997). *The religion of technology: The divinity of man and the spirit of invention.* New York: Knopf.

Ochse, R. (1990). *Before the gates of excellence: The determinants of creative genius.* Cambridge, England: Cambridge University Press.

Ogbu, J. U. (1978). *Minority education and caste: The American system in cross-cultural perspective.* New York: Academic Press.

Ogilvy, C. M. (1990). Family type and children's cognition in two ethnic groups. *Journal of Cross-Cultural Psychology, 21,* 319-334.

Ohlsson, S. (1993). Abstract schemas. *Educational Psychologist, 28,* 51-66.

Ohlsson, S. (1998). Spearman's g = Anderson's ACT?: Reflections on the locus of generality in human cognition. *The Journal of the Learning Sciences, 7*(1), 135-145.

Okagaki, L., & Frensch, P. A. (1994). Effects of video game playing on measures of spatial performance: Gender effects in late adolescence. *Journal of Applied Developmental Psychology, 15,* 33-58.

Olson, D. R. (1976). Culture, technology, and intellect. In L. R. Resnick (Ed.), *The nature of intelligence* (pp. 189-202). Hillsdale, NJ: Lawrence Erlbaum Associates.

Ong, W. J. (1982). *Orality and literacy: The technologizing of the word.* New York: Methuen.

Page, E. B. (1972). Physical miracle in Milwaukee? *Educational Researcher, 2,* 2, 4.

Page, E. B., & Grandon, G. M. (1981). Massive intervention and child intelligence: The Milwaukee Project in critical perspective. *The Journal of Special Education, 15,* 239-256.

Paisley, W. (1987, June). *Many literacies, many challenges.* Paper presented a the American Library Association Conference, San Francisco.

Pasamanick, B., Knobloch, H., & Lilienfeld, A. M. (1956). Socioeconomic status and some precursors of neuropsychiatric disorder. *American Journal of Orthopsychiatry, 26,* 594-601.

Pascarella, E. T., & Terenzini, P. T. (1991). *How college affects students: Findings and insights from twenty years of research.* San Francisco: Jossey-Bass.

Paul, R. (1993). *Critical thinking: What every person needs to survive in a rapidly changing world.* Santa Rosa, CA: Foundation for Critical Thinking.

Pea, R. D. (1993). Practices of distributed intelligence and designs for education. In G. Salomon (Ed.), *Distributed cognitions* (pp. 47-87). New York: Cambridge University Press.

Pederson, N. L., Plomin, R., Nesselroade, J. R., & McClearn, G. E. (1992). A quantitative genetic analysis of cognitive abilities during the second half of the life span. *Psychological Science, 3,* 346-353.

Pellegrino, J. W., & Glaser, R. (1979). Cognitive correlates and components in the analysis of individual differences. In R. J. Sternberg & D. K. Detterman (Eds.), *Human intelligence: Perspectives on its theory and measurement* (pp. 61-88). Norwood, NJ: Ablex.

Pentland, A. P. (1998). Wearable intelligence. *Scientific American, 9*(4), 90-95.

Perkins, D. N. (1992). *Smart schools: Better thinking and learning for every child.* New York: The Free Press.

Perkins, D. N. (1995). *Outsmarting IQ: The emerging science of learnable intelligence.* New York: The Free Press.

Perkins, D. N., Goodrich, H., Tishman, S., & Owen, J. M. (1994). *Thinking connections: Learning to think and thinking to learn.* Menlo Park, CA: Addison-Wesley.

Perkins, D. N., Jay, E., & Tishman, S. (1993). Beyond abilities: A dispositional theory of thinking. *Merrill-Palmer Quarterly, 39*(1), 1-21.

Perkins, D. N., & Salomon, G. (1987). Transfer and teaching thinking. In D. N. Perkins, J. Lochhead, & J. Bishop (Eds.), *Thinking: The second international conference* (pp. 285-303). Hillsdale, NJ: Lawrence Erlbaum Associates.

Plomin, R., & DeFries, J. C. (1998). The genetics of cognitive abilities and disabilities. *Scientific American, 278*(5), 62-69.

Polanyi, M. (1958). *Personal knowledge: Towards a post-critical philosophy.* Chicago: University of Chicago Press.

Pollitt, E., Gorman, K. S., Engle, P. L., Martorell, R., & Rivera, J. (1993). Early supplementary feeding and cognition: Effects over two decades. *Monographs of the Society for Research in Child Development, 58*(7, Serial No. 235).

Pressley, M., & Harris, K. R. (1990). What we really know about strategy instruction. *Educational Leadership, 44*(1), 31-34.

Ralph, J., Keller, D., & Crouse, J. (1994). How effective are American schools? *Phi Delta Kappan, 76,* 144-150.

Ramey, C. T., MacPhee, D., & Yeates, K. O. (1982). Preventing developmental retardation: A general systems model. In D. K. Detterman & R. J. Sternberg (Eds.), *How and how much can intelligence be increased* (pp. 67-119). Norwood, NJ: Ablex.

Ramey, S. L., & Ramey, C. T. (1992). Early cognitive intervention with disadvantaged children—to what effect? *Applied and Preventive Psychology, 1,* 131-140.

Rand, Y., Mintzker, Y., Miller, R., Hoffman, M. B., & Friedlender, Y. (1981). The instrumental enrichment program: Immediate and long-term effects. In P. Mittler (Ed.), *Frontiers of knowledge in mental retardation, Vol. 1: Proceedings of the fifth congress of IASSMDI—Social, educational and behavioral aspects* (pp. 141-152). Baltimore: University Park Press.

Reich, R. (1992). *The work of nations: Preparing ourselves for 21st-century capitalism.* New York: Vintage.

Reich, R. (1996, September 24). Casualties of the inflation war. *Financial Times of London*, p. 13.

Reinisch, J. M., Sanders, S. A., Mortensen, E. L., & Rubin, D. B. (1995). In utero exposure to phenobarbital and intelligence in adult men. *JAMA, 274*(19), 1518-1525.

Resnick, L. B. (Ed.). (1976). *The nature of intelligence.* Hillsdale, NJ: Lawrence Erlbaum Associates.

Resnick, L. B., & Glaser, R. (1976). Problem solving and intelligence. In L. B. Resnick (Ed.), *The nature of intelligence* (pp. 205-230). Hillsdale, NJ: Lawrence Erlbaum Associates.

Reuter-Lorenz, P. A., & Miller, A. C. (1998). The cognitive neuroscience of human laterality: Lessons from the bisected brain. *Current Directions in Psychological Science, 7*(1), 15-20.

Ricciuti, H. N. (1993). Nutrition and mental development. *Current Directions in Psychological Science, 2*(2), 43-46.

Rodriguez, O. (1992). Introduction to technical and societal issues in the psychological testing of Hispanics. In K. F. Geisinger (Ed.), *Psychological testing of Hispanics* (pp. 11-15). Washington, DC: American Psychological Association.

Rose, R. J., Harris, E. L., Christian, J. C., & Nance, W. E. (1979). Genetic variance in nonverbal intelligence: Data from the kinships of identical twins. *Science, 205*, 1153-1155.

Rowe, H. A. H. (1985). *Problem solving and intelligence.* Hillsdale, NJ: Lawrence Erlbaum Associates.

Rush, D., Stein, Z., & Susser, M. (1980). *Diet in pregnancy: A randomized controlled trial of nutritional supplements.* New York: Liss.

Ryle, G. (1949). *The concept of mind.* London: Hutchinson.

Salomon, G. (1983). The differential investment of mental effort in learning from different sources. *Educational Psychologist, 18*, 42-50.

Salomon, G. (1993). (Ed.). *Distributed cognitions: Psychological and educational considerations.* New York: Cambridge University Press.

Salomon, G., & Globerson, T. (1987). Skill may not be enough: The role of mindfulness in learning and transfer. *International Journal of Educational Research, 11*, 623-637.

Salovey, P., & Mayer, J. D. (1989-90). Emotional intelligence. *Imagination, Cognition and Personality, 9*, 185-211.

Savell, J. M., Twohig, P. T., & Rachford, D. L. (1986). Empirical status of Feuerstein's "Instrumental Enrichment" (FIE) technique as a method of teaching thinking skills. *Review of Educational Research, 56*, 381-409.

Scarr, S. (1981a). Genetics and the development of intelligence. In S. Scarr (Ed.), *Race, social class, and individual differences in IQ* (pp. 3-59). Hillsdale, NJ: Lawrence Erlbaum Associates.

Scarr, S. (1981b). Unknowns in the IQ equation. In S. Scarr (Ed.), *Race, social class, and individual differences in IQ* (pp. 61-74). Hillsdale, NJ: Lawrence Erlbaum Associates.

Scarr, S. (1992). Developmental theories for the 1990s: Development and individual differences. *Child Development, 63*, 1-19.

Scarr, S. (1997). Behavior-genetic and socialization theories of intelligence: Truth and reconciliation. In R. J. Sternberg & E. L. Grigorenko (Eds.), *Intelligence, heredity, and environment* (pp. 3-41). New York: Cambridge University Press.

Scarr, S., & Carter-Saltzman, L. (1982). Genetics and intelligence. In R. J. Sternberg (Ed.), *Handbook of human intelligence* (pp. 792-896). New York: Cambridge University Press.

Scarr, S., Pakstis, A. J., Katz, S. H., & Barker, W. B. (1977). Absence of a relationship between degree of white ancestry and intellectual skills within a black population. *Human Genetics, 39*, 69-86.

Scarr, S., & Weinberg, R. A. (1976). IQ test performance of black children adopted by white families. *American Psychologist, 31*, 726-739.

Scarr, S., & Weinberg, R. A. (1978). The influence of "family background" on intellectual attainment. *American Sociological Review, 43*, 674-692.

Scarr, S., & Weinberg, R. A. (1983). The Minnesota adoption studies: Genetic differences and malleability. *Child Development, 54*, 260-267.

Scarr-Salapatek, S., & Williams, M. L. (1973). The effects of early stimulation on low-birth-weight infants. *Child Development, 44*, 94-101.

Schank, R. C. (1986). Explaining intelligence. In R. J. Sternberg & D. K. Detterman (Eds.), *What is intelligence?* (pp. 121-131). Norwood, NJ: Ablex.

Scheiner, A. P., Hanshaw, J. B., Simeonsson, R. J., & Scheiner, B. (1977). The study of children with congenital cytomegalovirus infection. In P. Mittler (Ed.), *Research to practice in mental retardation* (pp. 261-268). Baltimore: University Park Press.

Schmidt, F. L., & Hunter, J. E. (1993). Tacit knowledge, practical intelligence, general mental ability, and job knowledge. *Current Directions in Psychological Science, 2*, 8-9.

Schmidt, F. L., & Hunter, J. E. (1998). The validity and utility of selection methods in personnel psychology: Practical and theoretical implications of 85 years of research findings. *Psychological Bulletin, 124,* 262-274.

Schmidt, W. H. O. (1960). School and intelligence. *International Review of Education, 6,* 416-432.

Schoenthaler, S. J., Amos, S. P., Eysenck, H. J., Peritz, E., & Yudkin, J. (1991). Controlled trial of vitamin-mineral supplementation: Effects on intelligence and performance. *Personality and Individual Differences, 12,* 351-362.

Schoenthaler, S. J., Doraz, W. E., & Wakefield, J. A. (1986). The impact of low food additive and sucrose diet on academic performance in 803 New York City public schools. *International Journal of Biosocial Research, 8*(2), 185-195.

Schooler, C. (1984). Psychological effects of complex environments during the life span: A review and theory. *Intelligence, 8,* 259-281.

Schooler, C. (1998). Environmental complexity and the Flynn effect. In U. Neisser (Ed.), *The rising curve: Long-term gains in IQ and related measures* (pp. 67-79). Washington, DC: American Psychological Association.

Schultz, T. W. (1981). *Investing in people: The economics of population quality.* Berkeley: University of California Press.

Secretary's Commission on Achieving Necessary Skills (1991). *What work requires of schools: A SCANS report for America 2000.* Washington, DC: U.S. Department of Labor.

Sewell, T. E., Price, V. D., & Karp, R. J. (1993). The ecology of poverty, undernutrition, and learning failure. In R. J. Karp (Ed.), *Malnourished children in the United States: Caught in the cycle of poverty* (pp. 24-30). New York: Springer.

Shockley, W. (1972). Dysgenics, geneticity, raceology: A challenge to the intellectual responsibility of educators. *Phi Delta Kappan, 53,* 297-307.

Shogren, E. (1999, August 3). EPA limits 2 pesticides, citing children's safety. *Los Angeles Times,* pp. A1, A6.

Shore, B. (1996). *Culture in mind: Cognition, culture, and the problem of meaning.* New York: Oxford University Press.

Shujaa, M. J. (1993). Education and schooling: You can have one without the other. *Urban Education, 27,* 328-351.

Sigel, I. E. (1993). The centrality of a distancing model for the development of representational competence. In R. R. Cocking & K. A. Renninger (Eds.), *The development and meaning of psychological distance* (pp. 141-158). Hillsdale, NJ: Lawrence Erlbaum Associates.

Sigel, I. E., Anderson, L. M., & Shapiro, H. (1966). Categorization behavior of lower- and middle-class negro preschool children: Differences in dealing with representation of familiar objects. *The Journal of Negro Education, 35,* 218-229.

Sigel, I. E., Stinson, E. T., & Kim, M.-I. (1993). Socialization of cognition: The distancing model. In R. H. Wozniak & K. W. Fisher (Eds.), *Development in context: Acting and thinking in specific environments* (pp. 211-224). Hillsdale, NJ: Lawrence Erlbaum Associates.

Simon, H. A. (1969). *The sciences of the artificial.* Cambridge, MA: MIT Press.

Simon, H. A. (1973). The structure of ill structured problems. *Artificial Intelligence, 4,* 181-201.

Simon, H. A. (1980). Problem solving and education. In D. T. Tuma & F. Reif (Eds.), *Problem solving and education: Issues in teaching and research* (pp. 81-96). Hillsdale, NJ: Lawrence Erlbaum Associates.

Simon, H. A. (1991, Fall). The cat that curiosity couldn't kill. *Carnegie Mellon Magazine,* pp. 35-36.

Simonton, D. K. (1984). *Genius, creativity, and leadership.* Cambridge, MA: Harvard University Press.

Simonton, D. K. (1996). Creative expertise: A life-span developmental perspective. In K. A. Ericsson (Ed.), *The road to excellence: The acquisition of expert performance in the arts and sciences, sports, and games* (pp. 227-253). Mahwah, NJ: Lawrence Erlbaum Associates.

Sinnott, E. W., Dunn, L. C., & Dobzhansky, T. (1958). *Principles of genetics.* New York: McGraw-Hill.

Skinner, B. F. (1938). *The behavior of organisms.* New York: Appleton-Century-Crofts.

Skinner, B. F. (1990). Can psychology be a science of mind? *American Psychologist, 45*, 1206-1210.

Sloboda, J. A., Hermelin, B., & O'Connor, N. (1985). An exceptional musical memory. *Music Perception, 3*, 155-170.

Smith, M. S., & Bissell, J. S. (1970). Report analysis: The impact of Head Start. *Harvard Educational Review, 40*, 51-104.

Snow, R. E. (1980a). Aptitude processes. In R. E. Snow, P.-A. Federico, & W. E. Montague (Eds.), *Aptitude, learning, and instruction, Vol. 1: Cognitive process analyses of aptitude* (pp. 27-63). Hillsdale, NJ: Lawrence Erlbaum Associates.

Snow, R. E. (1980b). Intelligence for the year 2001. *Intelligence, 4*, 185-199.

Snow, R. E. (with Yalow, E.). (1982a). Education and intelligence. In R. J. Sternberg (Ed.), *Handbook of human intelligence* (pp. 493-585). New York: Cambridge University Press.

Snow, R. E. (1982b). The training of intellectual aptitude. In D. K. Detterman & R. J. Sternberg (Eds.), *How and how much can intelligence be increased* (pp. 1-37). Norwood, NJ: Ablex.

Snow, R. E. (1986). On intelligence. In R. J. Sternberg & D. K. Detterman (Eds.), *What is intelligence?* (pp. 133-139). Norwood, NJ: Ablex.

Snow, R. E. (1991). The concept of aptitude. In R. E. Snow & D. E. Wiley (Eds.), *Improving inquiry in social science: A volume in honor of Lee J. Cronbach* (pp. 249-284). Hillsdale, NJ: Lawrence Erlbaum Associates.

Snow, R. E. (1992). Aptitude theory: yesterday, today, and tomorrow. *Educational Psychologist, 27*, 5-32.

Snow, R. E. (1996). Aptitude development and education. *Psychology, Public Policy, & Law, 2*, 536-560.

Snow, R. E., Corno, L., & Jackson, D., III. (1996). Individual differences in affective and conative functions. In D. C. Berliner & R. C. Calfee (Eds.), *Handbook of educational psychology* (pp. 243-310). New York: Macmillan.

Snow, R. E., Kyllonen, P. C., & Marshalek, B. (1984). The topography of ability and learning correlations. In R. J. Sternberg (Ed.), *Advances in the psychology of human intelligence* (Vol. 2, pp. 47-103). Hillsdale, NJ: Lawrence Erlbaum Associates.

Snow, R. E., & Lohman, D. F. (1984). Toward a theory of cognitive aptitude for learning from instruction. *Journal of Educational Psychology, 76*, 347-376.

Snow, R. E., & Lohman, D. F. (1989). Implications of cognitive psychology for educational measurement. In R.L. Linn (Ed.), *Educational measurement* (3rd ed., pp. 263-331). New York: Macmillan.

Solso, R. L. (1995). Turning the corner. In R. L. Solso & D. W. Massaro (Eds.), *The science of the mind: 2001 and beyond* (pp. 3-17). New York: Oxford University Press.

Sommer, R., & Sommer, B. A. (1983). Mystery in Milwaukee: Early intervention, IQ, and psychology textbooks. *American Psychologist, 38*, 982-985.

Sowell, T. (1995). Ethnicity and IQ. In S. Fraser (Ed.), *The bell curve wars* (pp. 70-79). New York: Basic Books.

Spaeth, J. L. (1976). Cognitive complexity: A dimension underlying the socioeconomic achievement process. In W. H. Sewell, R. M. Hauser, & D. L. Featherman (Eds.), *Schooling and achievement in American society* (pp. 103-131). New York: Academic Press.

Spearman, C. (1904). General intelligence, objectively defined and measured. *American Journal of Psychology, 15*, 201-293.

Spearman, C. (1927). *The abilities of man: Their nature and measurement*. New York: Macmillan.

Spearman, C., & Wynn Jones, L. (1950). *Human ability: A continuation of "The abilities of man."* London: Macmillan.

Sperry, R. W. (1995). The impact and promise of the cognitive revolution. In R. L. Solso & D. W. Massaro (Eds.), *The science of the mind: 2001 and beyond* (pp. 35-49). New York: Oxford University Press.

Spitz, H. H. (1986). *The raising of intelligence: A selected history of attempts to raise retarded intelligence*. Hillsdale, NJ: Lawrence Erlbaum Associates.

Staats, A. W., & Burns, G. L. (1981). Intelligence and child development: What intelligence is and how it is learned and functions. *Genetic Psychology Monographs, 104*, 237-301.

Stankov, L. (1986). Kvashchev's experiment: Can we boost intelligence? *Intelligence, 10*, 209-230.

Stanovich, K. E., West, R. F., & Harrison, M. R. (1995). Knowledge growth and maintenance across the life span: The role of print exposure. *Developmental Psychology, 31*, 811-826.

Starkes, J. L., Deakin, J. M., Allard, F., Hodges, N. J., & Hayes, A. (1996). Deliberate practice in sports: What is it anyway? In K. A. Ericsson (Ed.), *The road to excellence: The acquisition of expert performance in the arts and sciences, sports, and games* (pp. 81-106). Mahwah, NJ: Lawrence Erlbaum Associates.

Steele, C. M. (1999). Thin ice: "Stereotype threat" and black college students. *The Atlantic Monthly, 284*(2), 44-54.

Sternberg, R. J. (1977). *Intelligence, information processing, and analogical reasoning: The componential analysis of human abilities.* Hillsdale, NJ: Lawrence Erlbaum Associates.

Sternberg, R. J. (1980). Sketch of a componential subtheory of human intelligence. *Behavioral and Brain Sciences, 3*, 573-614.

Sternberg, R. J. (1985a). *Beyond IQ: A triarchic theory of human intelligence.* New York: Cambridge University Press.

Sternberg, R. J. (Ed.). (1985b). *Human abilities: An information processing approach.* New York: Freeman.

Sternberg, R. J. (1986). *Intelligence applied.* New York: Harcourt Brace Jovanovich.

Sternberg, R. J. (1989). Intelligence, wisdom, and creativity: Their natures and interrelationships. In R. L. Linn (Ed.), *Intelligence: Measurement, theory, and public policy* (pp. 119-146). Chicago: University of Illinois Press.

Sternberg, R. J. (1990a). *Metaphors of mind: Conceptions of the nature of intelligence.* New York: Cambridge University Press.

Sternberg, R. J. (1990b). Wisdom and its relations to intelligence and creativity. In R. J. Sternberg (Ed.), *Wisdom: Its nature, origins, and development. New York* (pp. 142-159). New York: Cambridge University Press.

Sternberg, R. J. (1994a). Answering questions and questioning answers. *Phi Delta Kappan, October*, 136-138.

Sternberg, R. J. (1994b). Intelligence. In R. J. Sternberg (Ed.), *Thinking and problem solving* (pp. 263-288). San Diego: Academic Press.

Sternberg, R. J. (1995). For whom the bell curve tolls: A review of *The Bell Curve. Psychological Science, 6*, 257-261.

Sternberg, R. J. (1996a). Costs of expertise. In K. A. Ericsson (Ed.), *The road to excellence: The acquisition of expert performance in the arts and sciences, sports, and games* (pp. 347-354). Mahwah, NJ: Lawrence Erlbaum Associates.

Sternberg, R. J. (1996b). Myths, countermyths, and truths about intelligence. *Educational Researcher, 25*(2), 11-16.

Sternberg, R. J. (1996c). *Successful intelligence.* New York: Simon & Schuster.

Sternberg, R. J. (1998a). Abilities are forms of developing expertise. *Educational Researcher, 27*(3), 11-20.

Sternberg, R. J. (1998b). A balance theory of wisdom. *Review of General Psychology, 2*, 347-365.

Sternberg, R. J. (1998c). How intelligent is intelligence testing? *Scientific American, 9*(4), 12-17.

Sternberg, R. J. (1999). The theory of successful intelligence. *Review of General Psychology, 3*, 292-316.

Sternberg, R. J., & Gardner, M. K. (1982). A componential interpretation of the general factor in human intelligence. In H. Eysenck (Ed.), *A model for intelligence* (pp. 231-254). Berlin: Springer-Verlag.

Sternberg, R. J., Nokes, K., Geissler, P. W., Prince, R., Okatcha, F., Bundy, D. A., Grigorenko, E. L., (in press). The relationship between academic and practical intelligence: A case study in Kenya. *Intelligence.*

Stevenson, H. W., Parker, T., Wilkinson, A., Bonnevaux, B., & Gonzalez, M. (1978). Schooling, environment, and cognitive development: A cross-cultural study. *Monographs of the Society for Research in Child Development, 43,* Serial No. 175.

Stewart, T. A. (1997). *Intellectual capital: The new wealth of organizations.* New York: Doubleday/ Currency.

Stoddard, G. D., & Wellman, B. L. (1940). Environment and the IQ. *Yearbook of the National Society for the Study of Education, 39*(1), 405-442.

Storfer, M. D. (1990). *Intelligence and giftedness: The contributions of heredity and early environment.* San Francisco: Jossey-Bass.

Tavris, C. (1995). A place in the sun. *Skeptic, 3,* 62-63.

Teasdale, T. W., & Owen, D. R. (1987). National secular trends in intelligence and education: A twenty-year cross-sectional study. *Nature, 325,* 119-121.

Terman, L. M. (1916). *The measurement of intelligence.* Boston, MA: Houghton Mifflin.

Tett, R. P., Jackson, D. N., & Rothstein, M. (1991). Personality measures as predictors of job performance: A meta-analytic review. *Personnel Psychology, 44,* 703-742.

Thomson, G. H. (1916). A hierarchy without a general factor. *British Journal of Psychology, 8,* 271-281.

Thompson, L. A., & Plomin, R. (1993). Genetic influences on cognitive ability. In K. A. Heller, F. J. Mönks, & A. H. Passow (Eds.), *International handbook of research and development of giftedness and talent* (pp. 103-113). Oxford, U.K.: Pergamon.

Thorndike, E. L. (1924). Mental discipline in high school studies. *Journal of Educational Psychology, 15,* 1-22.

Thorndike, E. L., & Woodworth, R. S. (1901). The influence of improvement in one mental function upon the efficiency of other functions. *Psychological Review, 8,* 247-261, 384-395, 553-564.

Thorndike, R. L. (1984). *Intelligence as information processing: The mind and the computer* [A CEDR monograph]. Bloomington, IN: Phi Delta Kappa.

Thorndike, R. M., & Lohman, D. F. (1990). *A century of ability testing.* Chicago: Riverside.

Thurow, L. C. (1985). *The zero sum solution.* New York: Simon & Schuster.

Thurstone, L. L. (1924). *The nature of intelligence.* Paterson, NJ: Littlfied, Adams.

Thurstone, L. L. (1938). Primary mental abilities. *Psychological Monographs, 1.*

Thurstone, L. L., & Thurstone, T. G. (1941). *Factorial studies of intelligence.* Chicago: University of Chicago Press.

Tishman, S., & Perkins, D. (1997). The language of thinking. *Phi Delta Kappan, 78,* 368-374.

Tizard, B., Cooperman, O., Joseph, A., & Tizard, J. (1972). Environmental effects on language development: A study of young children in long-stay residential nurseries. *Child Development, 43,* 337-358.

Tolman, E. C. (1932). *Purposive behavior in animals and men.* New York: Century.

Tuddenham, R. D. (1948). Soldier intelligence in World Wars I and II. *American Psychologist, 3,* 54-56.

U.S. Department of Commerce. (1997). *Statistical abstract of the United States.* Washington, DC: Bureau of the Census.

Vernon, P. A., & Mori, M. (1992). Intelligence, reaction times, and peripheral nerve conduction velocity. *Intelligence, 16,* 273-288.

Vernon, P. E. (1948). Changes in abilities from 14 to 20 years. *The Advancement of Science, 5*(18), 138.

Vernon, P. E. (1950). *The structure of human abilities.* London: Methuen.

Vincent, K. R. (1991). Black/White IQ differences: Does age make the difference? *Journal of Clinical Psychology, 47,* 266-270.

Vygotsky, L. S. (1978). *Mind in society: The development of higher psychological processes* (M. Cole, V. John-Steiner, S. Scribner, & E. Souberman, Eds. and Trans.). Cambridge, MA: Harvard University Press.

Vygotsky, L. S. (1986/1934). *Thought and language* (A. Kozulin, Ed. and Trans.). Cambridge, MA: MIT Press.

Wachs, T. D. (1993). Going beyond nutrition: Nutrition, context, and cognitive development. *Monographs of the Society for Research in Child Development, 58*(7), 101-110.

Wachs, T. D. (1996). Environment and intelligence: Present status, future directions. In D. K. Detterman (Ed.), *Current topics in human intelligence, vol. 5: The environment* (pp. 31-44). Norwood, NJ: Ablex.

Wade, N. (1976). IQ and heredity: Suspicion of fraud beclouds classic experiment. *Science, 194*, 916-919.

Waldman, I. D. (1997). Unresolved questions and future directions in behavior-genetic studies of intelligence. In R. J. Sternberg & E. L. Grigorenko (Eds.), *Intelligence, heredity, and environment* (pp. 552-570). New York: Cambridge University Press.

Wallman, J. (1994). Nature and nurture of myopia. *Nature, 371*, 201-202.

Warschauer, M. (1999). *Electronic literacies: Language, culture, and power in online education.* Mahwah, NJ: Lawrence Erlbaum Associates.

Watson, J. B. (1913). Psychology as the behaviorist sees it. *Psychological Review, 20*, 157-177.

Weiss, P. (1959). Cellular dynamics. *Reviews of Modern Physics, 31*(1), 11-20.

Weiss, B. (1997). Pesticides as a source of developmental disabilities. *Mental Retardation and Developmental Disabilities Research Reviews, 3*, 246-257.

Wheeler, L. R. (1970/1942). A trans-decade comparison of the IQ's of Tennessee mountain children. In I. Al-Issa & W. Dennis (Eds.), *Cross-cultural studies of behavior* (pp. 120-133). New York: Holt, Rinehart & Winston. [Originally published: (1942). A comparative study of the intelligence of east Tennessee mountain children. *The Journal of Educational Psychology, 33*, 321-334.]

Whimbey, A. (1975). *Intelligence can be taught.* New York: Dutton.

Whimbey, A., & Lochhead, J. (1991). *Problem solving and comprehension* (5th ed.). Hillsdale, NJ: Lawrence Erlbaum Associates.

White, B. Y. (1993). Thinkertools: Causal models, conceptual change, and science education. *Cognition and Instruction, 10*, 1-85.

White, R. W. (1959). Motivation reconsidered: The concept of competence. *Psychological Review, 66*, 297-331.

Wigdor, A. K., & Green, B. F. (Eds.). (1991). *Performance assessment for the workplace (vol. 1).* Washington, DC: National Academy Press.

Willatts, P., Forsyth, J. S., DiModugno, M. K., Varma, S., & Colvin, M. (1998). Effects of long-chain polyunsaturated fatty acids in infant formula on problem solving at 10 months of age. *The Lancet, 352*, 688-691.

Willerman, L., Naylor, A. F., & Myrianthopoulos, N. C. (1974). Intellectual development of children from interracial matings: Performance in infancy and at 4 years. *Behavior Genetics, 4*, 83-90.

Williams, C. J. (2000, January 21). *Breeding to further the Reich.* Los Angeles Times, pp. A1, A14.

Williams, P. A., Haertel, E. H., Haertel, G. E., & Walberg, H. J. (1982). The impact of leisure-time television on school learning: A research synthesis. *American Educational Research Journal, 19*, 19-50.

Willis, S. L., Blieszner, R., & Baltes, P. B. (1981). Intellectual training research in aging: Modification of performance on the fluid ability of figural relations. *Journal of Educational Psychology, 73*, 41-50.

Winner, E. (1996). The rage to master: The decisive role of talent in the visual arts. In K. A. Ericsson (Ed.), *The road to excellence: The acquisition of expert performance in the arts and sciences, sports, and games* (pp. 271-301). Mahwah, NJ: Lawrence Erlbaum Associates.

Witty, P. A., & Jenkins, M. D. (1934). The educational achievement of a group of gifted Negro children. *Journal of Educational Psychology, 25*, 585-597.

Witty, P. A., & Jenkins, M. D. (1936). Intra-race testing and Negro intelligence. *Journal of Psychology, 1*, 179-192.

Yudkin, J. (1991). Intelligence of children and vitamin-mineral supplements: The DRF study, discussion, conclusion and consequences. *Personality and Individual Differences, 12*, 363-365.

Zigler, E. (1979). Project Head Start: Success or failure? In E. Zigler & J. Valentine (Eds.), *Project Head Start: A legacy of the War on Poverty* (pp. 495-507). New York: The Free Press.

Zigler, E., Styfco, S. J., & Gilman, E. (1993). The national Head Start program for disadvantaged preschoolers. In E. Zigler & S. J. Styfco (Eds.), *Head Start and beyond: A national plan for extended childhood intervention* (pp. 1-41). New Haven, CT: Yale University Press.

Zwaan, R. A. (1999). Situation models: The mental leap into imagined worlds. *Current Directions in Psychological Science, 8*(1), 15-18.

Author Index

A

Ackerman, P. L., 30, 186, 193
Alborn, A.-M., 138, 198
Alexander, C. N., 73, 88, 193
Allan, K. M., 26, 197
Allard, F., 52, 211
Amos, S. P., 140–142, 209
Anastasi, A., 38, 42, 47, 69, 193
Anderson, J. R., 23–25, 30, 58, 193
Anderson, L. M., 119, 209
Angoff, W. H., 82, 193
Arbitman-Smith, R., 164, 201
Arlin, P. K., 60, 73, 193
Arvey, R. D., 2–3, 193
Atkinson, J. W., 190, 205
Atkinson, R. C., 21, 193

B

Baddeley, A., 21–23, 193
Balke-Aurell, G., 128, 193
Baltes, P. B., 57, 88, 138, 167, 193, 198, 213
Bandura, A., 84, 193
Barclay, C. R., 160, 167, 195
Barker, W. B., 103, 208
Barnard, K. E., 117–119, 194
Baron, J., 47, 68–69, 180, 193
Barrick, M. R., 185, 193
Bartlett, F. C., 23, 193
Behr, M., 23, 204
Belmont, J. M., 31, 59, 67, 159–161, 193
Benbow, C., 43, 78, 196
Benton, D., 19, 93, 140, 194
Bereiter, C., 29, 151, 167, 188, 194
Berends, M., 107–109, 120, 200
Berger, O. G., 144–145, 146, 198
Berlin, M., 113, 205
Bernstein, B., 120, 150, 194
Berry, J. W., 42, 72, 194

Bidell, T. R., 97, 123, 194
Binet, A., 3, 25, 67, 82, 126, 194
Birch, D. G., 116, 194
Birch, E. E., 116, 194
Bissell, J. S., 156–157, 210
Björk-Eriksson, T., 138, 198
Black, J. E., 44, 83–84, 200
Blagg, N., 163–164, 194
Blank, M., 167, 194
Blieszner, R., 138, 167, 213
Bloom, B. S., 46, 52, 190, 194
Bock, R. D., 82, 194
Bonnevaux, B., 133, 212
Boodoo, G., 64, 78, 83, 93, 121, 123, 206
Boring, E. G., 18, 36, 87, 194
Botkin, J. W., 6, 191, 194
Bouchard, T. J., 64, 77–78, 78, 83, 93, 121, 123, 187, 194, 206
Bower, G. H., 49, 194
Bowles, S., 119, 194
Boykin, A. W., 64, 78, 83, 93, 121, 123, 206
Bradley, R. H., 117–119, 194
Brandwein, P. F., 132, 173, 194
Bransford, J. D., 165, 167, 197
Breitmayer, B. J., 114, 124, 152, 194
Brody, N., 3, 14, 15, 64, 78, 83, 93, 106, 121, 123, 195, 206
Brooks-Gunn, J., 119, 195
Brown, A. L., 31, 159–161, 167, 195
Browning, H. L., 43, 72, 201
Bruer, J. T., 46, 195
Bruner, J. S., 49, 195
Buchsbaum, M. S., 43, 72, 201
Budoff, M., 167, 195
Bundy, D. A., 42, 211
Burns, G. L., 167, 187, 211
Burt, C., 15, 195
Butterfield, E. C., 31, 59, 159–161, 194, 195

K

Kamin, L. J., 81, 111, 203
Karmiloff-Smith, A., 42, 203
Karp, R. J., 139, 143–144, 201, 203, 209
Katz, S. H., 103, 208
Kaufman, M., 116, 203
Kaus, M., 81, 106, 109, 176, 203
Keating, D. P., 83, 203
Keller, D., 184, 207
Kermode, F., 183, 203
Kim, M.-I., 117, 119, 182, 209
Kirby, S. N., 107–109, 120, 200
Klaus, R. A., 150–151, 167, 203
Klebanov, P. K., 119, 195
Knapp, J. R., 14, 202
Knobloch, H., 101, 206
Kohler, S. S., 185, 204
Kohn, M. L., 86, 185, 203
Kornhaber, M. L., 34, 38, 58, 110, 175, 199, 204
Kosslyn, S. M., 64, 204
Krampe, R. T., 52, 56, 190, 198
Krugman, S., 116, 204
Kuhn, T. S., 54, 204
Kvashchev, R., 165–166, 204
Kyllonen, P. C., 22, 28, 64, 65, 204, 210

L

Lahart, C., 182, 205
Laird, J. E., 25, 58, 67, 204
Landy, F. J., 185, 204
Langer, E. J., 47, 73, 88, 193, 204
Larkin, J., 51, 204
Larson, G. E., 26–27, 29, 40, 204
Law, P., 116, 204
Lednar, W., 113, 205
Lesh, R., 23, 204
Lewontin, R. C., 80, 83, 88, 100, 204
Liaw, F., 119, 195
Lilienfeld, A. M., 101, 206
Lindzey, G., 95, 125, 204
Lochhead, J., 175, 213
Locurto, C., 121, 204
Loehlin, J. C., 64, 78, 83, 93, 95, 103, 121, 123, 125, 204, 206

Loftus, E. F., 23, 196
Lohman, D. F., 12, 23–25, 31, 32, 61, 63–64, 177, 204, 210
Lorge, I., 111, 126–127, 204
Lou, H. C., 113, 204
Loury, G. C., 98, 204
Lowell, E. L., 190, 205
Lubinski, D., 43, 78, 196
Lunneborg, C., 23, 27, 202
Lynch, G., 85, 139, 199, 204
Lynn, R., 90–91, 93, 139, 205

M

Mackworth, N. H., 59, 205
MacPhee, D., 152–153, 207
Malitza, M., 6, 191, 194
Marsh, D. O., 113, 205
Marshalek, B., 28, 210
Marshall, R., 189, 205
Marshall, S. P., 23, 205
Martínez, C., 124, 144, 184, 196
Martinez, M. E., 63, 66, 182, 205
Martorell, R., 124, 143, 207
Maslow, A. H., 58, 205
Mattson, S. N., 113, 205
Mayer, J. D., 48, 56, 205, 208
McClearn, G. E., 77, 87, 97, 207
McClelland, D. C., 190, 205
McDermott, J., 51, 204
McGue, M., 77–78, 194
McGuffin, P., 43, 78, 196
McPartland, J., 133, 196
Mealey, D. L., 179, 182, 198
Mehl, M. C., 164, 205
Meichenbaum, D. H., 48, 71, 205
Melnick, M., 115, 205
Messick, S., 15, 16, 37–38, 46, 55, 205
Miller, A. C., 46, 208
Miller, A. K. H., 93, 205
Miller, G. A., 21, 205
Miller, R., 162–165, 166, 198, 207
Mintzker, Y., 164, 207
Mitchell, S., 117–119, 194
Monk, T. H., 87, 199
Mood, A. M., 133, 196
Moon, T. R., 37, 55, 195

Subject Index

A

Academic Preschool, 151
ACT Theory, 23
Adoption Studies, 78-79, 102-103, 121-123
Analytical Intelligence, 38
Artificial Intelligence, 25
Automatization, 180-181

B

Barakumin, 98
Biological Theories of Intelligence, 43-46
Black-White IQ Gap, 98, 176
    blood group studies, 103-104
    closing, 106-109, 176-177, 190
    direct evidence, 102-106
    gifted Black children, 104-105
    indirect evidence, 100-101
    infant mortality, 101
    inequality theories, 98-100
    mixed-race children, 105-106
    social prospects 110-111
Brain Imaging, 43
Brain Responsiveness to Experience, 44-45
Breastfeeding, 116

C

Carolina Abecedarian Project, 152-153
Circadian Rhythms, 87
Club of Rome Report, 6
Cognitive Components Research, 28-29
Cognitive Correlates Research, 27
Cognitive Elite, 5, 50
Cognitive Information-Processing Theory, 21-25
    limits of, 48-49

Cognitive Interventions
    early childhood, 149-157
    infancy 148-149
    school age, 157-166
Componential Subtheory, 39, 55
Conscientiousness, 185-187
Contextualized Intelligence, 41-43
Creative Intelligence, 38-39
Creativity, 38-39, 51-54, 190-191
Crystallized Intelligence, 16, 18-19, 88-89, 179-180, 185-186
Culture and Intelligence, 40-43, 72
Cytomegalovirus, 114

D

Declarative Knowledge, 23
Deductive Reasoning, 63
Deliberate Practice, 51-52
Distributed Intelligence, 49-51
Docosahexaenoic Acid (DHA), 116

E

Early Training Project, 150-151
Economic Competitiveness, 88, 188-189
Economy, 1
Education
    economic reward, 3
    redefined, 6, 112, 145, 173
EEG and IQ, 43
Eindhoven Study, 129
Elementary Cognitive Processes, 25-27
Emotional Intelligence, 48-49
Efficient Quality of Intelligence, 60-65
English Canal Boat Children, 125-126
Entelic Quality of Intelligence, 58-60
Evaluative Quality of Intelligence, 66-68
Expertise, 51-52, 55, 186, 190